MONSTROUS CREATURES

Monstrous Creatures Copyright © 2011 by Jeff VanderMeer

Published by Guide Dog Books
Bowie, MD

First Edition

Cover image: Eric Orchard
Book design: Jennifer Barnes

Printed in the United States of America

ISBN: 978-1-935738-03-9

Library of Congress Control Number: 2010933090

www.GuideDogBooks.com

MONSTROUS CREATURES

Explorations of Fantasy through Essays, Articles and Reviews

Jeff VanderMeer

Acknowledgments

Thanks to everyone at Guide Dog for believing in this book and putting up with my schedule. Thanks to the editors at all of the publications and review websites who published many of these pieces originally. Thanks to my wife, Ann VanderMeer, for being a first reader for many of these pieces, and the last reader for the collection as a whole. Thanks to my fellow writers for being inspirational.

Table of Contents

Monstrous? Creatures? 9

Monstrous Thoughts 11
    The Third Bear 12
    The Language of Defeat 24
    An Anvil Is Not an Artichoke 28
    The Romantic Underground 31
    Politics in Fantasy 37
    The Triumph of the Good 43
    The New Weird – "It's Alive?" 46

Conversation #1: China Miéville and the Monsters 55

Appreciations of the Monstrous 65
    Prague: City of Fantasy 66
    Catherynne M. Valente's *The Labyrinth* 69
    Two Members of the Shadow Cabinet: Batchelor and McNaughton 71
    Making Her Own Light: Caitlín R. Kiernan 75
    Unsung Heroes of Science Fiction and Fantasy 79
    My Additional Misadventures with Engelbrecht 83
    Alasdair Gray and *Lanark* 87
    My Love-Hate Relationship with Clark Ashton-Smith 91
    Lovecraft Art: The Link Between Tentacles and Cosmic SF 99
    Alfred Kubin and the Tortured Triumph of *The Other Side* 103
    The "Black Books" of Derek Raymond 107
    A Giant of Literature, J.G. Ballard 122
    The Cosmology of Jeffrey Ford 126
    Five Years of Sfar and Trondheim's Dungeon Series 129
    How to Raise and Keep an Imagination: Joseph Nigg and the Power of Fantasy 132
    Authors in Praise of Beer 140

Conversation #2: Eaten by Bears—Margo Lanagan's *Tender Morsels* 148

Interrogating Other People's Monsters 153
    Prague Reimagined: Michal Ajvaz's *The Other City* 154
    The Perils and Triumphs of Transformation: China Miéville's *Un Lun Dun* 156
    Two New Anthology Series, Two Views of Comics 161
    Tove Jansson's Moomin Comics 166
    Bittersweet Fantasy: Kazu Kibuishi's *Amulet, Book One: The Stonekeeper* 168
    Dream Worlds: David B's *Nocturnal Conspiracies* 170
    Silence and Aversion: J. Robert Lennon's *Castle* 173
    Stairs to Nowhere: *House of Leaves*, Mark Z. Danielewski 176
    Future Past: Brian Francis Slattery's *Liberation* 179
    Not Good at Dying: *The Many Deaths of the Firefly Brothers* by Thomas Mullen 181
    Re-envisioning the West: Emma Bull's *Territory* 184
    Hollywood Punk: Steve Erickson's *Zeroville* 187
    Exchange Students Plot to Take Over America: Chuck Palahniuk's *Pygmy* 189
    Looking for Love: Alexander Theroux's *Laura Warholic, or The Sexual Intellectual* 191
    The Lost Girls of Alan Moore and Melinda Gebbie 193
    London's Last Stand: Jonathan Barnes' *The Domino Men* 197
    The Newt Speaks Volumes: Jack O'Connell's *The Resurrectionist* 200
    Not Enough Bite: Victor Pelevin's *The Sacred Book of the Werewolf* 202
    Hot Ice: Marcel Theroux's *Far North* 205
    Philosophy in Fiction's Clothing: Neal Stephenson's *Anathem* 207
    The Books of the Decade 212

Conversation #3: The Monstrous Capybara of Austin, Texas 219

Personal Monsters 225
    The Hannukah Bear 226
    Fantasy and the Imagination 229
    My Father's Pipe 232
    The Novella: A Personal Exploration 235
    Two Essays on Hiking 242

For Ann
&
For Caplin Rous, RIP

Monstrous? Creatures?

From an early age, I think I had an appreciation for a definition of "monstrous" that did not mean "hideous," "horrible," or "ghastly." Growing up in the Fiji Islands, if I came upon a lugubrious slug, it was cause for triumph and awe, not recoil. Similarly the defiantly ugly toads that would hop lethargic through the grass—I loved them and their jaded watchful but calm eyes. Tough old lobsters while snorkeling and snarling moray eels were better than bejeweled fish any day.

No surprise, then, that when I grew up, I pursued the monstrous with gusto. The insane micro-sinister of fungi attracted me, and I still find nothing more sublime than encountering a particularly monstrous mushroom, gnarled and gilled and enigmatic, shoving its way into our world from the trunk of a tree. A fascination with the sea followed me as well, so that giant squid and other cephalopods made a meal of me in hundreds of hours spent researching them and discovering their most monstrous secrets.

Mega-fauna, breadfruit, wolverines, sea cucumbers, sloths, rhinoceros beetles—the list of those things that I find amazing trends toward the monstrous. In this sense: to me, the monstrous is the intersection of the beautiful with the strange, the dangerous with the sublime. Things that seem to be continuously unknowable no matter how much you discover about them. That surround themselves with darkness. Sometimes, too, they are utterly terrifying, no matter how you try to keep that thought out of your head.

Books can be like that, too. The best fictions always have those qualities. They reveal dark marvels but they withhold some of their secrets as well. Monstrously ambitious. Monstrously odd. Monstrously wide and deep. Or even monstrously about monsters.

You could say that I've been seeking out the monstrous my entire life—and not just seeking it out, but running toward it. Wanting to explore it. Obsessively. Sometimes I might be running not toward a bear but toward the Third Bear, but that's okay too. Wonder and beauty need their opposites and sometimes are their own opposites.

This book collects some of the monstrous creatures I've encountered over the past few years. I hope you enjoy it.

—Jeff VanderMeer, Tallahassee, November 2010

MONSTROUS THOUGHTS

THE THIRD BEAR

From *Brothers & Beasts: An Anthology of Men on Fairy Tales (2007)*

I.

"Masha and the Bear"

The first bear may be uncouth, but not unkind, despite appearances. His English isn't good and he lives alone in a cottage in the forest, but no one can say he doesn't try. If he didn't try, if the idea of trying, and thus of restraint, were alien to him, the first bear wouldn't live in a cottage at all. He'd live in the deep forest and all anyone would see of him, before the end, would be hard eyes and the dark barrel of his muzzle. The third bear would be so much in him that no first bear would be left.

The first bear is a man's man, or, rather, a bear's bear: "golden brown, with enormous claws on his padded feet and sharp, pure-white fangs bigger than a person's hands, and eyes a startling blue." This bear smells like mint and blueberries, and his name is Bear.

One day, a girl named Masha gets lost in the woods. Bear finds her and takes her back to his cottage. He refuses to show her the way home, for his cottage is a mess and, as I may have mentioned, so is his English. Masha can help him with both disasters, although she isn't happy about the situation. She thinks Bear is the creature her parents warned her about when they told her not to go into the forest. But Bear is the first bear, not the third bear. In an odd way, Bear has saved her from the third bear.

Of course, Masha doesn't see it that way—and why should she? It's largely a matter of degree, and not just because she can't imagine what worse might happen to her. Bear is gruff with Masha, makes her work long hours, and ignores her pleas to be shown the way back to her village. As far as Masha's concerned, this is as bad as it gets.

This dynamic continues for awhile, with Masha afraid to run off blindly while Bear's not looking. But then an odd thing begins to happen to Bear: the longer he talks to Masha and grows fond of her company, his English improving every week, he begins to feel bad for her. He begins to understand how lost, alone, and cut off she feels—in part because he feels the same way. Still, Bear enjoys the captive audience so much he does not allow his concern for her well-being to override his need for companionship. He cannot bring himself to show Masha the way home, for surely that means he will lose her forever?

One day, Masha finds a huge bear-sized basket under a pile of Bear's dirty clothes and she has an idea.

She bakes some pies and tells Bear, "You need to let me go back to my village. I want to take my parents some pies to eat. I promise I'll come back. Just show me the way."

Bear just laughs and says, "Naw. That not happening. Who would clean all day? This place is mess."

Masha begins to cry and this is more than the Bear can, well, bear.

There's no real reason for him to do as Masha requests except that he cares for her. She's given him a way to help her without having to take the initiative, to be seen, somehow, as weak or vulnerable. Sometimes, that's all any of us need.

"Okay," Bear says. "I take pies to parents. But you stay here."

Masha smiles through her tears and says, "I will, Bear. I will! But I'm going to climb that tall tree outside of your cottage to keep an eye on you. I don't want you eating any of those pies along the way!"

Fine, says Bear, and when he lurches off for a few minutes to scratch his back against a pine tree, Masha hides herself in the picnic basket. Bear picks it up and off he goes, in his plodding, head-swaying bear way.

Every so often, Bear stops and, tempted, begins to open the picnic basket. Each time, Masha, supposedly seeing him from the top of a pine tree, shouts, "Remember, bear—those pies are for my parents! Don't eat them!" Each time, Bear, caught, sighs and continues on without opening the basket.

Or, rather, that's the traditional version. In the original version, too, Bear's English is fine from the beginning of the story. And not much of anything is revealed about Bear's internal reaction to Masha's pie delivery request.

But I didn't like the traditional version very much when I read it. I mean, I loved the description of Bear and the dynamic between Bear and Masha, but the picnic basket didn't make any sense. How dumb does Bear have to be to not know that Masha is in the basket?

No, Bear had to be in the know for any of that to work. In real life, in my version, Bear knows very well that Masha is in the basket. He's still a real bear, even if he's been anthropomorphized a bit. He can smell that Masha's in the basket. As for a bear's hearing and Masha's pathetic attempts to throw her voice, the less said the better—except that her attempts probably endear her to him all the more.

So:

"I see you!" Masha says. "I see you from my tree! Don't eat any of those pies!"

Bear grins a toothy grin. "Uh oh," he says loudly. "Masha must see me from the tall tree. I guess not eat pie."

In the original version, when Bear gets to the village, Masha's parents mistake Bear for the third bear they're always warning their daughter about and chase him away with a shotgun. Bear drops the basket and out jumps Masha, safe and found. Although the folktale doesn't tell us any more about what happens to Bear, I guess he must go back to his messy cottage, sad and lonely and embittered. Maybe one day, lacklorn, he wanders into the deep forest, encounters the third bear, and that's that.

I like Masha better than Bear in this folktale, even though I feel affection for the Bear because I recognize in him attributes of myself and my fellow males. After all, folktales have an odd way of stylizing violence and horrible actions by stripping them of their three-dimensional detail. In a sense, they sometimes function like those cartoons where the mouse hits the cat with a hammer. If it happened in real-life you'd recoil in horror.

Bear is perfectly cute in his role as shambling, inconsiderate ursine. Despite this, at base, Bear is a kidnapper who makes Masha into his work slave, no matter what his motivations. It is very nearly the stereotype of the unequal marriage or the unequal relationship in our culture. Most men have played the role of that bear at some time or another—the guy who doesn't want to appear weak, who needs a civilizing influence, who, at heart, is actually somewhat vulnerable and just needs someone to care about for that to come to the fore. Because, let's face it, Masha isn't Bear's daughter in this folktale. She's not quite his wife, either, thank god, but close enough.

Now, do you want to know what *really* happens to Bear? And what *really* happened at the end of the folktale?

In the *true* version that no one wants to talk about, Bear reaches the village at dusk, when he's able to walk down the streets without fear of discovery.

> Soon, he came to Masha's parents' house. He set the basket down and knocked on the door.
> Slowly, Masha's father opened the door and stared up at the great bear.
> "Who are you?" Masha's father asked. He didn't sound frightened, probably because Masha's mother was hidden behind the door holding a loaded shotgun.
> "I'm Bear," said Bear. "And I bring your daughter home, and pies. She's in basket right there. All in return is you help me more with English."

The parents accept Bear's proposal, once they see their daughter is unharmed. Bear becomes civilized and never returns to the forest. He even runs for mayor. Masha, meanwhile, grows up to become a smart, talented woman who forgives Bear and even becomes his friend—and definitely never gets lost in the forest again.

Bear never gets lost in the woods again, either. That third bear frightens him so much that sometimes his nightmares make it hard for him to breathe.

II.

"The Farmer's Cat"

The second bear isn't any tidier than the first. It's not that he's messy—it's that he carries his mess in his context. For many years, the second bear, whose name is Bear, doesn't realize he's a bear. He doesn't even think he's a cat. He thinks he's a human being. So there's the mess in his context, peeking out.

What am I talking about?

The second bear—Bear—inhabits a trickster tale involving a farmer and trolls. Every winter, the trolls smash down the door to the farmer's house and make themselves at home for a month. They eat all of his food, drink all of the water from his well, guzzle down all of his milk, break his furniture, and fart whenever they feel like it. Their leader, Mobhead, is a monstrous troll with an enormous head. It is so large that it has to be propped up with a head crutch.

The farmer has no choice but to let them trash his farm every year. Until one autumn, a traveling merchant comes by selling orphaned bear cubs. An idea forms in the farmer's head.

The next year, when the trolls come barreling through, they find the new cat.

One of the other trolls—a deformed troll, with a third eye protruding like a tube from its forehead—prodded the ball of fur with one of its big clawed toes. "It's a cat, I think. Just like the last one. Another juicy, lovely cat."

A third troll said, "Save it for later. We've got plenty of time."

The farmer, who had been watching all of this, said to the trolls, "Yes, this is our new cat. But I'd ask that you not eat him. I need him around to catch mice in the summer or when you come back next time, I won't have any grain, and no grain means no beer."

The misshapen troll sneered. "A pretty speech, farmer. But don't worry about the mice. We'll eat them all before we leave."

But the farmer gets Mobhead to swear to leave the cat alone. And Mobhead agrees, smug and secure in the omniscience of his enormous skull.

Now, in the original version of this tale the leader of the trolls doesn't have an enormous head—this is pure extrapolation on my part because I like the idea of head crutches—but the trolls are all such knuckleheads that the idea of them mistaking a bear cub for a kitten isn't that outlandish. The idea of their leader acquiescing to the farmer's request seemed slightly more outlandish. In my version of the tale, Mobhead grants the request, but says:

> Hmmm. I must admit I've grown fond of you, farmer, in the way a wolf is fond of a lamb. And I do want our winter resort to be in good order next time we come charging down out of the frozen north. Therefore, *although I have this nagging feeling I might regret this,* I will let you keep the cat. But everything else we're going to eat, drink, ruin, or fart on. I just want to make that clear.

Some characters in folktales just have a set role to play, regardless of logic or giant heads. A few of these characters, over time, develop a self-awareness about that role. However, that doesn't mean they can ever escape it.

At this point in the folktale, I stopped reading for awhile and I started thinking about that ball of fur curled up in the basket, the second bear, known as Bear. Here is an orphan that has never known its mother. Here is a bear sold to be a cat. Does the farmer raise Bear as a cat? Does the farmer raise Bear as a bear and just present him to the trolls as a cat? Exactly what sense of identity does the Bear have at this point?

The farmer's a sly character in the original folktale. The trolls are colorful and profane. But Bear is the interesting one because Bear has to perform multiple roles. The second bear is a kind of consummate actor—consummate in that he doesn't even know he's an actor.

Because it's pretty clear to me that, even if it's never stated in the folktale, the farmer raises Bear as if he were a human being with a bit of the third bear in him.

So, what happens next?

Two years later, the trolls come by and the farmer's "cat" is all grown up: "There rose a huge shadow with large yellow eyes and rippling muscles under a thick brown pelt. The claws on the shadow were big as carving knives, and the fangs almost as large." Bear savages the trolls, just like a bear.

> Suddenly they heard a growl that turned their blood to ice and set them to gibbering, and at their rear there came the sound of bones being crunched, and as they turned to look and see what was happening, they were met by the sight of some of their friends being hurled at them with great force.

Mobhead is furious with the farmer, but Bear is too much for the trolls. They won't be coming back.

In the traditional version from Norway, that's the end of the story: the farmer triumphant, the trolls vanquished. All is right in the world again. It is the classic trickster tale—one which often presupposes the stupidity of the opposition, unfortunately: a kind of brain-versus-brawn equation that allows for none of the clever complexity of, say, Roadrunner versus Coyote or Holmes versus Moriarty. And, again, we don't find out what happens to Bear afterwards. These bears are always falling off the map.

But when I finished reading, I was still thinking about Bear and his role in the story. If you look at it from Bear's perspective, what a screwed up childhood! He's orphaned. He's sold into the farmer's family under false pretenses. The farmer makes him part of the busy yet stable farm life—"The farmer and his cat would take long walks through the fields, the farmer teaching the cat as much about the farm as possible. And he believed that the cat even appreciated some of it."—but he also has to be a cold-blooded troll-killer when it comes right down to it.

The untold story within this folktale is about our place in the world. Where do we fit in? How much are we shaped by our environment, how much by our heritage? The farmer knows who he is, as do the trolls. They're more boring for it, but I'm sure Bear would prefer to be boring than unsettled and confused, the reader's boredom level rarely a concern of fictional characters. Bear is, in a sense, the classic teenager—neither fish nor fowl; capable of restraint and unbridled passion in almost the same instant.

So how does this folktale *really* end? How can it end, except with uncertainty?

Once inside, the farmer and the bear laughed.

"Thanks, Mob-Eater," the farmer said. "You looked really fierce."

The bear huffed a deep bear belly laugh, sitting back on its haunches in a huge comfy chair the farmer had made for him.

"I am really fierce, father," the bear said. "But you should have let me chase them. I don't like the taste of troll all that much, but, oh, I do love to chase them."

"Maybe next year," the farmer said. "Maybe next year. But for now, we have chores to do. I need to teach you to milk the cows, for one thing."

"But I hate to milk the cows," the bear said. "You know that."

"Yes, but you still need to know how to do it, son."

"Very well. If you say so."

They waited for a few minutes until the trolls were out of sight, and then they went outside and started doing the farm chores for the day.

Soon, the farmer thought, his wife and children would come home, and everything would be as it was before. Except that now they had a huge talking bear living in their house.

Sometimes folktales didn't end quite the way you thought they would. But they *did* end.

At least, this is the way *I* think the folktale should end. With Bear blithely unaware of the contradiction between third-bear bloodthirsty-ness and human boy frustration with chores. With the farmer realizing that the solution to one problem may have created another, altogether more deadly and personal problem.

Because, ultimately, the second bear is still a wild animal, not a human being at all.

III.

"The Third Bear"

The third bear is problematic. It doesn't think of itself as a bear. It doesn't want to be in this essay. The third bear is always waiting to be written so he can leap out and devour. He lives in the deepest of deep forest. He has no patience with human folktales. He lives rough and is all animal. No taint of human in this bear. He has no name, not even "Bear." He does sometimes exist at the edges of other folktales that are not about him at all—spore-dropping in the dark part of the woods; the sense of menace that forms the backdrop to some more brightly lit tale. You can just see him in the dark recesses of the foliage in the paintings of Rousseau. This is the bear Masha's parents warned her about. This is the bear that existed in the crunch of bone and spurt of blood when the second bear was slaughtering trolls.

But this is an essay about folktales, so let me put the third bear in that context.

Once upon a time...
One terrible stormy night...
There once was a...
Three bears once...

Once, there lived a creature that might have been a bear. This "bear" came to the forest near the village and soon anyone who used the forest trail, day or night, disappeared, carried off to the creature's lair. By the time even large convoys went through the forest, they would discover two or three of their number missing. A straggling horseman, his mount cantering along, just bloodstains and bits of skin sticking to the saddle. A cobbler gone but for a blood-soaked hat.

The villagers were distraught. Without using the trail through the forest, they couldn't bring in food from the farmers on the other side. Without that trail, they couldn't bring their goods to market. They were stuck in a nightmare.

Slowly, they realized that they couldn't wait for the third bear to devour them all. They had to strike back.

The village's strongest man, Clem, a blacksmith, volunteered to fight the beast. He had arms like most people's thighs. His skin was tough from years of being exposed to flame. With his full black beard he almost looked like a bear himself.

"I'll go, and I'll go willingly," he told the village elders. "I've not met the beast I couldn't best. I'll squeeze the 'a' out of him." And he laughed, for he had a passable sense of humor, although the village elders chose to ignore it.

Fitted in chain mail and leather armor, carrying an old sword some knight had once left by mistake in the village, Clem set forth in search of the third bear.

He left the path almost immediately, wandered through the underbrush to the heart of the forest, where the trees grew so black and thick that the only glimmer of light came reflected from water glistening on leaves. The smell in that place carried a hint of offal, so he figured he was close.

Clem had spent so much time beating things into shape that he had not developed a sense of fear, for he had never been beaten. But the smell in his nostrils did make him uneasy.

Clutching his sword, he came upon a hill and a cave inside. From within the cave, a green flame beckoned.

A lesser man might have turned back, but not Clem. He didn't have the sense God gave a donkey. Into the cave he went.

Inside, he found the third bear. And behind the third bear, arranged around the walls of the cave, the heads of the third bear's victims. The heads had been painstakingly painted and mounted on stands. They were all in various states of decay.

Many bodies lay stacked neatly in the back of the cave. Some of them had been mutilated. All of them had been defiled in some way. The wavery green light came from a candle the third bear had placed in the back of the cave, to display his handiwork. The smell was so horrible, Clem had to put a hand over his mouth. And as he took it all in, the methodical nature of it, the fact that the third bear had, in fact, not eaten hardly any of his victims, he found something inside of him tearing and then breaking.

"I...," he said, and looked into the eyes of the third bear. "I...."

Clem stood there, frozen, as the third bear disemboweled him and tore his head from his shoulders.

The third bear had no use for heroes. Except, possibly, as part of a pattern of heads.

A month later. Clem's head was found on the trail in the forest. Apparently, it hadn't fit the pattern. By then, four or five more people had been killed, one on the outskirts of the village. The situation had become desperate. Several villagers had risked leaving, and some of them had even made it through. But fear kept most of them in the village, locked into a kind of desperate fatalism that made their eyes hollow as they stared into some unknowable distance.

Over time, the village sent four or five of its strongest and most clever men and women to fight the third bear.

One, before the end, said to the third bear, "I think you were misunderstood as a child."

Another said, before fear clotted her windpipe, "You just need love."

A third, even as he watched his intestines slide out of his body, said, "Surely there is something we can do to appease you?"

The third bear said nothing. He had no snappy comebacks. No pithy sayings. No wisdom. His conversation was through his work, and he said what he wanted to say very eloquently in that regard.

The villagers became ritualistic and primitive and listless. They feared the forest so much that they ate berries and branches at the outskirts of their homes and never hunted wild game. Their skin became ever more pale and they stopped washing themselves. They believed the words of madmen and adopted strange customs. They stopped wearing clothes. They would defecate in the street. At some point, they lost sight of reason entirely and sacrificed virgins to the third bear. They took to mutilating their bodies, thinking that this is what the third bear wanted them to do. Some few in whom reason persisted had to be held down and mutilated by others. A few, during the winter, cannibalized those who froze to death, and others who had not died almost wished they had.

By the time the third bear finished his pattern and moved on, the remaining villagers had all become no different than him.

And they all lived happily ever after.

***

There are always carious eyes peering out from the forest in a certain kind of folktale. Something hidden in the middle distance. Readers often think they are wolf eyes. But they are not the eyes of wolves. They are the eyes of the third bear. Peering from darkness into darkness.

The original folktales often served as literal warnings against wolves, bears, and other threats prevalent in a pre-industrial world. When the folktales became civilized, they developed more refined subtexts about human predators or dangerous situations. They began to impart advice, in a sense, that had to be extracted from that subtext. We've become quite adroit at infusing and extracting this subtext as writers and readers. We add postmodern twists to our folktales—updating them for what we feel the modern world needs from them. In the process, we ironically enough sometimes make them more distant and less visceral than they need to be to work for us in the modern world.

But the smell of the third bear gives him away. It's the smell of piss and blood and shit and bubbles of saliva and of half-eaten food. It's what we forget is always with us no matter now big our cities get, how advanced our civilization. To say the third bear is all bear is to miss the point. To say that the third bear needs no symbolism but is simply himself is also to miss the point.

Sometimes I think modern fairy tales should be horror tales, that to encompass all of the ferocity and animal intensity at the core of the past century's excesses, we need a little bit of the third bear in everything we write.

But, at the very least, when we re-invent our folktales, we need to acknowledge the third bear, even if only by his absence.

Sometimes the author has no recourse. Sometimes, there is nothing I can do.

The Language of Defeat
Clarkesworld Magazine, 2008

I have heard, more times than I care to admit, what I call the language of defeat. I've heard it on panels and on blogs, at genre conventions, at books festivals, and at academic conferences over the past decade.

This language of defeat has to do with accepting a paradigm of the fiction world as "us" versus "them," of "mainstream" versus "genre." I use quote marks around "genre" and "mainstream" because I do not believe these terms are as monolithic or as meaningful in practice as we think of them in theory. The "mainstream" and "genre," if we must subdivide in this way, are both various, rich, and fecund traditions, with many strands and diverse lineages. (In many cases, the two intertwine in such an incestuous way that separating them from each other is a job for a trained genealogist.)

In most cases using this kind of language leads to a bemoaning of the lack of acceptance by the "literary mainstream." It also leads to a certain resentment on the part of "genre" writers, especially centered on the idea that some "mainstream" writers get away with writing "genre" books. We've seen this attitude a lot lately—focused on writers like Margaret Atwood for her *Onyx & Crake*, Jeanette Winterson for *The Stone Gods*, Cormac McCarthy to a lesser extent for *The Road*, and even the work of Jonathan Lethem in a general way, once accused of abandoning his "genre" roots. The negative attitudes toward these books and authors have three layers or premises: (1) that it is somehow inherently wrong and *rude* for these writers to write in what is so clearly a "genre" milieu (without asking first?), (2) that these authors' cliché comments disavowing their books as "Science Fiction" or "Fantasy" somehow reflect negatively on the quality of the actual texts, and (3) that these forays into forbidden territory are written with no regard for or knowledge of "genre" predecessors.

All of these assumptions tie into the language of defeat because they constitute a kind of wall or barrier in people's minds to acceptance of the work *as it exists on the page*. And what I mean by this being the language of defeat is that it pre-loads any discussion to appear self-pitying and shrill, weighted down with envy. It also severs the link of responsibility, in that we are no longer talking about individuals or individual institutions, individual gatekeepers, but instead a shadowy *them*—an enemy without a face, as amorphous as mist.

The language of defeat also requires participants to wade through decades of grudges, jealousies, and insecurities passed down through the generations in the form of received ideas, anecdotes, and assumptions that constitute genre's least useful heirloom.

In fiction, received ideas (which manifest as cliché) are death, but we seem unable to think except in terms of generalizations when it comes to the frustrations and concerns of the writing life. It is much easier to take on the language and ideas of the supposed oppressor and exist in a world where our failures are someone else's fault, and where if only the roadblocks were removed, the ivory towers razed, the truculent, generic, nameless gatekeepers executed, and their heads put on spikes, everyone would get their proper due.

This then is the language of defeat, the acceptance of one's status as victim whilst mouthing the words of dead people from panels past—even being willing to channel the syntax of our defeat, as if we were all pessimistic travelers from the past.

I would like to see a few things change in the future. I would like to see less hyperbole and angst about so-called "mainstream" forays into the "ghetto" of genre. I would like to see all writers make a better effort to see the work of their fellows with eyes unfettered by received ideas as conveyed through whatever label has been slapped on a particular book or author. If we wrote fiction the way we talk about genre and mainstream most of the time, we would all be *hacks*, our prose full of the most crass and belabored clichés. Yet we persist in outdated, dangerous generalizations, and allow them to color our perceptions of reality. We refuse to engage with the individual in front of us, to communicate, and instead create badly-made fictions about them.

I remember clearly one panel at a Slipstream conference in Georgia that included the iconic SF figure of Bruce Sterling and first novelist Mary Doria Russell, who had written *The Sparrow*, a SF book marketed to the mainstream. Sterling dismissed Russell's legitimacy throughout the panel, mostly because of a sense of profound insecurity. This work was not from genre, therefore it was not genre. Later, Russell revealed that her chief mentor and first reader had been the famous *Analog* magazine editor Stanley Schmidt, who had commented on several drafts.

On another panel, I remember genre writers bemoaning their inability to sell fiction to the prestigious literary magazines—the literary world was ignoring them. Someone asked them how often they submitted to literary magazines. After some hemming and hawing, they all admitted that they rarely submitted to such publications. Later on, one even admitted that he wouldn't submit to most literary magazines because genre magazines paid better.

So, in short, the literary world was thwarting them from achieving wider success by not sneaking into their homes, figuring out their computer passwords, and checking out the drafts on their hard drives.

There are similar stupidities perpetrated on the mainstream side of things. For example, when a reviewer pitched a review of my novel *Shriek: An Afterword* to a prestigious literary journal, the answer was "why would we want to promote some genre novel?" The review was published, but only after the reviewer was forced to add language amounting to "even though this is genre, it's worth your time." But, again, this was *one* publication, one editor, and to extrapolate from that single point of anecdotal contact some larger commandment applying to some mythical "literary mainstream" constitutes a form of madness.

As for equivalent jealousies on the "mainstream" side, your average "literary" writer, even some Pulitzer Prize winners, might sell, at best, three or four thousand copies and look across the aisle enviously at a mid-list SF writer selling fifteen thousand copies, with a correspondingly higher advance. They—and already you can see how I enter into the dangerous territory of generalities just by using a pronoun—can also be envious of the ease with which much genre material makes the transition into pop culture, and into media such as movies, comics, and television.

The fact is, we all have our wounds, our defeats, our Waterloos. We all look up ahead at some person or group that seems to be doing better than us in some way. The trouble occurs when we perpetuate cliché and stereotype and received ideas as if they were immutable truth, or commonsense, or even, god forbid, wisdom.

Do you know why? Because when enough people keep saying something, the weight of those words becomes a kind of *perceptional or operational reality*, and not only do we lose opportunities to build something unique and fresh, but we also make the world a duller, less interesting place. We deny the true complexity of the world, and our place in it.

But perhaps just as importantly, the continual perpetual motion machine of this kind of approach wastes our time and saps our energy. It is a quintessentially negative message that moves the average reader, not versed in the stylized symbolism of the ghetto, to two main reactions: pity for the downtrodden and a desire to help the poor victim do better, usually with lots of helpful suggestions that have been trotted out and tried a thousand times before. (Besides, the panelists tackling such questions at conventions often don't really want answers—they just want to wallow in the lovely misery of being victims.)

When that happens, the messenger and the receiver of the message become trapped in the old paradigm. Instead of a genuine and articulate discussion that is, as much as possible, about the books or authors being examined, we enter into an argument that is mostly about defenses, battlements, territorialism, and pettiness.

It is easy to fall into cynicism and become fatalistic. Sometimes, there are perfectly honest catalysts that create an outlook of this kind. But that doesn't mean we have to live in that place, or make other people live there.

An Anvil Is Not an Artichoke
Bookslut, 2006

For the past few months, I've been absorbing the comics and graphic novel scene in a much more systematic way than ever before, and it's gotten me to thinking about quite a few issues.

One of the main questions I keep going back to is: Why do many reviewers and people associated with comics feel the need to equate *graphic novels* and *novels* when they're different creatures? This phenomenon is not necessarily found only in the comics subculture. For an example close to home, note the Bookslut guest blogger who called *The Wire* HBO series her favorite novel of the year. No, *The Wire* is her favorite *television program* of the year, although I understand at least one of the points she's trying to make. In her lexicon, a novel is automatically a superior art form. To love something as much as she loves *The Wire* is to wish for it the legitimacy that the novel form automatically possesses. The implication is that television usually is a debased form and that the complexity of *The Wire* must, therefore, be *something else*. And I think this is one of the reasons some people in the comics field want, sometimes with seeming desperation, to have their works or the work they love compared to "literature." A sense of wanting to be taken seriously pervades comics as pungently as it pervades the field I come from, fantasy and horror fiction.

However, in equating novels and graphic novels, an essential point about taxonomy is being missed. As soon as a proactive graphic element exists as part of the overall experience of reading and viewing—a graphic element that isn't purely illustrative in purpose, i.e., not merely a reaction to a text that does not need art for the integrity of its form—the experience becomes different from that of reading a novel. It's almost like calling the sky blue to point this out, but the difference is that when reading a novel, the images, that most central anchor of the reader's experience—be they characters, objects, settings, or whatever—are not immutable. The reader creates those images in his or her mind. That is the essential interconnectivity of the novel—that the reader must do much more of a particular kind of work, generally, than when viewing a sculpture or a painting or comic. Description in a novel is not a closed system. You can never describe something thoroughly enough for two different readers to create the exact same set of images in their heads. This is a very important distinction—it speaks to the heart of why we read novels even though we have plenty of visual media to choose from.

Sculptures, paintings, and comics have their own reading or viewing protocols that are just as complex but in their essential nature *different*. For example, although a novel can play with time and space, it cannot do it in quite the lithe way as a graphic novel or comic. (I can't, for example, see any way to gracefully replicate Rebecca Dart's multi-thread panel approach in *RabbitHead* in novel form.) Graphic novels allow for juxtapositions that would be cumbersome in novel form. They allow for that wonderful confluence of image and word (if words are involved) in which each carries its own very particular weight, with image playing off of word, word playing off of image. The difference between the two forms may not interest the general reader who picks up a graphic novel or novel and just wants to read an entertaining story, and yet that difference still exists, regardless. Neither form is superior to the other, but they are undeniably *not the same thing*.

Which brings me to one of the bigger news stories in the comics field last year: *American Born Chinese* by Gene Luen Yang (First Second) was a National Book Award finalist in the Young People's Literature category. Dynamic, direct, and complex, *American Born Chinese* is a great graphic novel. That kind of quality definitely should be recognized, and many people in the comics field seemed to feel vindicated by its inclusion.

But let's look at what actually happened in terms of process. A couple of judges, or maybe even three, loved this particular graphic novel. Maybe those judges looked at one or two or even three dozen other graphic novels, but at best I can't imagine they performed anything other than a random, ad hoc analysis of the best work coming out of the graphic novel field in reaching their assessment.

Worse, the judges didn't nominate any graphic novels in the adult category. Does this mean that there wasn't a single adult graphic novel the equal of the best adult novels published in 2006? Absolutely not. What it means is that no systematic review occurred because such a review was outside of the judges' brief with regard to the categories. The National Book Award is set up to reward fiction, nonfiction, poetry, etc. That a judge or two or even three managed to shoehorn *American Born Chinese* into a finalist slot in one category means only that, in 2006, *American Born Chinese* was shoehorned into a finalist slot in the young adult category. Which is to say, the phenomenon is like snow in Tallahassee, Florida, where I live: it occurs about every decade for a few minutes, and then it's gone again until the next random occurrence. That's not a milestone. That's not a sign of graphic novels being taken seriously. That's the subjective interpretation of a category that was not meant to contain graphic novels.

If the National Book Award wants to be inclusive of graphic novels, it should create a separate category and acknowledge the art form as a vibrant and unique creative endeavor. Then, too, you would see systematic discussion and consideration of all graphic novels in the context of the award, not just one or two bright baubles alighted upon by some magpie of a judge.

I'm not one of those cultural elitists outraged that a graphic novel was named a finalist in a novel category. As should be clear, I love graphic novels and I love novels. But every art form must reach its maturity and find its respect by understanding and celebrating that which makes it unique, not by stressing similarities by association or by touting ad hoc exceptions. (For this reason, I love the fact that a large publishing company thinks comics are important enough to do a *Best American Comics* series, or that Yale University Press would want to do editor Ivan Brunetti's survey of comics in a handsome hardcover.)

Put another way, can you imagine a *novel* being a finalist for the Eisner Award? Absurd, right? And why? Because a novel is a not a comic, is not a graphic novel, in the same way that an artichoke is not a pear, and a pear is not an ostrich, and an ostrich is not an anvil.

Nor would most people want their pear to be an ostrich. Nor think less of either for being pear not ostrich, ostrich not pear.

The Romantic Underground
(An Exploration of a Non-Existent and Self-Denying Non-Movement)
Nebula Awards Showcase 2005

Although the phrase "the romantic underground" is often attributed to Shelley and his minor poem "The Assignation of Lapels" (1819), the Romantic Underground actually began as an offshoot of the Decadent Movement in France.[1] The first text identified with the Romantic Underground was Gustave Flaubert's *The Temptation of St. Anthony* (1874), since claimed by the Symbolists.

Flaubert vehemently denied that his book was a Romantic Underground text; in fact, he denied the existence of the movement altogether. This has been a recurring refrain in the development of the Romantic Underground: every author identified as an adherent of the movement has denied this fact. No text has long remained part of the Romantic Underground because no living author has allowed it to for very long. (In some cases, another movement has made a better case in claiming a particular text, as well.)

Some of the authors "outed" as "Romantic Underground-nistas" in those early years included Remy de Gourmont, Oscar Wilde, August Strindberg, Emile Zola, Alfred Kubin, Andre Breton, and Ronald Firbank. Some have even claimed that Breton himself formed the surrealists as an offshoot of the Romantic Underground, not as a reaction to Dada, Futurism, and the proto-magic realists.

Regardless, the enduring properties of the Romantic Underground remain a lack of membership by those authors cited and a general lack of identifying characteristics. At first, reading between the lines of critical texts from the period—some from the infamous *Yellow Book*—the Romantic Underground apparently formed a "loose umbrella" around certain authors, attempting to provide a critical and imaginative landscape in which creativity could have free,

---

[1] The author is unable to confirm or deny whether any actual "RU" research has been done for this essay.

albeit vague, reign. Authors, being skittish at best, most apparently saw the umbrella as more of a gaping maw and escaped without their names ever being connected to rumors of a vast but secret literary organization dedicated to the antithesis of anything popular, tidy, or, indeed, logical.

Chroniclers of the Romantic Underground lost track of it during the 1920s and most of the 1930s, when the group may have decided to form "literary guerilla cells of single individuals, with no communication between any two cells." It is supposed that Jorge Luis Borges joined the movement in the 1940s, but only a reference to "the underground romantic with his hopeless beret" in his short story "The Immortal" (1962) suggests any active participation. Fellow South Americans Pablo Neruda and Gabriel Garcia Marquez may have joined the movement in the 1960s and 1970s, but, again, both deny the existence of the movement and any participation in it—thus seeming to substantiate the rumors, since this behavior is all too indicative of Romantic Underground members.

During the science fiction New Wave movement of the 1960s, the Romantic Underground again came to the fore, with many literary critics, including Brian Stableford and Colin Wilson, claiming that the New Wave was nothing more or less than an especially visible cell of the Romantic Underground. *New Worlds* contributor Rachel Pollack, however, called this "bullshit" at the time, while *NW* editor Michael Moorcock later wrote in his book *Wizardry and Wild Romance* (1986) that "there was nothing romantic or underground about the New Wave. We had no time for sentimental tripe nor did we want to remain part of some invisible subculture. We were very much in the public eye."[2]

In the 1980s, writers such as Rikki Ducornet, Angela Carter, Edward Whittemore, and Alasdair Gray all denied being part of the Romantic Underground movement. At this point, noted critic John Clute, in a footnote to a review of Iain M. Banks' Culture novel *Consider Phlebas* (*Interzone*, 1987), wrote "The sole criteria of the so-called Romantic Underground movement?

---

[2] However, Moorcock added almost a decade later, "I refer you to Capek's subtle RUR (Romantic Underground Revival) in which he introduced the word 'robot' to the world. Also the 'Apocalypse' movement of the 30s and 40s. The Welsh 'Coven of 12' which included Henry Treece, Ruthven Todd, Dylan Thomas, and was connected to the so-called Wenlock Coven of which Alan Garner was probably the most prominent member. All have equally denied the existence of the RU while exhibiting many familiar characteristics of membership. 'RU RU if so Y ?' as the familiar text message reads."

The conscription of idiosyncratic writers dragged without their consent to the renunciation block, where they proceed to deny entrapment in anything as clandestine and formless."

In this respect, the Romantic Underground seems to mirror the Slipstream list put forth by Texas technophile Bruce Sterling.[3] Sterling published his list in a magazine called *SF Eye* (July 1989). For several years, publishers, some writers, and fewer readers mouthed the word "slipstream" whenever confronted by any text that did not fit a tidy definition of "genre fiction." It seems clear today that Sterling, depending on his mood, meant his term "slipstream" more as a joke or the approximation of a joke, given the Catholic qualities of the list. In many respects, Sterling may thus be considered an agent of chaos—or, perhaps, a Romantic Underground mole ordered by the RU elites to create misdirection and mischief, all with the purpose of directing attention away from the RU. Sterling's repeated denial of this accusation only makes his actions all the more suspicious.

Still, the ultimate effect of Sterling's coined term—competition from a movement just as ill-defined, composed of writers who refused to call their work "Slipstream" in the same way earlier generations refuted "Romantic Underground"—appears to have irritated the invisible elites of the RU's command and control. For many years, throughout the 1990s, in fact, no further word was heard from the Romantic Underground.

For example, the Splatterpunk movement raised not a single hackle in the form of an implied reference to the Romantic Underground or even a nonconsecutive footnote number in a *New York Review of SF* article (which might have suggested the suppression of a reference to the Romantic Underground). It is possible, of course, that the blood-and-alcohol-soaked Splatterpunks—with a "no limits" slogan that apparently meant "no limits to the badly-written material we'll champion"—were not seen as a threat by the "shadow cabinet" (as I have come to think of the Romantic Movement's hidden elites).

However, in this new century, hints of the Romantic Movement have again come into the light—a glimmer of an old coin at the bottom of a fountain

---

3 Sterling was also part of a cheerfully dysfunctional literary movement called "cyberpunk" that falls outside of the scope of this essay. All that survives of this movement today is the pairing of advanced technology and dark sunglasses with badly woven sweaters, as exemplified by the Matrix movies.

pool, the suggestion of a shadow watching from a vine-entangled forest. More specifically, the Interstitial Movement, which has taken up the task of defining the indefinable, appears to have some of the characteristics of the Romantic Underground movement. Could the Interstitial Movement be a new and subversive way of leveraging the Romantic Underground into the public eye while leaving its shadow cabinet once again unknown?

At first glance, it would appear that this could be the case. Certainly the Interstitial Movement, much like the Romantic Underground movement in the 1890s, believes in forming an "umbrella" for a motley assortment of idiosyncratic writers, most of whom have nothing in common, some of whom are not in fact interstitial at all, and many of whom do not identify themselves as interstitial, even though "pegged" as such by the Interstitial Arts Foundation.[4] This would be a typical Romantic Underground tactic. Similarly, the Interstitial strategy of continuing to insist that "we are not a movement" would appear to mirror the Romantic Underground's propensity for general denial.

However, a closer examination of the Interstitial reveals too many clashes with the presumed agenda of the Romantic Underground. First of all, no Romantic Underground writer—or Surrealist writer, for that matter—would tolerate for one moment the presence of so many writers of an easily-definable nature; writers whose work is identifiable as belonging to one genre and, while often excellent, does not in fact "cross boundaries" (the clarion call of the Interstitial). Nor do the Interstitial writers graze far from the pastures of genre itself, whereas the Romantic Underground has always included members of the literary mainstream who could smugly and steadfastly deny their involvement in the movement.

Finally, it would take any Romantic Underground writer every bit of self-control he or she possessed to say, definitively, "I am an Interstitial writer," since the very essence/core of a Romantic Underground writer cries out for disassociation with any formal group of any kind. And yet, most "Interstitial" writers blithely bleat out their allegiance at the slightest provocation, or wear

---

4 Certainly, the IAF's inclusion of a contingent of mythopoetic writers raises questions. Can a group with its own National Public Radio outlet, pop culture guru (Joseph Campbell), and a convention sponsored by Krispy Kreme Donuts really be considered to "cross borders" in an edgy way?

bright buttons proclaiming this fact. (Most damning, however, may be a certain lack of cohesion within the Interstitial Arts Foundation, completely at odds with the almost sinister, yet beautiful, organization and knack for secrecy the Romantic Underground movement has demonstrated for over one hundred years.)

Another movement put forward in recent years comes from the United Kingdom—the New Weird, espoused by China Miéville and, to some extent, M. John Harrison. An oddity in the brave new world of computers and the Internet, the New Weird is unaffected by modern communication and modern "online communities," for, as has been repeatedly stated, this movement is a uniquely *British* phenomenon.[5] It cannot be found elsewhere; it's something in the soil, akin to the inability in Florida to grow anything but grapes for the sweetest of wines.

The New Weird also preaches a return to the pre-postmodern world. This is an earnest world in which irony does not exist, a world in which John Barth and his ilk took up carpentry rather than writing—building houses with three roofs and twelve balconies—Barth's hugely idiosyncratic novels consigned to the trashcan of *might have been*. In this world, ironically enough, the *Argentine* writer Jorge Luis Borges has often been heralded as the godfather, since his work predates the formal postmodern experimentation that was based in part on his stories.

Although the irony inherent in a movement that abhors irony indicates the presence of individual RU cells, the New Weird does not represent the new clandestine rise of the Romantic Underground. For one thing, the Romantic Underground would never insist on its members hailing from one particular country or group of countries. This would be too limiting to an international organization that relies on literally thousands of writer-members from over one hundred nations to maintain the strict secrecy that allows it to continue to deny that it has ever existed.

Further, no Romantic Underground writer would ever deny him or herself the right to employ postmodern technique where appropriate. Would an artist be taken seriously if he or she said that a particular type of brush, a particular color of paint, a particular thickness of canvas would never again be used in the service of art? As a very secret self-denying organization, the Romantic Underground <u>does not have the</u> luxury of denying itself every tool at its disposal.

5 Except when it's not.

Therefore, I reluctantly tip my hat to the cleverness of the Romantic Underground movement. It appears once again to have relegated itself to single-author cells, none of which are in communication with any other, similar cells. Although writers such as Angela Carter, Edward Whittemore, and Vladimir Nabokov, as well as such contemporary authors as Edward Carey, Peter Carey, A.S. Byatt, Thomas Pynchon, Martin Amis, Ursula K. LeGuin, Jack Dann, M. John Harrison (a double-agent), Kelly Link (another double-agent, working for both the Interstitial and RU), Paul Di Filippo, Zoran Zivkovic, Gene Wolfe, Jeffrey Ford, K.J. Bishop, Liz Williams, Nalo Hopkinson, Michael Cisco, Stepan Chapman, Rhys Hughes, Ian R. MacLeod, and myself have at one time or another been associated with the Romantic Underground movement—depending on the tone or theme or style of a particular book—none of us has ever admitted belonging to such a movement (either while living or after death). The Romantic Underground, it would appear, retains its crafty self-denying ability even one hundred years after its non-formation and the non-creation of its non-rules. In short, dear reader, the Romantic Underground, like many so-called movements, *does not exist*.[6]

---

[6] That said, it is worth noting the recent discovery of a new journal entry by Angela Carter. This entry may finally cut through the fog of denials to the core of the Romantic Underground movement. In the text, Carter scrawled a list of points that seem uncannily like the recipe for the perfect literary movement. Could this be the manifesto of the Romantic Underground-nistas? It reads as follows:

1 - It should focus on individual works.
2 - It should include no works that do not fit its manifesto or mission statement.
3 - It should appeal to both the heart and the head, inciting passion and thought in equal measure.
4 - It should be blind to, but inclusive of, gender, race, and nationality.
5 - It should separate commerce from art and only operate at the level of art.
6 - It should encourage creativity and experimentation.
7 - It should partake equally of high and low culture.
8 - It should partake equally of high and low literature.
9 - It should do no harm to any writer.
10 - It should be both humble and arrogant, as appropriate.
11 - It should deny its own existence at all times.
12 - It should exist in the soul and spirit, heart and brain, of one individual writer at a time.
13 - It should express the bittersweet confluence of seriousness and humor, honesty and deception, that we all experience in life.

Politics in Fantasy
Emerald City, 2006

Politics is as personal as religion. Current events should have an impact on writers and resonate in their fiction. Activism has a place in the writing of fantasy fiction. Characters, plots, story structures all benefit from a careful consideration of, and dialogue with, the political world.

Two decades ago, I would have been horrified by statements like these—statements I now believe in deeply. In my teens and early twenties, I very much saw fiction as Art with a capital "A," and Art was above the fray of the everyday, and, therefore, politics. I didn't yet see that the Surrealists' statement of "convulsive beauty in the service of liberty" was a political call-to-arms.

At the same time, however, my *fiction* conflicted with my conscious thoughts about writing. On a subconscious level, on the level of inspiration, politics and the consequences of political decisions entered my fiction on a regular basis. I wrote about Latin American dictatorships and the legacy of the Conquistadors. I wrote about the erosion of personal liberties. I wrote about the impact of war on individuals and groups. I wrote about the effects of colonialism.

My short fiction was awash in politics and political positions. Sometimes it was so embedded that to cut it out of a story would have required killing the story. Sometimes it was superficial. Sometimes it was probably too didactic.

I think this last possibility—that the fiction could become too preachy—made me believe that writing as Art should somehow be separate from the current world, and therefore the messiness of politics. Fiction should come out of character and situation. Anything from the ordinary day-to-day should be included solely in the form of specific detail. The way light struck a window frame. The particular lilt to a woman's speech. The smell of coffee curling out from a sidewalk café.

I believe this position on fiction explains why many of my stories had a stylized quality. I almost thought of them as paintings: beautiful but static, emblematic and symbolic, solemn and visionary, the passion grounded in the so-called "universal," which had no place for the temporal.

Writing about my imaginary city of Ambergris changed all of that. As a place, it had to encompass nitty-gritty detail at street level. It forced me to think about politics on all sorts of levels. A city can't remain stylized and be real—that would be like denying oxygen to someone, or depicting everyone in mid-step, forever frozen. A city also can't be above politics because politics forms its beating heart—its institutions, its government, and the personal politics of its individual citizens, their personal interactions.

I remember that Brian Stableford once said of Angela Carter that her work had risked sliding into mere rote symbolism before its exploration of gender politics became wedded to a fantasy setting. She risked not allowing enough air into her work for readers to breathe.

For me, the secondary world fantasy of Ambergris let more of the real, unstylized world into my writing—and that meant those echoes of the real world that concerned politics as well. I found myself thinking about how conflict arises on a micro and macro level. How do ruling elites come into being? How do they stay in power? What are the consequences of colonialism and pogrom on both the oppressor and the oppressed? Who fills a power vacuum when it occurs, and why?

In Ambergris, merchant clans serve as stand-ins for the corporations of our world. A merchant oligarchy more or less rules Ambergris, aided by a hodge podge of revered artists and other creative people. These are the people who lend legitimacy to or withhold it from the rulers.

Of course, there is also a strong vein of anarchy running through Ambergris, a sense that the city could descend into chaos at a moment's notice, even if the annual festival serves as a release of violence that helps stave off every-day anarchy.

Is this much different than the world I live in as an American? I don't think so. We have our own aggression-relief festivals in the form of sports events, for example. And, when an event like Hurricane Katrina occurs, or election irregularities, or, as happened in Florida recently, rival state agencies have an armed stand-off over the fate of a person in a vegetative state, we begin to realize that we are much closer to the edge than we would like to think, anesthetized as we are by our technophiliac gadgets and our selfish pursuit of creature comforts.

Not only are we closer to the total or partial breakdown of civilization than we think we are, we do not understand how close we exist to potential atrocity. In Ambergris, pogrom and counter-pogrom occur as the result of greed, ignorance, and fear. The gray caps, a native people driven underground by the founders of the city, exist in that dynamic shared by every group of oppressors and the oppressed. (The plot of such events varies in its details—whether in Rwanda or the Balkans, Cambodia or Germany—but the results are the same: a mass psychosis and individual indifference to suffering that leads to mass bloodshed.)

But "politics" in fiction is not just about using a backdrop of war or atrocity or city dynamics at the macro level to explore questions that affect us in a longer-term, broad way. It is also about understanding that *all* people are political in some way, even those who seem apathetic, because politics is about gender, society, and culture. Every aspect of our lives is in some way political. So if we don't, at some point during our writing, think about this consciously—if we simply trust our instincts as writers—we may unintentionally preserve cliché, stereotype, and prejudice.

Carol Bly, in her amazing writing book *The Passionate, Accurate Story*, makes a compelling case for the inclusion of the political—and thus real-world ethical, moral issues—in the creation of character. She gives the example of a character who happens to be an executive for a company that produces a harmful product or whose factories pollute the environment. The story's emphasis may have nothing to do with the character's job, but it is still incumbent on the writer to ask, *What is the character's relationship to his or her job? Does the character think about the ethics of supporting harm to others, even if indirectly? What are the character's politics, and how do they reflect or not reflect the character's actual actions? How does the character justify both personal and political decisions?*

Asking such questions is part of creating fully rounded characters. A character's politics—public and private—may be inconsistent or, again, irrelevant to the main story being told, but the writer still needs to think about such issues.

The questions still need to be part of the conversation the writer has with him or herself about the character.

When writing about characters in Ambergris, I try to position them in relation to events such as the Silence (when 25,000 people disappeared from the city, possibly because of the gray caps), or a war between rival political groups the Reds and the Greens, or on how they feel about the merchant-ruler Hoegbotton & Sons. Not because all of these thoughts will make it onto the page as part of character, but because somehow even just considering them rounds out the character, influences other things about the character that do make it onto the page.

Just as every day we make potentially dozens of small decisions that reflect our thought or lack of thought about the world around us, so too does a fictional character of any weight exist in a world of such daily decisions, such thoughts. Otherwise, the character becomes less than real. Even small decisions have consequences in the real world, because we live in a world where politics matter, where politics can get you killed or knighted, often for the same action in a different context.

As part of the whole of a character, these types of attributes, internalized, expressed at the most basic level can make the difference between good fiction and great fiction, but, also, perhaps as importantly, the difference between fiction that is relevant and fiction that is not.

But is it important for fiction to be "relevant"? Does it affect what we think of as "classic" fiction fifty years from now? Relevance may, in certain types of fiction, create a kind of "temporally regional" form of literature—fiction that contains outdated references to issues no longer of consequence in the future, consigning a novel or story to that gray, half-lit, half-dark world where fiction is primarily read for its historical importance.

However, there is at least one area of fiction in which the idea of relevance today leading to potential anachronism tomorrow doesn't have as much truth to it: that loose grouping of types of settings or a way of seeing the world often labeled "fantasy," and, in particular, secondary world fantasy.

Seen through the mirror of a fantasy setting that allows the real world to be reflected in it, a writer can perhaps more easily be relevant—in the short term—without running the risk of becoming dated in the long term.

In my new novel, *Shriek: An Afterword*, I wrote several war sequences during the most horrifying phases of the Iraq War and the conflict in Afghanistan. Are those scenes making a comment on U.S. involvement in the Middle East? No. Any aspects of those events become fictionalized and conflated with a number of other wars, until the specific detail I've gleaned from my nonfiction reading and television viewing is subsumed by the creative process into something that is both timely in one sense and timeless in another. Thus the current war becomes a catalyst for a relevant mood, for a *way in* to writing about a fictional war—an indirect influence.

A more pointed example might be a movement in *Shriek* called Nativism that reflects our country's head-in-the-sand attitude toward Iraq, while still being fantastical enough that it can be read any number of other ways as well. In a similar way, the stranglehold corporations have on the politics practiced in Washington, D.C., becomes, as previously mentioned, warring merchant clans' stranglehold on Ambergris. Even climate change is addressed in *Shriek*, in an off-kilter way. None of these elements of *Shriek* will be dated in fifty years, or one hundred years. All of them can be read on the surface level or on a subtextual level in a way that has nothing to do with "current events"—even though any reader today would easily recognize those events embedded within the novel.

(Did I intend all of these points of common reference originally? No. I wrote most of *Shriek* or at least planned out most of it well before 9-11 and all that occurred thereafter. But an organic novel, a novel that is alive, has at least one inherent trait during the writing of it: it devours the world. It is wide enough, deep enough, and enough about the entirety of life that it envelopes the real world and distills it out the other side in fictionalized form.)

Incorporating such issues from a through-the-looking-glass angle also allows for the possibility of presenting a heated current political situation in a non-confrontational context. This doesn't mean that the *ideas* aren't still threatening, but that the remove from reality allows for possible acceptance of those ideas by readers who originally did not share in that same system of beliefs. In other words, on some level, even if subconsciously, you may begin to change the world, one reader at a time. Even better, at least in *Shriek*, the politics of the setting do not overshadow the characters, but instead are expressed through the characters, and the emphasis in the novel is on other matters entirely. (The defeatist would say that, in fact, the opposite is true—for example, many right-wingers listen to, say, The Clash, and enjoy the music while ignoring the lyrics.)

However, no matter what I intend, the success of that intention depends on reader reaction and interpretation. Sometimes the reader has a responsibility—and in the case of the political, that responsibility includes not screaming "didactic!" any time a writer raises important issues in his or her work. Readers who care about writing need to recognize that sometimes the entertainment value of a piece must be weighed against the depth of what is being said, that sometimes a story may need a certain slow pace in a section, may need to build, and may even need to, yes, lecture, to achieve its full effect.

Now, after stating all of this, you may realize I haven't yet answered the question I posed before: Is it important for fantasy, or fiction generally, to be relevant in this way? The answer is a resounding *No, it isn't*. The instinctual idea I had as a teen and young adult about Art for Art's sake, the idea that character and situation are paramount, that some truths transcend politics—that's all valid.

But, for me, not because of 9-11 but because of everything since then—the hypocrisy, greed, and evil of government leaders, institutions, and private individuals—I cannot *not* react in a different way than before. These issues permeate our world, and if you do not internalize that, if it *doesn't* affect your writing, then it lies like an unhealing wound in your heart, and you go a little bit crazy.

If there's one thing I've learned in the post 9-11 world, it is that everything we do matters—*every little thing matters*—even if we sometimes feel like we're drowning, going down for the third time.

I'm not a political activist. I'm just a writer. But in doing what you love most—writing—and in observing the state of the world you love so much and have such curiosity about—with its insane assortment of sad, beautiful, ugly, evil, wonderful people—how can you not write these kinds of things into your fiction?

The Triumph of the Good

Ecstatic Days, October 2007

There has been much talk recently about the death of short fiction, or the lack of interest in short fiction—generally in the context of "genre"—and I'd like to suggest, hypothetically, that perhaps ideas of comfort, quirkiness, and politeness come into play. I have been reading countless stories over the past couple of years and, despite finding some excellent material, I have at various times felt as if something was wrong that I couldn't quite articulate, some elusive sense of being *in danger*. Not danger *in* the fiction, but a danger *to* fiction.

Sometimes when this happens it is entirely personal, related to my own writing: I have repeated myself or have come close to being rote, in process, in technique, in content. (This is an issue separate of the relative success or failure of the fiction in question.) But the more I've thought about it, the more I feel that my general apathy when reading a lot of fantasy short fiction today is a sense of middle class professionalism that I find profoundly disturbing. The magazines and anthologies are dominated by what I'd call centrist fiction that simply drowns in competence. It's good—it's just not great. It's clever—it's just not trying to do more, or it does reach for more, but in familiar ways.

As I thought about this more, I visualized a story mill, similar to a puppy mill. An endless churning sound as thousands of writers typed and handwrote the first drafts of stories destined from conception to be *good enough*. Good enough for publication. Good enough to pass muster. Good enough to earn an appreciative nod. It was a depressing thought.

I kept coming back to words like *rough* and *wild* and *pushing* and *punk* and *visionary*. Words for what I was reading were more like *twee, comfortable, recycled, reasonable, well-rounded, whimsical, unoriginal, well-behaved,* and *fuzzy*.

Maybe it's always been this way. Maybe I just haven't been looking in the right places.

I was reading through an old batch of *Interzones* and *New Worlds* while Ann and

I selected stories for the *New Weird* anthology, and I thought I caught a glimpse of something different. Perhaps I'm wrong, perhaps it's a myopic nostalgia for some golden age that never existed, but just bear with me for the sake of argument.

What I seemed to find in those old magazines sometimes overreached, or crashed into and sank on the rocks of evangelical experimentalism…but, at its best, that fiction was altogether more *adult* than much of what I've read recently. It seemed sharper and more balanced between intellect and emotion. There was ample intelligence behind it, sometimes a cruel and enervating intelligence. It was often bracing, unexpected, and jagged.

It also seemed to take the self-determination of its characters more seriously and had things to say about and to observe about adult relationships that I'm just not sure I see in short fantasy fiction much any more. Hard choices, hard made.

Now, I know this comparison is blatantly unfair to some extent. I'm talking about impressions. I'm not naming names. I may just be expressing my own restlessness. But what I'm getting at is this: it's just possible that, for whatever reason—perhaps the co-opting of counterculture by all-powerful pop culture, or the rise of delightful but ultimately popcorn influences on TV and the movies, or the proliferation of editors as interested in gathering the same old "names" as publishing excellent anthologies, or perhaps because space aliens have eaten our brains—a lot of today's fiction is *soft*, too vapid, without the requisite intellect behind it, with too many stories that don't go far enough, and too few stories that come from the margins, the fringes, the places that lie outside of suburban, middle-class America or England or wherever. (Can you imagine the gaping hole, for example, if no one "retold" another fairy tale for the next thirty years?)

Perhaps also there is too much comfort in our own lives, and too many distractions that contribute to this softness, making it easy for us to be satisfied with what we've done: content, content, content. Happy with the well-rounded sentences, the fulfilling character arc, the recursive plot. Patting ourselves on the back for miracles never earned, epiphanies bartered for with trinkets and trifles. Thrilled just to have a beginning, a middle, and an end.

I'm sure many would say it's the same as it ever was, or, more likely, that we live in a golden age of cross pollination, and that we should be happy to have so many great writers working today. Most people in the field have a stake in supporting this idea—that this is *the* moment, and this, and this, and the next. Can you imagine if most of the reviews of stories and novels were mixed or indifferent or negative? Yet more than ninety-eight percent of all fiction published in 2007 will be forgotten within two to five years. How is this possible when reviewers tell us every year that so much great material has been published *every year*? And why is there never a year when a year's best anthology announces there was only enough good fiction to put out a 30,000 or 50,000-word edition? (The International Horror Guild suggested this with regard to fiction anthologies a year ago, by not nominating any, and caused an uproar only slightly less volatile than if they'd advocated shoving babies onto spikes.)

So I'm not sure this is a golden age. I'm not sure that the field isn't oddly familiar and similar, that the differences aren't more like the facile differences between Republicans and Democrats, and that, in fact, most of us are telling the same story, all the time, everywhere.

Maybe it is, in fact, just a change in my own tastes, or the rise of the power of the adolescent—who, exactly, are we writing for these days?—or the cop-out that the world is too terrible or complex now for most writers or readers to engage it head-on in short fiction.

But my gut tells me that, regardless, we need more of a punk aesthetic, and the courage—because it does take courage these days—to continually renew our faith in fiction as art and not as product. To know that words matter, and that characters in our stories matter in the sense that if we're going to commit to writing fiction in the first place, then we need to commit *all the way*, whether we think we're writing literature or "only" entertainment. The problem isn't, as some have said, that we don't have enough stories that try to entertain, but that too much of our entertainment isn't good enough. "Art" and "entertainment" are not at odds, except when put into conflict by those with an agenda or a general misunderstanding of fiction.

Perversely, though, thinking about all of this makes me want to write, even as I know the solution might be fewer stories in the world, not more. It makes me want to write something bold and different. It makes me want my reach to *always* exceed my grasp. Because, for every writer, there is always another story, and it doesn't have to be even close to the one you told before.

The New Weird — "It's Alive?"

Originally published as the introduction to the anthology *The New Weird*, 2008

Origins

The "new weird" existed long before 2003, when M. John Harrison started a message board thread with the words: "The New Weird. Who does it? What is it? Is it even anything?" For this reason, and this reason only, it continues to exist now, even after a number of critics, reviewers, and writers have distanced themselves from the term.

By 2003, readers and writers had become aware of a change in perception and a change in approach within genre. Crystallized by the popularity of China Miéville's *Perdido Street Station*, this change had to do with finally acknowledging a shift in *The Weird*.

Weird fiction—typified by magazines like *Weird Tales* and writers like H. P. Lovecraft or Clark Ashton Smith back in the glory days of the pulps—eventually morphed into modern-day traditional Horror. "Weird" refers to the sometimes supernatural or fantastical element of unease in many of these stories—an element that could take a blunt, literal form or more subtle and symbolic form and which was, as in the best of Lovecraft's work, combined with a visionary sensibility. These types of stories also often rose above their pulp or self-taught origins through the strength of the writer's imagination. (There are definite parallels to be drawn between certain kinds of pulp fiction and so-called "Outsider Art.")

Two impulses or influences distinguish the New Weird from the "Old" Weird, and make the term more concrete than terms like "slipstream" and "interstitial," which have no distinct lineage. The New Wave of the 1960s was the first stimulus leading to the New Weird. Featuring authors such as M. John

Harrison, Michael Moorcock, and J. G. Ballard, the New Wave deliriously mixed genres, high and low art, and engaged in formal experimentation, often typified by a distinctly political point of view. New Wave writers also often blurred the line between science fiction and fantasy, writing a kind of updated "scifantasy," first popularized by Jack Vance in his *Dying Earth* novels. This movement (backed by two of its own influences, Mervyn Peake and the Decadents of the late 1800s) provided what might be thought of as the brain of New Weird. The second stimulus came from the unsettling grotesquery of such seminal 1980s work as Clive Barker's *Books of Blood*. In this kind of fiction, body transformations and dislocations create a visceral, contemporary take on the kind of visionary horror best exemplified by the work of Lovecraft—while moving past Lovecraft's coyness in recounting events in which the monster or horror can never fully be revealed or explained. In many of Barker's best tales, the starting point is the acceptance of a monster or a transformation and the story is what comes after. Transgressive horror, then, repurposed to focus on the monsters and grotesquery but not the "scare," forms the beating heart of the New Weird.

In a sense, the simultaneous understanding of and rejection of Old Weird, hardwired to the stimuli of the New Wave and New Horror, gave many of the writers identified as New Weird the signs and symbols needed to both forge ahead into the unknown and create their own unique re-combinations of familiar elements.

The Shift

Nameless for a time, a type of New Weird or proto-New Weird entered the literary world in the gap between the end of the miniature horror renaissance engendered by Barker and his peers and the publication of *Perdido Street Station* in 2000.

In the 1990s, "New Weird" began to manifest itself in the form of cult writers like Jeffrey Thomas and his cross-genre urban *Punktown* stories. It continued to find a voice in the work of Thomas Ligotti, who straddled a space between the traditional and the avant garde. It coalesced in the David Lynchean approach of Michael Cisco to Eastern European mysticism in works like *The Divinity Student*. It entered real-world settings through unsettling novels by

Kathe Koja, such as *The Cipher* and *Skin*, with their horrific interrogations of the body and mind. It entered into disturbing dialogue about sex and gender in Richard Calder's novels, with their mix of phantasmagoria and pseudo-cyberpunk. It could also be found in Jeffrey Ford's Well-Built City trilogy, my own Ambergris stories (*Dradin, In Love*, etc.), and the early short work of K. J. Bishop and Alastair Reynolds, among others.

Magazines like Andy Cox's *The Third Alternative*, my wife Ann's *The Silver Web*, and, to a lesser extent, David Pringle's *Interzone* and Chris Reed/Manda Thomson's *Back Brain Recluse*—along with anthologies like my *Leviathan* series—provided support for this kind of work, which generally did not interest commercial publishers. Ironically, despite most New Weird fiction of the 1990s being skewed heavily toward the grotesque end of the New Wave/New Horror spectrum, many horror publications and reviewers dismissed the more confrontational or surreal examples of the form. It represented a definite threat to the Lovecraft clones and Twilight Zone döppelgangers that dominated the horror field by the mid-1990s.

Flash Point

The publication of Miéville's *Perdido Street Station* in 2000 represented what might be termed the first commercially acceptable version of the New Weird, one that both coarsened and broadened the New Weird approach through techniques more common to writers like Charles Dickens, while adding a progressive political slant. Miéville also displayed a fascination with permutations of the body, much like Barker, and incorporated, albeit in a more direct way, ideas like odd plagues (M. John Harrison) and something akin to a Multiverse (Michael Moorcock).

Miéville's fiction wasn't inherently superior to what had come before, but it was *epic*, and it wedded a "surrender to the weird"—literally, the writer's surrender to the material, without ironic distance—to rough-hewn but effective plots featuring earnest, proactive characters. This approach made *Perdido Street Station* much more accessible to readers than such formative influences on Miéville as Mervyn Peake's Gormenghast novels or M. John Harrison's Viriconium cycle.

The truth of this accessibility also resides at the sentence and paragraph level, which in Miéville's case house brilliant, often startling images and situations, but do not always display the same control as those past masters (by Miéville's own admission, and not meant as a pejorative here). Yet, by using broader brushstrokes, Miéville created much more space for his readers, a trade-off that helped create his success. Ultimately, Miéville would also serve as an entry point to work that was more ambitious on the paragraph level. In a neat time traveling trick, one of his own touchstones, M. John Harrison, would benefit greatly from that success.

Quite simply, Miéville had created just the right balance between pulp writing, visionary, surreal images, and literary influences to attract a wider audience—and serve as the lightning rod for what would become known as New Weird.

The Debate

But Miéville wasn't alone. By the time Harrison posited his question "What is New Weird?" it had become clear that a number of other writers had developed at the same time as Miéville, using similar stimuli. My *City of Saints & Madmen*, K. J. Bishop's *The Etched City*, and Paul Di Filippo's *A Year in the Linear City*, among others, appeared in the period from 2001 to 2003, with Steph Swainston's *The Year of Our War* published in 2004. It seemed that something had Risen Spontaneous— even though in almost every case, the work itself had been written in the 1990s and either needed time to gestate or had been rejected by publishers—and thus there was a need to explain or name the beast. The resulting conversation on the Third Alternative public message boards consisted of many thousands of words, used in the struggle to name, define, analyze, spin, explore, and quantify the term "New Weird." The debate involved more than fifty writers, reviewers, and critics, all with their own questions, agendas, and concerns.

By the end of the discussion it wasn't clear if New Weird as a term existed or not. However, over the next few years, with varying levels of enthusiasm, Miéville (and various acolytes and followers) promulgated versions of the term, emphasizing the "surrender to the weird," but also a very specific political component. Miéville thought of New Weird as "post-Seattle" fiction, referring to the effects of globalization and grassroots efforts to undermine institutions like the World Bank. This use of the term "New Weird" was in keeping with Miéville's idealism and Marxist leanings in the world outside of fiction, but, in my opinion, preternaturally narrowed the parameters of the term. This brand of New Weird seemed far too limiting, unlike the type envisioned by Steph Swainston in the original message board discussion; her New Weird seemed almost like a form of literary Deism, a primal and epiphanal experience.

The passion behind Miéville's efforts made sure that the term would live on—even after he began to disown it, claiming it had become a marketing category and was therefore of no further interest to him. Despite Miéville's lack of interest, by 2005 the term "New Weird" was being used with some regularity by readers, writers, and critics.

That the term, as explored primarily by M. John Harrison and Steph Swainston, and then taken up by Miéville, has since been rejected or severely questioned not only by the initial Triumvirate but by several others speaks to the fact that most New Weird writers, like most New Wave writers, are various in their approaches over time. They are not repeating themselves for the most part. Cross-pollination—of genres, of boundaries—occurs as part of an effort to avoid easy classification—not for its own sake, or even consciously in most cases, but in an attempt to allow readers and writers to enter into a dialogue that is genuine, unique, and not based on received ideas or terms.

Miéville attempted to place this political element within a complex, multifaceted context, but the reality of how ideas are transmitted meant that this complexity was stripped away as the thought spread and was re-transmitted, each time more constraining and less interesting. The constant flux-and-flow of support and lack of support for New Weird in the same individuals would be taken as "waffling" in a politician. In a writer, it is part of the necessary testing and re-testing connected to one's writing, as well as part of the need to continually be open to and curious about the world.

I myself reacted adversely to the idea of New Weird in 2003—in part because it seemed that some writers wanted to claim it, falsely, as a uniquely English phenomenon; in part because I continue to champion artistic discussion and publication of "genre" and "literary" work within one context and continuum; and in part because it did seem limiting inasmuch as the term was most useful applied to specific works rather than specific writers (almost impossible to "enforce," given how labeling works).

In retrospect, however, my rejection of the term seems premature—because as used in the message board discussion, "New Weird" was just a term on which to hang an exploration and investigation of what looked like a sudden explosion of associated texts. While much of the discussion may have been surface, much of it was also incisive, rich, and deep. With less concern about holding onto "territory" and control, from everyone, those discussions might have led to something more substantive.

Effects in the "Real" World

The other reality about the term "New Weird" has little to do with either moments or movements and more to do with the marketplace: Miéville's success, through his own efforts and those of his followers, became linked to the term New Weird. A practical result of this affiliation is that it became easier for this kind of fiction to find significant publication. It wasn't just "find me the next Miéville"—firstly impossible and secondly corrosive—but "find me more New Weird fiction." As an editor at a large North American publishing house told me two years ago, "New Weird" has been a "useful shorthand" not only when justifying acquiring a particular novel, but also when marketing departments talk to booksellers. Confusion about the specifics of the term created a larger protective umbrella for writers from a publishing standpoint. Many books far stranger than Miéville's have been prominently published as a result. By now, this effect may have begun to fade, like all marketing trends, but the writers blessed by its effects now have careers autonomous from the original umbilical cord.

I know that without New Weird, it would have been harder for me to find publication by commercial and foreign language publishers. This is probably doubly true for writers like K. J. Bishop, who had not already had books out by 2001. In a trickle-down effect, I also believe this atmosphere has helped decidedly non-New Weird writers like Hal Duncan, whose own brand of weirdness is much more palatable in the wake of the "New Weird explosion." (Inasmuch as there is a "Godfather" or "protective angel" of New Weird, that person would be Peter Lavery, editor at Pan Macmillan, who took a chance on Miéville, Bishop, Duncan, me, and several other "strange" writers.)

The other truth is that even though heroic fantasy and other forms of genre fiction still sell much better than most New Weird books, New Weird writers partially dominated the critical and awards landscape for almost half a decade.

In a similar way, New Weird has become shorthand for readers, who don't care about the vagaries of taxonomy so much as "I know it when I read it." For this reason, writers such as Kelly Link, Justina Robson, and Charles Stross have all been, at one time or another, identified as New Weird. These reader associations occur because when encountering something unique most of us grab the label that seems the closest match so we can easily describe our enthusiasm to others. (The result of both carefree readers and some careless academics has been to make it seem as if New Weird is as indefinable and slippery a term as "interstitial.")

The effect of New Weird outside of England, North America, and Australia has been various but often dynamic. New Weird has, in some countries, already mutated and adapted as an ever-shifting "moment"—as well as a potent label for publishers. In some places "New Weird" has become uniquely independent of what anyone associated with the original discussion in 2003 now thinks of the term and its usefulness. For example, in Finland you can say without equivocation that Kelly Link *is* New Weird. (At the same time, New Weird has largely failed to penetrate the awareness of the literary mainstream, probably because of its secondary-world nature, which is almost always a barrier to breaking out of the genre "ghetto.")

In addition, as alluded to earlier in this introduction, many of the writers associated with New Weird and collected in this volume are already transforming into something else entirely, while new writers like Alistair Rennie (whose story is original to this anthology), have assimilated the New Weird influence, combined it with yet other stimuli, and created their own wonderfully bizarre and transgressive recombinations.

This speaks to the nature of art: as soon as something becomes popular or familiar, the true revolution moves elsewhere. Sometimes the writers involved in the original radicalism move on, too, and sometimes they allow themselves to be left behind.

A Working Definition of the New Weird

Following the aftermath of all of this discussion, research, and reading, the opportunity to create a working definition of twenty-first-century New Weird now presents itself:

> New Weird is a type of urban, secondary-world fiction that subverts the romanticized ideas about place found in traditional fantasy, largely by choosing realistic, complex real-world models as the jumping off point for creation of settings that may combine elements of both science fiction and fantasy. New Weird has a visceral, in-the-moment quality that often uses elements of surreal or transgressive horror for its tone, style, and effects—in combination with the stimulus of influence from New Wave writers or their proxies (including also such forebears as Mervyn Peake and the French/English Decadents). New Weird fictions are acutely aware of the modern world, even if in disguise, but not always overtly political. As part of this awareness of the modern world, New Weird relies for its visionary power on a "surrender to the weird" that isn't, for example, hermetically sealed in a haunted house on the moors or in a cave in Antarctica. The "surrender" (or "belief") of the writer can take many forms, some of them even involving the use of postmodern techniques that do not undermine the surface reality of the text.

This definition presents two significant ways in which the New Weird can be distinguished from Slipstream or Interstitial fiction. First, while Slipstream and Interstitial fiction often claim New Wave influence, they rarely if ever cite a Horror influence, with its particular emphasis on the intense use of grotesquery focused around transformation, decay, or mutilation of the human body. Second, postmodern techniques that undermine the surface reality of the text (or point out its artificiality) are not part of the New Weird aesthetic, but they are part of the Slipstream and Interstitial toolbox.

This Anthology

We hope that this anthology will provide a rough guide to the moment or movement known as "New Weird"—acknowledging that the pivotal "moment" is behind us, but that this moment had already lasted much longer than generally believed, had definite precursors, and continues to spread an Effect, even as it dissipates or becomes something else. (And who knows? Another pivotal "moment" may be ahead of us.)

Ann and I still have reservations about the term New Weird, but in our readings, research, and conversations, we have come to believe the term has a core validity. The proof is that it has taken on an artistic and commercial life beyond that intended by those individuals who, in their inquisitiveness about a "moment," unintentionally created a movement. It is still mutating forward through the work of a new generation of writers, as well.

Finally, anyone who reads the initial New Weird discussions will find that the term arose from a sense of curiosity, of play, of (sometimes bloody-minded) mischievousness, and from a love for fiction. We offer up this anthology in the spirit of the best of that original discussion.

New Weird is dead. Long live the Next Weird.

CONVERSATION #1:

CHINA MIÉVILLE AND THE MONSTERS
Weird Tales, 85th Anniversary Issue, 2008

The publication in 2000 of China Miéville's second novel, *Perdido Street Station*, galvanized and challenged the fantasy field with its potent mix of pulp and literary influences, fantasy, horror, and SF, its commitment to "the Weird," and its epic scope. Since then Miéville has published two more novels set in his New Crobuzon milieu, *The Scar* and *Iron Council*, along with a YA novel, *Un Lun Dun*. Along the way, he has won the Arthur C. Clarke Award, the British Fantasy Award, and been a finalist for the World Fantasy Award and the Hugo Award, among others. Many critics consider Miéville's contribution to modern Weird fiction (and the "New Weird moment") as important as Clive Barker's in the 1980s with the *Books of Blood*. Recently, I talked to Miéville about Weird fiction and many other topics via instant messenger.

What does the word "weird" mean to you?
I've been thinking about this a lot recently. I'm teaching a course in Weird Fiction at the University of Warwick, so this has come up a lot. Obviously it's kind of impossible to come to anything like a final answer, so I approach this in a Beckettian way—try to define/understand it, fail, try again, fail again, fail better...I think the whole "sense of cosmic awe" thing that we hear a lot about in the Weird tradition is to do with the

sense of the numinous, whether in a horrific iteration (or, more occasionally, a kind of joyous one), as being completely embedded in the everyday, rather than an intrusion. To that extent the Weird to me is about the sense that reality is always Weird.

I've been thinking about the traditional notion of the "sublime," which was always (by Kant, Schopenhauer, et al) distinguished from the "Beautiful," as containing a kind of horror at the immeasurable scale of it. I think what the Weird can do is question the arbitrary distinction between the Beautiful and the Sublime, and operate as a kind of Sublime Backwash, so that the numinous incomparable awesome slips back from "mountains" and "forests," into the everyday. So…the Weird as radicalised quotidian Sublime.

So theoretically people should see "the weird" in every day life. But most don't see it—or aren't prepared to see it, possibly because they're too inward-turning, not really experiencing the world moment-to-moment? Is that what you mean? Or is that too New Age-y for what you're talking about?

I'm talking about it as a literary/aesthetic effect—my impression is that a lot of us do experience it quite a lot, in everyday life. But given that part of its *differentia specifica* is that it is AWEsome, beyond language, expressing it is very difficult. I think a lot of what we admire in Weird Fictioneers is not that they see, but that they make a decent fist of expressing.

That's the theory side, in a sense, but expressed on a more personal level, what appeals to you most about the weird tale?

The awe, the ecstasy. I was reading Blackwood's "The Wendigo" the other day, and the moment when Defago is taken by the Wendigo and wails from above the trees this astonishing moment of unrealistic speech, "oh, oh, my burning feet of fire! This height and fiery speed!," the strange poetry of it, I found very affecting. Of course we all have our favourite iterations of Weird, and for me it dovetails a lot with a love of teratology, so I also hugely love when the Weird is expressed by radical monster-making, the strangeness of strange creatures, but some of my favourite Weird Tales contain no monsters at all. It's the awe and ecstasy that gets me.

But not necessarily epiphany? I.e., this awe and ecstasy is a cumulative effect of the story or it's what it culminates in?

I don't think I can distinguish [between] the two. I think for me the best Weird fiction is an expression of that awe, which permeates the whole thing, but because you can't structure a story as a continual shout of ecstasy (at least not and expect many readers to stick with you) it sort of pretends to be an epiphany. But I think it's the epiphany of realisation—that the real is Weird—rather than change or irruption—that something Weird occurs. Lovecraft for example is always back-projecting his mythos into history. We don't know it, unless we're one of the select unlucky few in his story, but it's not that these things have suddenly arrived to mess about with previously stable reality, but that we're forced to realise—there's the epiphany, it's epistemological, rather than an ontological break—that it was always Awesome.

But you are talking about visionary fiction to some extent—some of it is hardwired with ecstasy, and that's why the best examples are short stories, no? Because you can't sustain that "reverie"?

I think that's true—it's much harder to maintain Weird, or, certainly, ecstasy, over a longer form. Which is why these stories are about the revelation—not because it's a surprise (we expect it) but because it's a necessary kind of bleak Damascene moment. There are Weird novels and some brilliant ones, but they're harder to sustain.

What do you think most surprises your students studying weird tales?

I think for a lot of people who don't read pulp growing up, there's a real surprise that the particular kind of Pulp Modernism of a certain kind of lush purple prose isn't necessarily a failure or a mistake, but is part of the fabric of the story and what makes it weird. There's a big default notion that "spare," or "precise" prose is somehow better. I keep insisting to them that while such prose is completely legitimate, it's in no way intrinsically more accurate, more relevant, or better than lush prose. That adjective "precise," for example, needs unpicking. If a "minimalist" writer describes a table, and a metaphor-ridden adjective-heavy weird fictioneer describes a table, they are very different, but the former is in absolutely no way closer to the material reality than the latter. Both of them are radically different from that reality. They're just words. A table is a big wooden thing with my tea on it. I think they also are surprised by how much they enjoy making up monsters.

Who doesn't? But you say they're surprised? They think that's too childish to start?
Yes, to some extent. It's something you need to grow out of. Or your monsters are only legitimate to the extent that they "really mean" something else. I spend a lot of time arguing for literalism of fantastic, rather than its reduction to allegory. Metaphor is inevitable but it escapes our intent, so we should relax about it. Our monsters are about themselves, and they can get on with being about all sorts of other stuff too, but if we want them to be primarily that, and don't enjoy their monstrousness, they're dead and nothing.

Right—nobody likes a monster piñata.
Yeah—it's what Toby Litt brilliantly called the "Scooby Doo Impasse"—that people always-already know that they'll pull the mask off the monster and see what it "really" is/means. The notion that that is what makes it legitimate is a very drab kind of heavy-handedness.

Do you think a lot of writers create monsters, though, that they don't mean literally? I mean, do you think writers sit down and go, when writing the rough draft, "This is going to be a metaphor for 9-11?" Or is it just that readers and academics think they do?
Well I think this is one of the big distinctions between genre and non-genre traditions. I think, for example, that when Margaret Atwood invents the "pigoons" for *Oryx & Crake*, part of the problem with them for me is I think they are primarily a vehicle for considering genetic manipulation, and only distantly secondarily scary pig monsters. I think plenty of monsters get hobbled by their "meaning." The Coppola Bram Stoker's *Dracula* vampire had to shuffle along, so weighed down was he by bloated historical import. None of this is to say that monsters don't mean things other than themselves—of course they do—but that to me they do so best when they believe in themselves.

Good point—and of course writers often look at their rough draft and like oracles pull things out that look like they have meaning…This does actually bring me to one of those "weird" questions I'm contractually obligated to ask for this interview: What's the weirdest (in any sense) movie you've ever seen?

Weirdest movie? Probably either a Jan Svankmajer—*The Flat*—and/or a Jean Painlevé, *Le Vampire*. Also, *Terror in a Texas Town*. [Regarding] *Pan's Labyrinth*—this is spoiler territory—but I know a lot of people who said they thought the end was a lovely escape into the healing power of fantasy and I was thinking OH REALLY?!?! I had a similar argument with those people who thought the ending of [Stephen Spielberg's] *AI* was "sentimental." I was thinking, fuck, did we see the same film? That was some sadistic shit I just saw. Not that I much enjoyed AI, but I was fascinated by the astoundingly cruel last half-hour.

Do you find that some readers, related to what you're saying, don't recognize a monster, a human monster, when they see one? And I agree—*AI* is a very cruel movie, unnecessarily so. Whereas *Pan* is cruel only because it has to be.

I totally agree—*AI* sadistic, *Pan's Labyrinth* politically unsentimental. Very different. What do you mean [about not recognizing a monster]?

I have a current theory that writers become so in love with their characters that they don't always recognize when they've written a sociopath, for example. And then their enthusiasm blinds readers who aren't careful and who go along with the ride, thinking "oh this person is great."

Ah. It's an interesting question, and I've not thought of it in those terms. I've certainly been aware of the consideration of certain characters as admirable, or, in other ways, as despicable, when read from a different optic, they are not. I loathed *Tess of the Durbervilles* because I got the strong impression that Hardy and I disagreed about Tess. Similarly Simmons' *The Terror*, with several of his characters.

Did you like *The Terror*?

No. I kept wanting to find out what the giant polar bear was. When I discovered it was, indeed, a giant polar bear, I was deflated. I found it fairly page-turny, but I found it much too long, too bogged down with its historical research for its narrative, its disclosures and teratological money-shots too contingent to its narrative, and its embedded politics—particularly vis-à-vis homosexuality—offensive.

You don't believe those embedded politics were part of the historical research?

No, because I'm not talking about the politics of the characters, but about the politics of the text, as I read it. Specifically, the obsessive locus of the evil character's evil in the fact that he was an engager in anal sex. I know lots of people point to the fact that there's a "sympathetic" gay character too (who reads, incidentally, to me, very like someone invented because an editor said "we really need a counterbalance to the evil gay") but that character is explicitly defined as a goody because he doesn't have sex on the ship. That's nothing to do with historical research or attitudes (and parenthetically the idea that in a crew that size two men only would be fucking is ludicrous) but to do with the text's pathological Terror of anal penetration which is (spoiler!—hello *The Sparrow*) the usual way culture gets to have a deep-seated pathologising of gay sexuality alongside putatively liberal attitudes to desexualised gay men.

You've just ruined the innocence of perhaps 85% of Weird Tales readers.

Hurrah! My work here is done.

Please take a bow. I really liked the book, but I didn't catch the subtext you're talking about, in part, probably, because I was turning pages too quickly.

I'm very aware, by the way, that loads of readers of this may think I'm being a humourless or po-faced dick about it. This is how it reads to me, and I have a big problem with it. And I think arguments about "what the writer really means" or thinks are very point-missing, because this stuff isn't reducible to "intent."

True, but—and I'm not saying in this case—but in some cases, don't you have to be forgiving?

It depends of what. Give me an example?

For example, Philip K. Dick was often a raging misogynist. But if you unravel the stuff about his work that is bad in that sense, you also unravel the good stuff. In a sense I'm playing devil's advocate because I do believe writers should think these things through, because it reflects on whether they've really created well-rounded characters as opposed to stereotypes.

This is not about pissing and moaning just because I disagree with the writer's politics—I love passionately Gene Wolfe's work, for example, far more than the writing of many people whose politics are more congenial to me. It's about saying that as a matter of reading, of literary response, when the politics or concerns or whatever of a particular text impinge on it in certain ways, make it pull in certain directions, interfere with other aspects of it, etc. etc., and in my opinion make it not just politically objectionable but work less well as a text, then I feel perfectly free to criticise it on those (politico-literary) axes.

Sure—I mean, what you're saying about *The Terror* makes sense in that— does it make any difference whether the evil guy is gay or not? To the story? Not really. So then you have to ask yourself why it's there.

I don't think there's such a thing as "the story" disembarrassed of the other stuff, basically. That's why I think about "texts' or works rather than the story, versus/and/or the writing, versus/and/or the characters, etc. In art these things are intertwined. Not reducible to each other, sure, but not little just-add-and-stir packets of sauce that you can choose one but not the other. Did I want to get to the end of *The Terror* and see the bear? Sure. Still, though, I stand by what I said, and I think there's no contradiction. I don't mind people disagreeing at all, of course, that's the point of debate. I do get frustrated when—and maybe it's my fault for not being clear—people take what I'm saying as "he doesn't like books by people he doesn't agree with." As the Lovecraft, Celine, Machen, Blackwood, Ewers, James, Cordwainer Smith, Blyton, et many al, on my shelves indicate, this isn't so. And it can operate the other way round too. For me *The Sparrow* was a big thing there—that's obviously a book that intends to be very progressive about homosexuality, but in my opinion it, whatever Russell's beliefs and intents, is deep-structured by anal-penetration panic.

Since we seem to be approaching this territory anyway, here's another contractually obligated question. What's the weirdest book you've ever read?

God, that's a merciless question.

All the weirdest questions are merciless.

Un Semaine de Bonté, by Max Ernst. Which means that "read" is a bit of a tendentious verb in this context, but fuck it, I'm sticking with my answer.

Okay, so we've talked about weird books and movies. What's the weirdest place you've ever been?

Probably the East Anglian coast, where M.R. James set loads of his ghost stories, and which I have a long family connection with. Very freaky places—Cove Hithe, Dunwich, Walberswick. Second, the outskirts of a big factory in the outskirts of Bulawayo in Zimbabwe. But places are all SO weird, that's a real embarrassment of riches. Ever been to the coast of the Netherlands? Weird.

On that note, let's wrap things up with a "weird" speed round or two. I'm going to list two "weird" writers at a time and you'll tell me which you like better with maybe a sentence on why, if you want. Ready?

Okay, cool. I *love* the either/or game. People who say "ooh can't I have both" are terrible cheats.

Here goes. Jack Vance or Robert E. Howard?

Vance because of *DYING EARTH*. Dying. Earth. And big dying sun.

Vance or Lovecraft?

Lovecraft: (also damn you for making me choose!) Because i) the monsters are revolutionary, and ii) the prose is totally weird. And Weird.

Lovecraft or Clark Ashton Smith?

Lovecraft. Because CAS, to whom all honour and respect go, has a post-

Dunsanian sort of slightly sentimental archaic singsongism that doesn't freak me out as much as Lovecraft's hysteria.

Surprise! Lovecraft or Ursula K. LeGuin OR Ray Bradbury?

A Troika? That's cheating surely! Lovecraft ow sorry sorry Le Guin and Bradbury. Because he reshaped a form more radically than either of them (to whom infinite burnt offerings and love go).

Lovecraft or Tennessee Williams (both of whom appeared in *Weird Tales*)?

(NO! REALLY???) Lovecraft. Though TW closes up close for that weird play where the guy gets eaten by children—*Suddenly Last Summer*. Also, William Hope Hodgson is pulling ahead of Lovecraft in my head, increasingly recently, workmanlike prose or not. But that's another discussion.

And, finally, mammals or reptiles?

Please. PLEASE. Mammals Schmammals. In ascending order, it goes Mammals and birds equally, Reptiles, Amphibians, Insects, Fish, Cephalopods.

APPRECIATIONS
OF THE MONSTROUS

Prague: City of Fantasy

Locus Online, March 2009

"If you look at Prague from up here, as her lights flicker on one by one, you feel you would gladly plunge headlong into an unreal lake in which you had seen an enchanted castle with a hundred towers [as] the evening chimes on that black lake of starry roofs." —Vítězslav Nezval, co-founder of the surrealist movement in the Czech Republic

To my wife Ann and me, there may be no more fantastical city than Prague, the capital of the Czech Republic, situated on the banks of the Vltava River. Its roots in fantasy go much deeper than Franz Kafka, who once lived in a room in the city's walls. They also go deeper than the tale of the Golem, one of Prague's most famous fictitious exports.

A penchant for the fantastical seems to come naturally to Czechs, perhaps nowhere more in evidence than Jaroslav Hasek's tales of the good soldier Svejk. In these absurd stories, Svejk's fabrications become ever more bizarre and grandiose, and yet fool everyone with the sincerity and detail of their telling. In one particular tale, Svejk claims to have discovered such oddities as the Sulphur-Bellied Whale, the Edible Ox, and Sepia Infusorium, a kind of sewer rat.

Indeed, Frank Blei, a member of Franz Kafka's writing circle, must have been taken by the spirit of Prague when he was moved to describe his colleague as part of an imaginary bestiary: "*The Kafka*. The Kafka is a magnificent and very rarely seen moon-blue mouse, which eats no flesh, but feeds on bitter herbs. It is a bewitching sight, for it has human eyes."

Prague has always been a haven for creative people—it had a Cubist art scene second only to Paris in the 1920s—and remains the home of many fine artists and filmmakers, including the animator Jan Svankmajer, whose *Alice* tells a decidedly macabre version of the classic by Lewis Carroll. Svankmajer was heavily influenced in his choice of career by receiving a toy puppet theater as a Christmas gift in 1942. His Gamba Gallery sits on a cozy street just north of the castle that overlooks the city. A humble white-washed exterior with iron-barred windows hides rooms full of wonders, as most of Prague's more surreal creators have exhibited there.

It was the streets around the Gamba Gallery that we made us realize that some of the more fantastical paintings of Hawk Alfredson were based on reality. On the streets around the gallery, you will find houses with inward curving walls, delicate slanted ceilings, and tiny doors that look like they came from faeryland.

In addition, one of the earliest influences on Alfredson's oil paintings was Prague writer Gustav Meyrink's *The Golem*. Another painting echoes the texture of Wallenstein Palace's Grotesquery in Prague, a strange "forgery" of the walls of a limestone cave, complete with stalactites.

Much of Prague's playfulness also has an edge to it. For example, with the fall of communism Prague was left with a few ugly reminders of that repressive era—like the local television station. Looking a little like a steel cactus, this grim structure fulfilled all of the unimaginative requirements of the Soviet era. But, rather than tear it down, the Czechs commissioned a sculptor to create large "space babies," which were then attached to the sides of the building. This solution is fun but also offers a mocking comment on the prior regime.

The television station is one of the few instances of Czechs having to beautify an ugly structure. As *The Rough Guide to Prague* states, the city represents "some six hundred years of architecture almost untouched by natural disaster or war...the city retains much of its medieval layout and the street facades remain smothered in a rich mantle of Baroque, Rococo, and Art Nouveau." We couldn't go anywhere in the Old Town section of Prague without encountering seemingly magical buildings with flying buttresses, ramparts, and clock towers. Some of the modern structures also seemed not of this world, including the famous Dancing House, also known as "Fred and Ginger." Doors are also a highlight of Prague, which boasts entrances that can rival or surpass such fictional marvels as the Mines of Moria door in the *Two Towers* Lord of the Rings movie.

Modern Prague continues to exhibit this sense of sly playfulness, as evidenced by a major gallery exhibit at the Kampa Museum of Modern Art consisting of huge plastic bears and rabbits, along with a huge wicker chair by the river, suitable for a giant. Not to mention a fine memorial to John Lennon opposite the Old Town, where thousands of people a year come to pay tribute.

As a modern, thriving metropolis, Prague by day or by night contains so many imaginative surprises that even cynical travelers can be amazed by it. Walking around a corner in the evening, with the old town area lit up like some fairy tale setting, we have stumbled across impromptu concerts, street theater, puppetry, and stunning exhibits of international photography.

But one discovery exemplified for us the magical nature of Prague. Walking through the gardens overlooking the city, we heard faint music coming from a high hedge. We soon found a narrow break in the shrubbery that led to a little beer bar with a radio and seats made from tree stumps with green felt as upholstery. Although it was the summer, holiday lights had been woven through the gnarled trees. In the back lay a delicate gazebo set amidst a forest of vines and strange metal sculptures.

It's hard indeed to top the reality of Prague, in any art form. This might be why the best history of Prague is *Magic Prague* by Angelo Maria Ripellino. He captures the city by combining fiction and nonfiction. His account begins, "To this day, every evening at five, Franz Kafka returns home to Celetna Street (Zeltnergasse) wearing a bowler hat and black suit." Throughout, he interweaves characters and situations from novels with the actual events that have defined the city's rich life. As Ripellino writes near the end of his fascinating account: "The fascination of Prague, the life of Prague has no end. Its gravediggers will vanish into the abyss."

Anyone who loves the fantastical will find Prague—its arts, its history, and its tall tales—a fascinating delight. It may come as no surprise, then, that when Czechs voted, along with other European Union members, on a famous person to best represent their country, their selection was a little different. Every other country chose a real person. Czechs chose a fictional character featured in a series of well-known national plays.

Catherynne M. Valente's *The Labyrinth*
Introduction to the first edition, 2007

Flying doorways that "appear in the morning like dew-dampened butterflies, manic and clever." "Latinate clams" that clatter in the water, "their vulgate symphony of clicking nails and meaningless morse code…" Voices "like a rustling of linden leaves, like sand becoming a pearl." A great hare that speaks, a "handsome golden macaque with a bodhisattva face," a decapitated Queen—all this and more awaits you in Catherynne M. Valente's small jewel of a novel, *The Labyrinth*.

Have we been here before? Yes and no—we've seen these mountains, those valleys, before (at least from afar), but that makes no difference. Every time language dislocates and damages us with the intensity of its unexpected beauty, and the truth of that beauty, we undergo a similar transformation—and we return so we can be dislocated and beautifully damaged once again, albeit in a slightly different way.

Tapping into the same wellspring of charged imagery as the Decadents and the Surrealists, *The Labyrinth* displays a confidence and sophistication of language rare in a first novel. That the author is drunk with words belies the control with which she uses them. The reader will be reminded of such monstrous creations as Latreaumont's *Maldoror*, *Alice in Wonderland*, and Angela Carter's more surreal fiction, but at the same time, Valente's voice is unique, her style her own. Metaphors and similes crowd the page, some literal, some figurative. Each sentence has the ability to surprise. Many have the ability to inflict damage.

Valente is certainly as fearless as any of the great non-linear, ur-logical Surrealists or Decadents—for her, language is not a balancing act, but the equivalent of flinging oneself off of a cliff, determined to sprout wings before hitting the rocks below. Most of the time, Valente does grow wings well before annihilation. Or, rather, I should say, *writes herself wings*.

But what of the tale? Is it secondary to the prose? No, not so much secondary as fused to the prose—this is one book where the story cannot be separated from the way in which it has been told, which is all to the good. Our nameless narrator navigates her way through a labyrinth as much metaphysical as sensual, as much dream-like as empirical (despite the sharply empirical nature of its many lovely descriptions).

Some works simply require savoring at the level of language. *The Labyrinth* is one of these works, best enjoyed paragraph by paragraph, word by word. So many fictions are inert at the level of language—as lifeless as an old shoe—that I found it wonderful to be reminded of the possibilities. The best analogy I can make is to a beach at low tide, rich with tidal pools. The beach as a whole is quite satisfactory, but the tidal pools, which from a distance are just mirrors of the sky, prove to be even more compelling: look into each one and you discover that each teems with life, each its own self-sufficient community. The same with Valente's fiction: each paragraph is self-sufficient and contains an entire world. You can lose yourself in a paragraph in *The Labyrinth*, which is, perhaps, fitting.

As for the author, Valente is only—astonishingly enough—24 years old, wrote this novel in 10 days, and has had a book of poetry published already. I'm not surprised by this last fact, however, since in some ways *The Labyrinth* is an extended prose poem.

Two Members of the Shadow Cabinet: Batchelor and McNaughton
Heliotrope, Fall 2007

Shadow Cabinets are the great equalizers, the great communicators. It is only within the dark confines of a Shadow Cabinet, like certain Cabinets of Curiosities, that books and authors with little in common find themselves shoved up against one another, under glass. Like the eccentric elements in photographs by Rosalind Purcell, juxtapositions create their own classifications.

Thus, the subjects of this column: two books, two authors, who traveled in completely different circles, and yet wound up in the same place: John Calvin Batchelor and his *The Birth of the People's Republic of Antarctica* (1983) and Brian McNaughton and his *The Throne of Bones* (1997). The former is a devastating but ultimately compassionate examination of the savage brutality of human nature. The latter is a dark fantasy story cycle set in Seelura, a place that while uniquely its own also evokes Robert E. Howard and classic-era *Weird Tales*. Both constitute exceptional accomplishment, and both are now largely forgotten.

1

"I am Grim Fiddle. My mother, Lamba, first spied me in her magic hand-mirror late in the evening of the spring equinox of 1973. She was dancing by herself at the time, in the rear of a shabby beer hall called The Mickey Mouse Club, located in the foreign quarter of Stockholm, the capital of the Kingdom of Sweden. She was midway between the music box and the bank of telephone booths. She was not under the influence of any drug, though my maternal grandfather was a Lutheran preacher. There is no further explanation of Lamba's vision forthcoming. Mother was Norse sibyl."

—The opening paragraph of *The Birth of the People's Republic of Antarctica*

A product of the 1960s and 1970s, John Calvin Batchelor had what many writers would consider a very good career. Between 1981 and 1994, he had eight novels published from large publishers like Henry Holt. Almost all of these books received some kind of critical acclaim and coverage. However, around the mid-1990s, Batchelor fell off the map, only to reappear as a radio host in New York City after 2000.

The truth is, Batchelor could be uneven. I always preferred his more exotic work to the American novels like *Gordon Liddy Is My Muse*. He also could be too derivative of Thomas Pynchon. He could be difficult in a frivolous way. But at his best, he deserved better than he got. Batchelor's work has a fierce intelligence, a deep and abiding interest in the issues of the contemporary world, and an incisive view of the individual's place in that world. He took chances, sometimes leaping off the edge. He could tell a cracking good story, too, supported by a quirky and rich and brave imagination. (For all I know, he still possesses these qualities, but his books are out of print and he hasn't published anything new for over a decade.)

The Birth of the People's Republic of Antarctica is, in my opinion, his best novel. I remember the first time I read it, picked up randomly because I liked the title. As I began to read, I realized I had something unique in my hands, something that was about to blow the top of my head off. Beleaguered freighters full of plague victims set adrift by governments unwilling to deal with sick refugees, fated to roam the seas? A future of religious war and conflict over limited resources? A man named Skallagrim Strider, larger than life and outside of the law, who leads these refugees to a new life in a free republic in Antarctica? And all of this recounted by an observer both uncanny in his observations and a fool.

The very act of writing *The Birth* was, to my mind, audacity of the first order, showing the kind of nerve you wish you'd see more often. Further, in retooling parts of the myth of *Beowulf*, Batchelor had created a mythic resonance that made the whole thing seem timeless—even as it didn't need that, was as timely then as it is now in its warnings and its revelations.

Parts of this novel, merciless in its execution and intent, made me cry. Parts of it reminded me of John Brunner's *Stand on Zanzibar*. Parts of it were literally like nothing I'd ever read before. Batchelor's observations on the frailty, cruelty, futility, and bravery of human life horrified me and moved me. Somehow, he managed to use summary more often than scene and get away with it (something that influenced me in writing *Shriek: An Afterword*), juxtaposed scenes both terrifying and funny, and never let the reader or his characters off the hook.

But, honestly, I don't think I can put it any better than whoever wrote the description on the back cover of the trade paperback edition: "Batchelor has written a stunning lament about the beastliness in man and the violence in nature, about the darkness of hope abandoned and the blood-price of hope regained. It is a bewitching work of profound and prophetic vision."

And now forgotten, at a time when it is most relevant, when many other fictions I read seem childlike in comparison.

2

"Even if they were not immediately eaten by their mothers, the offspring of ghouls would be short-lived, for they are typically formless things that seem less the product of parturition than pathology. It therefore roused great envy among the mining community when one of their number gave birth to a perfectly formed baby boy; who would have looked rosy, had anyone been so perverse as to light a lamp in the dank niche where he was born."
—the opening of "The Ghoul's Child" from *The Throne of Bones*

Brian McNaughton achieved his greatness after a lifetime of anonymity and toiling in the corpse-filled trenches of the horror field. McNaughton first started publishing horror in the 1960s, at a time when there was no recognizable horror field as such. The only big authors working in horror were people like Robert Bloch. McNaughton got by with a newspaper day job and writing pulpy mass market paperbacks. Then, when things got worse, in the 1970s, he wrote, as he put it, "a lot of books with the word 'Satan' in the title." He also wrote for men's magazines.

When he reappeared in the early 1990s, McNaughton was only about a decade away from his own death. At this point, he was working full-time jobs in factories, unable to find a publisher for his work. He had stopped writing.

Then, for some reason, he started writing again. This time, though, something was different, or at least seems different from my perspective. He had a vision, and he appeared to be writing solely for himself. He sold his first new stories of Seemura to magazines in the now-resurgent horror field, places like *Terminal Fright, TEKELI-LI*, and *Weird Book*. The Seemura stories had the look and feel of odd adult swords-and-sorcery tales. They had an originality and seriousness to them that bypassed the easy wit of Fritz Leiber's Fafhred & The Grey Mouser series. McNaughton was Old School, in some cases seemingly Old Testament. He was Clark Ashton Smith without the pretty. He was Lovecraft exiled to a foreign, murderous land. McNaughton's pulp roots provided the grit and grime for these stories, enhancing their verisimilitude. Visceral and extreme, they could be moody, atmospheric, and touching. Necromancers and sorcerer kings, shamans and lovely princesses—all of these elements should have seemed familiar, and yet in McNaughton's hands they became exotic, fundamentally strange, and original again.

When McNaughton's collection of the Seemura stories, *The Throne of Bones*, appeared in 1997, it received acclaim in the horror field, even won the World Fantasy Award. Then came a trade paperback edition. Then that went out of print. And then came a second collection, not as good as *Throne*. And then McNaughton died, and now, except among some hardcore horror fans, no one remembers McNaughton, or his one remarkable book.

Two writers. One a child of the literary mainstream, with pedigree, the other a pulp author for much of his life, touched by sudden vision, sudden clarity.

There was a time in the mid-1980s when Batchelor was golden. There was a time in the mid-1990s when McNaughton had a modicum of fame and attention. At both times, for both men, to readers and reviewers, it must have seemed as if they were fated to advance from strength to strength.

This did not happen. Instead, one petered out and died and the other stopped writing.

Making Her Own Light: Caitlin R. Kiernan
Introduction to *The Ammonite Violin & Other Stories*, 2010

Some writers cannot help themselves. Some writers, by the sheer complexity and reach of their imaginations will always be somewhat unclassifiable. For this reason, it's their view of the world we value, not the category in which a publisher places them. These are the writers who create what they find to be perfectly normal, only to be told it is strange. Such writers I value the most, for they are *sui generis*. Caitlin R. Kiernan is one of these writers, and in *The Ammonite Violin & Others* she goes to very strange places, indeed.

In effect, she has created a collection that positions supernatural elements of myth and folktale in a place far more primal than even their original context. In a radical move that no doubt came to her as naturally as a dolphin takes to swimming, Kiernan has managed, through texture and point of view, to show us the *reality* of these archetypes. Angela Carter in a collection like *The Bloody Chamber* reclaimed iconic stories for feminism, but still used her lush prose in a stylized way that mimicked the flatness of tales, which are generally two-dimensional compared to short stories. Kiernan has accomplished something more subversive—hers is a kind of dirty, modern lyricism. Like many of the Decadents, her prose is, yes, lush, but it's also muscular, allows for psychologically three-dimensional portraits of her characters, and has the flexibility to be blunt, even shocking. Mermaids, selkies, vampires, and fairies all make appearances in this collection. However, the method of description and storytelling creates a sheer physicality and alien quality to the context for these creatures that both humanizes them—in the sense of making them real, if not always understandable—and makes it impossible to see them—so often the case when writers describe "monsters" as just people in disguise or as caricatures we can dismiss because they exist solely for our passing frisson of unease or terror.

Part of this authenticity, part of the reason I find them disturbing, comes from the simple fact that the people in these stories don't really survive their encounters with the supernatural. Whether in, among others, "Madonna Littoralis" or the two "Metamorphosis" stories, this inability to survive can be literal or figurative, or both—and it occurs because the supernatural isn't so much something terrifying in Kiernan's view. It can be, but that's not the true point. The supernatural to Kiernan is also something beautiful and unknowable in intent, and often wedded to the natural world. In a sense, trying to know something unknowable will always destroy the seeker.

In almost all of these stories, too, the characters seem to encounter the supernatural as part of a need for connection, even if the thing they connect with is Other and will be the death of them. And, once the connection is made, the implications of that *passing over* are never what they might have seemed to be before the crossing. For example, the powerful, controlled yet intensely interior narrative "The Cryomancer's Daughter (Murder Ballad No. 3)" burns with its description of an obsessed, unequal relationship: "...she reaches out and brushes frozen fingertips across the space between my shoulder blades. I gasp, and at least it is *me* gasping, an honest gasp at the pain and cold flowing out of her and into me." That there is often a graphic sexual component to these stories shouldn't come as a surprise—it supports this idea of trying to connect, even if the connection can turn from erotic to grotesque, the two elements co-mingling until it's not always clear which is which.

Kiernan also discards the typical plots that you see in fantasy or supernatural fiction. There are few twists here, little action in the conventional sense. Such artifice would form a barrier to getting at truths about the relationships in these stories, some of which function as intricate snapshots of dysfunction and the attempt to communicate, underscoring that even in normal human relationships, we are all encased in our separate skulls and, ultimately, unknowable.

This focus contributes to the sense that we're reading something *new* here, even though these stories fit comfortably within Kiernan's overall oeuvre—something that is unrelenting in peeling away layers of falsehood in an attempt to get somewhere real. It's not just the characters but *readers* who receive what seem like true glimpses of what it might be like to encounter the inexplicable, with all blinders off, stripped of any niceties. I won't lie—Kiernan's approach can be brutal at times, the true fodder for nightmares, but it's also brave and true.

"Untitled 23" exemplifies these qualities, with its depiction of a faerie girl mistreated by the Faerie Queen. She's trapped by the Queen when she chases a lizard—"verdant, iridian, gazing out at me with crimson eyes"—through the forest and becomes a slave, and then even less than that.

The descriptions in this story, which serve to underscore the themes, are devastatingly brilliant. The Queen is "fashioned of some viscous, shapeless substance that is not quite flesh, but always there is the dim impression of leathery wings, as of some immense bat, and wherever the Queen brushes against the girl, there is the sensation of touching or being touched by matted fur and the blasted bark of dying, lightning-struck trees." The girl sits on a "black bed far below the forest floor," while the "Queen of Decay moves across her like the eclipse of the sun," surrounded by "mirrors hung on bits of root and bone and the fishhook mandibles of beetles."

Here, then, is the true terrible *unknowableness* of that which is often sanitized or only brought forward for our amusement, revealed as terrible because we cannot truly fathom it. Even more important, perhaps, is the sense that this is all part of the natural cycle from the Faerie Queen's point of view, as much as the pattern of the seasons, and that the natural world around us is a deeply alien place, even though we try so hard to control it. Thus, it's appropriate that the story ends with the lizard that led the girl to her fate. The lizard is the real main character in "Untitled 23," the secret sharer: that which we forever chase without realizing the depths of what we chase. It's a stunner of a story, and it's one that only Kiernan could have written.

Throughout *The Ammonite Violin & Others*, these moments proliferate, mixed with moments of pure horror—"It's loose in the room with us," "I cannot look away"—that always serve to support something beyond just unsettling us. These stories are, ultimately, driven by deeply human, deeply humane, deeply secret moments.

In the first story in *The Ammonite Violin & Others* the beleaguered narrator tells the reader, "There are things that are born into darkness and live their entire lives in darkness, in deep places, and they've learned to make whatever light they need. It sprouts from them, lanterns of flesh to dot the abyss like bare bulbs strung on electrical cords, and I wish I could make my own light at the bottom of the walls of the earth."

Caitlín R. Kiernan creates her own light in this remarkable collection, and shines it on dark places. In doing so, she gives us gritty, lyrical, horrible, beautiful truths.

Unsung Heroes of Science Fiction and Fantasy

Bantam magazine, 2008

Underrated. Obscure. Cult. Idiosyncratic. These words describe writers who haven't really gotten their due, but that readers somewhere, passionate about their favorites, offer up to their friends and post about on blogs. Sometimes, it's a one-book author who never did anything else. Sometimes, it's a writer with a reputation in the literary mainstream who remains an enigma to genre readers. Sometimes, it's just a writer who never got the luck, or the breaks, necessary to make it to wider recognition.

The great thing, though, is that you never know when an unsung hero might just walk into the limelight. Case in point: George R.R. Martin, who, despite success in short stories, experienced a certain amount of commercial resistance to his early novels. If not for Hollywood and his subsequent success, I might be trying to convince you to read *his* work.

Need another example? The SF/horror writer Jeffrey Thomas would have made my list if his Punktown novels hadn't been picked up for commercial publication in 2007.

So, with all of that in mind, I'm offering up four "unsung" heroes who deserve your reading attention.

Stuart Gordon: Victim of the New Age Fad?

After a series of pulpish novels like *The Bike From Hell* (under the pen name Alex Stuart) and an interesting fantasy series, Stuart Gordon turned to alternative history science fiction, resulting in the cult classic novel *Smile on the Void (1981).*

Smile on the Void, issued by Berkley in mass market paperback, was labeled "the stunning novel of the coming millenium" and featured praise from *Newsday* and many others. (It subsequently inspired the album Smile on the Void by the Los Angeles band A Produce.) The novel purports to be the autobiography of Ralph M'Botu Kitaj, who starts out as an arms dealer and winds up founding a religion, before disappearing in Venice in front of one hundred thousand of his followers—after having promised to return when most needed. Kitaj's story of his rough early years, his transformation from a life of crime and other bad deeds, is rendered in realistic, believable detail. From Poland to East Africa to California, Kitaj's life journey ironically ends where it started: wanted by the police, but now because of the religion that has grown up around him.

Smile on the Void is often mystical without being cloying. It is funny, heartbreaking, and beautifully written. Berkley clearly thought it would be a huge hit, one that they could leverage by using terms more familiar to nonfiction readers at that time, like "new-consciousness." Unfortunately, this strategy backfired when the New Age boom came to an end. As a result, a writer who should have entered the pop culture zeitgeist as thoroughly as Thomas Pynchon has gotten scant attention since. Gordon qualifies as an unsung hero because he wrote a novel unique in the history of genre fiction, never since duplicated, that, in some alternate universe, is still on top of the bestsellers list.

Rikki Ducornet: Invisible to Genre Readers?

Unlike Stuart Gordon, Rikki Ducornet could never be considered a one- or two-book author. She has a large body of consistently excellent fiction and has been recognized in some quarters as the finest American surrealist of the past thirty years. What she has not had, however, is much of a profile among genre readers, despite having written some of my favorite fantasy.

Her best novels include *Entering Fire* (1986), *The Fountains of Neptune* (1989), *The Jade Cabinet* (1993), and *The Fan-Maker's Inquisition*. However, *Phosphor in Dreamland* (1995), which relates the fantastical history of an imaginary Caribbean island, may be the best entry point for new readers. The novel details the attempts of a man named Phosphor to document the island in photographs, while having a series of wonderful, sometimes startling adventures. Evoking Swift in its sharp satire and relevant to current issues like climate change and species extinction, *Phosphor in Dreamland* is, above all else, a towering work of the imagination. As an ambassador of fantasy in the mainstream literary world, and for her other numerous excursions into editing, painting, poetry, and nonfiction, Ducornet gets my vote for the most well-rounded unsung hero, forging paths for others to follow. If you enjoy the work of Angela Carter or Kelly Link, you'll love Rikki Ducornet.

Rhys Hughes: Hurt by His Devotion to Short Fiction?

Referred to by some as "the mad Welshman," Rhys Hughes creates fiction that plays with reality and with language, showing the influence of such diverse writers as Jack Vance, Italo Calvino, Michael Moorcock, and Stanislaus Lem. Although he's written novels, Hughes' strength lies in the short form. He's written more than five hundred short stories, resulting in nine collections. Some of his fiction is experimental, some humorous, and some riffs off of traditional Welsh tales. Almost every story has a supernatural or absurd element that places it firmly in the fantasy or horror category. Featuring pirates, bards, explorers, hopelessly lost lovers, mazes, underground fantasy worlds, mad inventors and moving houses, Hughes consistently comes up with some of the most imaginative creations in genre.

At one time considered on a course for a major career, Hughes has thus far wound up marginalized by his devotion to the short form, and to idiosyncratic storytelling—which is a shame given the high level of entertainment Hughes provides to a reader in even his most mundane short story. Even internet junkies may find it difficult to track down original editions of Hughes' best short fiction, collected in *The Smell of Telescopes* (2000) and *Stories From a Lost Anthology*, (2002), which first appeared in lovely limiteds from Tartarus Press.

For his tireless devotion to, and innovation within, the short form, Rhys Hughes deserves not only our praise, but the designation of unsung hero.

L. Timmel Duchamp: Too Daring for Her Own Good?

Although known for short fiction in, among others, *Asimov's SF Magazine*, L. Timmel Duchamp's major work, the Marq'ssan Cycle—*Alanya to Alanya* (2005), *Renegade* (2006), *Tsunami* (2007), and *Blood in the Fruit* (2008)—remains relatively unknown. Highly praised by Samuel Delany, these novels chronicle a near-future Earth in which people in the United States are divided into executive and service classes ruled by a repressive government. Then the Marq'ssan, an advanced race of aliens, arrive and change everything by frying all electronics and giving aid to anyone willing to fight for independence from the existing power structure. In the resulting chaos, Seattle breaks off as a free zone, among other interesting extrapolations. The novels follow Kay Zeldin, a history professor who works for the government and is one of Duchamp's more inspired characters. Zeldin is genuinely conflicted—not sure if she should continue to support the government, or throw her lot in with the aliens.

Although the first novel has some clunky moments, the series gains strength as it progresses, offering a truly unique vision of the future that is also relevant to our society today. At the same time, these novels often have the pacing and tension of thrillers, the message embedded in wild plot twists and very real characters caught up in extraordinary times. Considering the ferocity and bravery displayed by Duchamp in the Marq'ssan Cycle, she deserves the title of unsung hero for her bravery in going where so many fear to tread.

My Additional Misadventures with Engelbrecht
Introduction to *Engelbrecht Again!*, Rhys Hughes, 2008

My first encounter with Engelbrecht the Dwarf Surrealist Boxer, in all of his eccentric glory, occurred when I received *The Exploits of Engelbrecht*, a lavishly illustrated tome from Savoy Books purporting to be the work of one Maurice Richardson, the stories originally published in *Lilliput Magazine*. As I entertained myself with tales of dog opera, sports on Mars, witch shoot-outs, and plant theater, I soon came to realize that "Maurice Richardson" must be a portmanteau nom de plume for a garrulous and various *collection* of ne'er-do-wells and drunkards who had come up with the character of "Engelbrecht" in a bar and proceeded to do an Album Zutique project, as per the French Decadents several generations before. Certainly, this would explain the frequent references to the "Surrealist Sportsman's Club," no doubt a phantasmagorical version and vision of whatever worn and seedy pub had originally housed the miscreants responsible as they mapped out their insane adventures on napkins, tablecloths, and the labels of a multitude of wine bottles.

Such was the exoticism of the visions laid out before me. Single authorship seemed not only *not* credible, but *in*credible. Of course, this issue soon fell from my mind, erased by the originality and fleet-footedness of the collection...only to return when, upon finishing the last story, "Unquiet Wedding," I realized that short of erasing my memory, I would never again freshly encounter Engelbrecht. Never again would I have those initial moments of innocent and not so innocent discovery.

So imagine my delight when Dead Letter Press delivered to my door a manuscript by a mad Welshman, one Rhys Hughes, purporting to be *Engelbrecht Again: Being the Further Adventures of Engelbrecht*. Those multitudinous authorial phantoms concocting Engelbrechtian illusions whilst imbibing absinthe, nepenthe, and things much stranger, apparently had been hard at work in the intervening years—not just creating new tales, but also re-creating a new pen name; one more believable for being Welsh and for having already resurrected the obscure Argentine dwarf/juggler Jorge Luis Borges in convincing fashion for *A New Universal History of Infamy*.

With trembling hand and twitching eye (a familial tic familiar to my familiar), I perused the pages with a strange mixture of dread and anticipation. I longed to learn more of Engelbrecht's exploits, but was this authorial collective named "Rhys Hughes" as talented or as lunatic as that previously labeled "Maurice Richardson"? Would the multi-brain multi-verse of "Hughes" read as if it came from lithe *Lilliput* or from its distorted mirror brother, the uncouth *Blefuscudia*?

I decided to make a first pass through the manuscript during which I skimmed the surface, collecting phrases. If this went well, I would delve deeper, as they say, and commit myself to further exploration. If it went poorly, I would disengage and throw the manuscript in the fireplace, there to join the chipmunks, voyeurs, and Jehovah's Witnesses. Among the sentences I surgically flensed from the narrative without becoming mired in guerilla warfare or anything similarly time-consuming were the following:

> Not that I wanted him transformed into a mineral, you understand, but it seemed ludicrous to waste such an easy opportunity to recoup my earlier loss.

> Among the many two-wheeled events sponsored by the Id, the most taxing, physically and psychically, is the annual Tour de Trance.

> We expected a tapeworm parade, which the Id always prefers to the tickertape version, but celebrations were muted.

> The Roulette Wheel was large and terrible, carved from uranium and powered not by a croupier but jagged lightning which gushed from the ceiling down a copper cable to a hidden motor under the device. There were plenty of headless corpses strewn around the table, in sundry states of decay, which was strange considering this was the Casino's opening night.

The embryonic Romantic had been regrown in one of Dr Sadismus's accelerated incubators, though he was still too fresh to be a proper youth.

and, finally, the tantalizingly obscure

With the puppets, our strength totaled 77,777 arms and the back of our line wasn't visible from the vicinity of the pit.

It was this last mystery that proved my undoing, as I abandoned my structured skim and dove headlong into the story, titled "Tug of Worlds," and just barely managed to avoid falling, there being so much rope in the story I had no choice but to hang on. From there I pulled myself back up to "The North Face of the Ego" and, realizing I was in it for the duration, went down to the pub and ordered lunch and some good German beer.

Several days later, buttocks calcified upon my stool, I had encountered not only the monkey for all seasons but also a mermaid supper, an Atlantean tango, the Borges twins, and some very odd argonauts, among a million and one other things.[1] During this somewhat confused time (I went in wearing an overcoat, sweater vest, undershirt, shorts, and long sockless boots but came out, squinting against unwanted sunlight, in the full moon-cluttered robes of a high-level freemason), I came to a sudden conclusion.

Whereas I still believed "Maurice Richardson" was an amalgamation of a possible dozen talented half-wits, "Rhys Hughes" was incontrovertibly a single individual talented half-wit. No one piece of evidence supported this conclusion, but something in the tone, something in the post-absurdist *bent* of the stories—the underlying mischievous subtext, the cheeky rhythm of the (much longer) paragraphs, the refusal to ever use the word "y'all," even in

---

[1] My only regret during this reading adventure is that I somehow managed to misplace one tale entitled "Engelbrecht and the Ultimate Secret of Tlon and the Mad Arab" during an extended drinking session with a giraffe of my acquaintance. I remember a munching from above I thought was innocent at the time. The manuscript sent to me being the original, and Rhys Hughes' memory being much diminished from years of eating baby food laced with laudanum, the story could not be reconstructed for publication here.

dialogue, the weird logic, even more insane than in the original volume—convinced me of this truth.

Further evidence appeared when, during some spring cleaning, I unearthed two volumes from behind a very irritated bear, itself wearing a bear suit with lobster claws for hands: *The Smell of Telescopes* and *Stories from a Lost Anthology*. Both of these handsome collectible Tartarus hardcovers contained stories that, despite mentioning Engelbrecht, appeared to be conveying his adventures regardless. The truth of this is hard to convey, but in re-reading "Journey Through a Wall," "The Macroscopic Teapot," "The Squonk Laughed," and "A Girl Like a Doric Column," among others, I began to feel as if *Engelbrecht* might have written these tales. That in some perverse sense, Rhys Hughes *was* Engelbrecht, in his later years, having retired from his sporting endeavors and taken up fiction.

No matter what the literal or figurative truth of this sensation, it has haunted me, dear reader, ever since, in ways most unexpected and uncanny. I wake up in strange places with peculiar books piled up beside me. I mouth odd phrases to passersby and can barely bring myself to water the fish or clean the snails from the carpet. For now I, too, write Engelbrecht stories, and have no clue who or what I am channeling.

But, of course, this is none of your concern. For you, this book shall be a delight, an entertainment, a fancy ball, a surrealistic assortment of carefully crafted desserts. *For you, dear reader, the only important detail is that Engelbrecht lives once more!*

Alasdair Gray and Lanark

In Alasdair Gray's terrible afterworld of Unthank, giant mouths descend from the sky to devour the main character, Lanark, a cold wind rising "with the salty odour of rotting seaweed, then a hot one with an odour like roasting meat." As Lanark is swallowed up, so is the reader.

Gray's visions in his masterwork *Lanark* (1981) are as apocalyptic as they are political, and when the fantastical becomes entwined with themes of social iniquity, the critic who attempts to pull them apart risks being devoured himself. "I believe there are cities where work is a prison and time a goad and love a burden," Lanark says. Yet embossed on the hardcover first edition of Gray's novel *Poor Things* (1992) are the words "Work As If You Live In The Early Days Of A Better Nation." Dragon hide, "as common as mouths or softs or twittering rigor" in Unthank, encrusts the limbs of citizens in a "glossy cold hide," the color "an intensely dark green" that causes people to act out their hidden nature: "Lanark saw that his dragon fist was clenching to strike her. He thrust it into his pocket where it squirmed like a crab." At the same time, many, like Lanark, seek the light in a lightless place, even as the dragon hide conspires to take them into darkness. On the level of prose, at the sub-atomic level, does Gray make his intentions clear through the words of Lanark's eventual enemy, Sludden?

> Metaphor is one of thought's most essential tools. It illuminates what would otherwise be totally obscure. But the illumination is sometimes so bright that it dazzles instead of revealing.

Lanark's success may lie in the use of metaphor in prose as tall and true as the title of his second short story collection. Gray's genius, however, stems from his ability to portray the struggle of the individual against dysfunctional institutions in dual personal and fantastical terms. The entry point for Gray's exploration of this theme is the centuries-long struggle of the Scots against the English (and, admittedly, against their own shortsightedness). As Gray said in an interview:

> My approach to institutional dogma and criteria—let's call it, my approach to institutions—reflects their approach to me. Nations, cities, schools, marketing companies, hospitals, police forces, have been made by people for the good of people. I cannot live without them, don't want or expect to. But when we see them working to increase dirt, poverty, pain, and death, then they have obviously gone wrong…Everyone suffers for it, so it is an ingredient in all fiction except the most blandly escapist.

The novel centers around Lanark's life in the underworld of Unthank and that of his previous incarnation in the "real" world, Duncan Thaw. Thaw, a sensitive artist, attempts to create great art; failing, he commits suicide after first possibly murdering a female friend. A decaying Glasgow of the 1940s and 1950s, similar to that of Gray's own childhood, serves as the backdrop to the plot.

Lanark arrives in Unthank with no memory of his past as Thaw. As he attempts to discover his identity, Lanark makes his way across a grossly exaggerated mirror of a city, in which all the vices and problems of the "real" world have been magnified and distorted. Once Lanark regains his memory of his life as Duncan, he embarks on a frenetic attempt to save the city of Unthank from destruction. In some of the most surreal scenes, he has a son with his girl friend, Rima, while traveling through a kind of time warp. Rima leaves him for his old enemy, Sludden, but Lanark continues to soldier on—as always hoping to one day experience "light," although he may not be certain what "light" means.

Gray purposefully divides his novel into four "Books." However, he begins with Book Three, the first Lanark section. The most pragmatic reason for this chronological dislocation is to introduce the reader to the fantastical underworld of Unthank first. The novel must exist within the fantastical frame. Given the intensely realistic—even grimly so—quality of the Glasgow sections, the surrealism of Unthank would be too jarring to the reader. Instead, Gray takes the calculated risk that the realistic sections will seem more integrated if they occur later. In a perverse sense, Gray, by using this order, makes the naturalistic scenes fantasy because they are fantasy to the inhabitants of Unthank. It is, perhaps, a truly alternative interpretation to think that Glasgow is the hell and Unthank the reality.

Lanark has been called many things by many reviewers. Anthony Burgess praised it as a masterpiece. John Crowley and Michael Dirda (to a lesser extent) both praised the book's tremendous vision and the brilliance of individual scenes, while criticizing the increased allegorical content of the novel's latter half.

The novel does veer toward abstraction in Book Four, the ratio of dialogue to exposition increasing dangerously. Gray also devotes a chapter to cataloging Gray's theft from long-dead writers. While the chapter displays Gray's signature wit, it slows the momentum of the narrative.

But in the case of *Lanark*, such criticism is largely irrelevant for the same reason that criticism of the whaling chapters in Herman Melville's *Moby Dick* is irrelevant. The correction of these "flaws" would rob both books of their unique genius. The hallmark of original, eccentric writers is that what makes the writer different, even in a maddening sense, cannot be separated out from what makes the writer good. Gray's rough edges are the rough edges of what can only be termed *prophecy*.

More importantly, in terms of the fantastical content, *Lanark* provides a unique example of the use of fantasy in a social commentary. Unlike *Animal Farm* (1945), *Candide* (1759), or *Gulliver's Travels* (1726), *Lanark* is not intended primarily as parody, satire, or parable.

Whether in *Lanark* or faux Victorian romps such as *Poor Things*, fantasies of the mind like *1982 Janine* (1984) or via the futuristic satire of *The History Maker* (1996), Gray writes "regional" literature with such ferocity and skill that it transcends its Scottish origins to become universal. If Gray tends to incorporate fantasy or science fiction, he does so to make full use of all relevant tools—and because such elements of an unshackled imagination represent the writer's own seeking of the light. Although not a surrealist, Gray does ascribe to the idea of convulsive beauty: beauty, even grim beauty, in the service of liberty.

If discussion of Gray's work begins and ends with *Lanark*, it is for the simple reason that all of his other fiction exists within the borders of its imagination. The black sense of humor, the obsession with social injustice, the difficult acts of communication between the sexes, the homage, even in altered form, to Glasgow—all manifest themselves fully in *Lanark*. The novel represents the absolute limits of Gray's eccentricity, postmodern inquiry, and what can only be termed a kind of *rough genius*. No writer should have to live up to such a book. That Gray has produced other novels almost as profound indicates a remarkable tenacity on the part of the author.

My Love-Hate Relationship with Clark Ashton-Smith
Introduction to Bison Books editions, 2006

Lost Worlds

I've had a love-hate relationship with Clark Ashton Smith's work for as long as I can remember. The lovely visions of other worlds and other places linger in my memory, but so too do the hyper-elevated prose style, the grimly formal dialog, and the sometimes stiff, ritualistic scenes.

In re-reading *Lost Worlds*, however, I'm struck by how little these latter tendencies interfere with my enjoyment of many of the stories. I thought this might have something to do with my close reading of Decadent literature in the interim, because I can finally see how Smith's work weds pulp and Decadent-Symbolist writing with the sensibilities of an outsider artist. I'm not sure Smith's fiction always succeeds—nor am I convinced that Smith's aesthetic is the result of conscious intent—but the attempt makes for interesting work. Some of these tales have only historical significance now; however, many of them still hold great imagistic power.

Lost Worlds collects, as one might expect, Clark Ashton Smith's "lost world" stories, from Hyperborea to Atlantis, Zothique to Averoigne. The collection immerses the reader in a sensibility that is foreign but also familiar. Readers will recognize these settings from countless movies, other pulp writers, and the work of Sir Arthur Conan Doyle, although Smith has a somewhat different take on the subject matter.

Unlike most other approaches to "lost worlds," Smith's fiction tends to eschew the framing structure in which modern-day people come across the "lost" place. Instead, he treats his settings not as lost worlds at all, but as vibrant, living locales peopled with picturesque, oddly ritualistic characters. There is no modern world existing on the "outside." There is no "outside" at all, and for this reason these tales might well be classified as "secondary world" in nature (or even "primary world," as Smith's fanatical devotion to his visions seems to eliminate our world altogether).

The descriptions in these tales are somehow altogether more useful than in his tales set in the "real" world. Their intensity does not seem as out of place, their length seems appropriate when describing milieus that depend so much for their existence on the stuff of myth and rumor.

"The Tale of Satampra Zeiros" exemplifies this approach. Like many of the Lost Worlds stories, Smith tells it entirely in summary with a few attempts at half-scene. At first, the layering of description, as the narrator embarks on his quest, seems excessive. The reader waits for the story to begin…and then begins to understand that the description *is* the story. This is not necessarily a bad thing, but it is unusual in this sense: such an approach usually fails. Creative writing instructors generally advise beginning writers to focus on showing not telling, and for good reason. In Smith's case, it works more often than not, due to his pseudo-poetic stylings:

> There were no birds nor animals, such as one would think to find in any wholesome forest; but at rare intervals a stealthy viper with pale and heavy coils glided away from our feet among the rank leaves of the roadside, or some enormous moth with baroque and evil-colored mottlings flew before us and disappeared into the dimness of the jungle. Abroad already in the half-light, huge purpureal bats with eyes like tiny rubies arose at our approach from the poisonous-looking fruits on which they feasted, and watched us with malign intention as they hovered noiselessly in the air above.

Some may note the carelessness of the vague "evil-colored," among other examples, but on the whole the intensity of such prose serves Smith well. The reader has little choice but to believe in the world described, even if the reader may not always believe in the story being told. Less lush prose would cause the descriptions to crumble, the reader left with the banal, rendered in bland summary.

However, in areas where a possible Decadent influence gives way to the undigested hyberbolean in-exactnesses of his Lovecraftian influence, Smith falters badly. Later in the story, for example, tentacles come into play:

> What unimaginable horror of protoplastic life, what loathly spawn of the primordial slime had come forth to confront us, we did not pause to consider or conjecture. The monstrosity was too awful to permit of even a brief contemplation; also, its intentions were too plainly hostile, and it gave evidence of anthropophagic inclinations.

Critics of Smith's prose style may miss the mark in their assignation of the word "purple" to Smith's writing. I think it is more that he writes at such an elevated, poetic level that when called upon to put special emphasis on an event, Smith has no option but to engage in near histrionics. These histrionics are then accompanied by a lack of specific detail, as if the need to be mouth-frothing has inhibited his descriptive abilities. In such cases, Smith devolves into what can only be called pastiche.

(One is driven to wonder why in almost all of these stories the natural world is such a horribly cruel and evil place, one in which men—there are no women of note in these stories—must struggle against not just indifferent nature but "evil" nature. Certainly, this may reflect the view of some Decadents, but it is not a point of view necessarily prevalent in Smith's contemporaries.)

In similar fashion, the slightly more scene-laden "The Door to Saturn" contains scenes of beautiful description, but also dialogue like "'Detestable sorcerer! Abominable heretic! I arrest you!' said Morghi with pontifical severity." What are we to make of such camp? Is it intentional? Is it intrinsic to writing this kind of story? I don't know the answer. I only know Smith must have found it necessary, and readers must forgive him for that necessity if they want to enjoy the stories.

As a counterbalance, certain passages ring with true intrigue, as when his character meets "the Ephiqhs, who hollow out their homes in the trunks of certain large fungi, and are always having to hunt new habitations because the old ones crumble into powder in a few days. And they heard the underground croaking of that mysterious people, the Ghlonghs, who dread not only the sunlight but also the ring-light, and who have never yet been seen by any of the surface dwellers."

I am captivated by paragraphs like these, so much so that I sometimes feel that Smith was either writing summaries of stories he planned to write at some time in the future, or was filing reports from places he'd visited as a tourist.

Ultimately, stories like "The Door to Saturn" work due to that mystery, but also because of the sense of scale. Smith is forever putting his stories in a deeper perspective. When this works, the effect can be grand-eloquent yet not grandiose, as at the end of "The Door to Saturn":

> As a consequence of this belief, the faith of Yhoundeh declined, and there was a widespread revival of the dark worship of Zhothaqquah throughout Mhu Thulan in the last century before the onset of the great Ice Age.

In such passages, Smith's sincerity and earnestness shine through, illuminating the story. Although there can be an arch tone to his writing—especially in his dialogue—on the whole Smith seems to believe in his worlds so completely that he makes the reader believe in them, too.

Smith may not have had the perfect comic timing and sense of humor that elevates Fritz Leiber's Grey Mouser tales above the ordinary. Nor did he have Tolkien's completist sense of history. But in the combination of extraordinary detail, sincerity, and grand scale, Smith managed to carve out a unique place for himself in the canon of fantasy fiction. This is a somewhat singular achievement, as many other pulp-era writers, similarly self-taught, similarly obsessed with presenting a unique worldview through the cracked mirror of their technique, are now literally pulped and forgotten.

In the final analysis, "visionary" is perhaps the best word to describe these tales, in the same way that much outsider art is "visionary"—in that the vision is sometimes clouded by the writer's lack of formal training. Ultimately, this is both Smith's blessing and his curse.

Out of Space & Time

When Clark Ashton Smith was twenty, Marcel Proust published *Swann's Way* and D. H. Lawrence published *Sons and Lovers*. By the time Smith was twenty-five, James Joyce had written *Dubliners*, Virginia Woolf had written *The Voyage Out* and Spengler had completed *The Decline of the West*. Throughout his thirties and forties, Smith could have encountered new works by Pirandello, Eliot, Mansfield, Hemingway, Kafka, Breton, Faulkner, and even Nabokov.

However, it doesn't appear *any* of these writers, with the possible exception of Kafka, exerted any influence on Smith's own work whatsoever. Instead, he focused on French Symbolists, already well in decline by the time he became an adult—although it is possibly more honest to say he focused on the French Decadents as well. (Many of the "Symbolists" were identified as "Decadents" before academia legitimized them.)

This identification with a literary group that influenced other important writers but that largely did not reflect the mainstream of American literature is one reason why Smith remained obscure during his lifetime. Another reason, of course, was his love for pulp fiction, in the form of H.P. Lovecraft, among others. Is it any surprise that aligning himself in his writing with two "outsider" groups led to his own obscurity? He might have been rescued by the Beat Poets, who had a certain sympathy for the aesthetic of the Decadents, if he hadn't stopped writing well before they came into being.

We can find evidence of Smith's dual highbrow-lowbrow sensibility even in his life. As August Derleth pointed out in the original introduction to *Out of Space and Time,* Smith was:

> …the descendent of Norman-French counts and barons, of Lancashire baronets and Crusaders. One of his Ashton forebears was beheaded for his part in the famed Gunpowder Plot. His mother's family, the Gaylords, came to New England in 1630—Huguenot Gaillards who fled persecution in France after the revocation of the Edict of Nantes. Smith's father, Timeus Smith, was a world-traveler in his early years, but settled at last in Auburn, where he died less than a decade ago.

At the same time, Smith's own life as "journalist, a fruit picker and packer, a woodchopper, a typist, a cement-mixer, a gardener, a hard-rock miner, mucker, and windlasser," was hardly aristocratic; quite the opposite. Just because in his prose he used a diverse, archaic, and formidable vocabulary does not mean readers should assume that Smith was an erudite man of letters. It is precisely his overgrasping for literary authenticity in some of his stories that shows us he was not.

And it is in a proletarian, pulp mode that Smith has been rescued from complete obscurity—through genre publications and publishers, which initially resulted in his work being discussed in terms of other pulp writers, or with vague generalizations and waves of the hand toward the Symbolists (who perhaps more specifically influenced his poetry).

This pulp-genre comparison seems valid in terms of the purported "purple" quality of Smith's prose. At first glance, and sometimes second, Smith's writing does seem overwrought. Thus, it's easy to dismiss it as amateurish, much as others have dismissed Lovecraft's writing in the past. I don't believe that this conclusion is false so much as incomplete.

First of all, Smith's prose is not always lush—it tends to become that way the more descriptive passages infest a particular story. In scenes dominated by dialog, the lushness is pushed to the background and the action tends to be better paced as a result.

Secondly, we read Smith precisely *for* his prose escapism, for those flights of fancy that some critics condemn. (Is it too odd to suggest that the French seem to like Smith because in translation a translator can flense those flights that are just a bit too fanciful?)

In the more banal tales, this sense of prose poetry is restrained, as in "A Rendezvous in Averoigne," which, with its chateaus and chivalry, exists all too clearly in a recognizably real world. While lovely, the descriptions of a "purling brook," a "tarn of waters that were dark and dull as clotting blood," and "skeletons of rotting osiers" seem oddly muted in the context of the story. There is no real resonance to the images—they do not seem illuminated from within but curiously immutable, mere description. Conversely, in "The City of the Singing Flame," trans-dimensional travel interferes with Smith's effectiveness because of his need to explain, or attempt to explain, through his narrator, with passages like:

> I had read a number of transdimensional stories—in fact, I had written one or two myself; and I had often pondered the possibility of other worlds or material planes which may co-exist in the same space with

ours, invisible and impalpable to human senses. Of course, I realised at once that I had fallen into some such dimension…

Or: "My brain reeled before the infinite vistas of surmise that were opened by such questions." Or: "Inevitably, I began to speculate as to the relationship between the columns in this new dimension and the borders in my own world."

All of this "business," as one would say in the world of theater, dilutes the poetic quality of the prose, dilutes the reader's sense of wonder. Regardless of whether this criticism is merely symptomatic of the difference in focus between weird fiction from that period and modern weird fiction—few writers today would bother with much in the way of explanation or extrapolation about the transdimensional factor—this is one reason Smith can seem dated. Conversely, his ability to ignore the niggling need for such explanation at other times preserves the transcendent quality of some of his stories.

Once Smith feels comfortable with the idea that, for example, the reader will not reject his initial premise he relaxes into the story and the narrative begins to exert an inexorable power.

> I returned to the town; and once again I sought to make my presence known to the inhabitants, but all in vain. And after awhile, as I trudged from street to street, the sun went down behind the island, and the stars came swiftly out in a heaven of purpureal velvet. The stars were large and lustrous and innumerably thick: with the eye of a practiced mariner, I studied them eagerly; but I could not trace the wonted constellations, though here and there I thought that I perceived a distortion or elongation of some familiar grouping.

The difference between Smith trying to defend his creations and Smith just living comfortably inside of them is often the difference between success and failure. At times, I get the sense from these stories that Smith would like nothing better than to discard the pulp shapings of his plots, abandon the cardboard cut-outs of his first person narrators, and dive head-first into the worlds themselves, to immerse himself in them without need to conform to the needs of narrative.

Luckily, the core of *Out of Space and Time* consists of stories like "A Night in Malneant," "The Chain of Aforgomon," "The Last Hieroglyph" (with its many delights, such as a talking salamander guide), "The Vaults of Yoh-Vombis," and others in which the need to explain is generally subsumed by the need to visualize a world or wondrously alien place.

In re-reading these stories, I did begin to feel that Smith's strengths and his weaknesses might be so intertwined that surgery would have to be performed to separate them. It's a theory—some would say an excuse—that writers like China Miéville have put forth about several pulp-era writers, including Lovecraft. But it has a ring of truth to it, in that Smith is a classic example of "outsider art" in the literary arena. Self-taught, everything Smith did outside of writing (sculpture, drawing) had an amateur sheen to it—a sincerity and originality that went hand-in-hand with a kind of unfinished or rough draft quality. Why should we assume his writing was any different?

Both of Smith's purported centers of influence—pulp-genre and Symbolist/Decadent—have, at one time or another, been on the outside looking in: illegitimate, disreputable. (Sometimes this reflected the desire or aims of the writers associated with both groups, sometimes not.) What ties this all together in Smith's case is that he truly *was* an outsider artist. I don't mean "outsider" in the narrow European definition of art or writing by the mentally disturbed, but the broader definition that includes folk art and creative endeavors by those with no formal training.[1]

In support of this, I would offer that there are few writers who seem to write so wholly for themselves, who seem so enraptured in a vision only they can see that they sacrifice accessibility for that vision. Smith, it seems to me, is an outsider precisely because, in pursuit of his own gratification, he makes the reader an outsider, looking in. This is what attracts readers to Smith's writing—that voyeuristic sense of peering in on a world and worldview never meant for us—and at the same time can repel us from it. I do not believe Smith cared one way or the other about the reader, so long as he could write what he wanted to write, in the way he wanted to write it. His visions may thus be incomplete, sometimes cloudy, but they are also to readers today, ironically enough given his pulp origins, undiluted by any appreciable commercial taint.

---

1 Per *Wikipedia*: "Outsider Art was coined by art critic Roger Cardinal in 1972 as an English synonym for Art Brut (which literally translates as "Raw Art" or "Rough Art"), a label created by French artist Jean Dubuffet to describe art created outside the boundaries of official culture."

Lovecraft Art: The Link Between Tentacles and Cosmic SF

io9, June 2008 (with Ann VanderMeer)

> The spread of the tentacle—a limb-type with no Gothic or traditional precedents (in "Western" aesthetics)—from a situation of near total absence in Euro-American teratoculture up to the nineteenth century, to one of being the default monstrous appendage of today, signals the epochal shift to a Weird culture.... The "Lovecraft Event," as Ben Noys invaluably understands it, is unquestionably the centre of gravity of this revolutionary movement; it's defining text, Lovecraft's 'The Call of Cthulhu,' published in 1928 in Weird Tales. —from China Miéville's "M.R. James and the Quantum Vampire," *Collapse IV*.

Tentacular horrors, unnamable evils, and quests to the edges of such alien-landscapes-on-earth as Antarctica were just some of the beautifully bizarre qualities of H.P. Lovecraft's weird fiction. Recently enshrined by the Library Series of America alongside Philip K. Dick, Lovecraft has had an enormous influence on readers and writers. (Remember the Call of Cthulhu RPG?)

But what about the art? Ever since the first pulp covers showcasing Lovecraft's fiction, a multitude of visual creators have been interpreting those tentacular horrors, unnamable evils, and odd quests. It is arguably one of the most enjoyable and yet tortuous tasks an artist could have, especially as version after version of images from iconic stories accumulate over the decades, making original riffs that much more difficult.

Now, Centipede Press has issued one of the most audacious hardcover art books ever created: *The Art of Lovecraft: Artists Inspired by Lovecraft*. About the size of a thick tombstone, including over 400 pages of mostly full-color art, with nonfiction by Harlan Ellison, Thomas Ligotti, and others, this absolute stone-cold classic is a testament to the publisher's attention to detail and Lovecraft's enduring influence.

It also provides a wonderful gallery setting for H.R. Giger, Bob Eggleton, John Coulthart, Michael Whelan, Lee Brown Coye, Virgil Finlay, Ian Miller, Gahan Wilson, John Picacio, Harry O. Morris, J.K. Potter, and many others.

Often, the images in the book mix fantasy with Lovecraft's take on "cosmic horror," the idea that the universe is hostile and inert.

In SF-nal terms, Bob Eggleton interprets that cosmic horror as alien influence: "Lovecraft's elder gods, unspeakable ones, shamblers and so on...were all in reality malevolent aliens from other worlds. They were ancient and evil, but the fact they're from another world is lost in the mists. His stories had references to astronomy, astrology and science and yet took this 180 turn into something scary and dark. Nigel Kneale, for instance, wrote the Quatermass series in much the same way. *Quatermass & The Pit* was truly Lovecraftian."

John Coulthart notes, too, that "the young Lovecraft was a keen astronomer who became acquainted at an early age with a sense of cosmic scale, the vastness of the universe and so on. This combined with a natural pessimism, and his later atheism gave him a strong sense of human insignificance in the face of cosmic enormity. 'We live on a placid island of ignorance in the midst of black seas of infinity,' as he says at the opening of *The Call of Cthulhu*."

Not exactly the most uplifting of messages, but definitely powerful—and revolutionary within genre at the time.

"His problem as a writer was that most Western supernatural fiction up to that point had some kind of Christian dimension to it, even if this wasn't directly stated," Coulthart says. "That was obviously a problem for an atheist writing a form of fiction which needed something malevolent at its core. His solution was to replace the Devil and the Christian idea of evil with vast extra-dimensional entities which disturb or threaten us because we mean as much to them as microbes do to human beings."

Disappointingly (to us at least), Harry O. Morris rules out a literal cephalopodic element to the idea of cosmic horror: "[It's] not a giant squid descending from outer space, but rather an all pervasive sense of dread that permeates everything we think we know, including our faces in the mirror and the knives and forks at the dinner table."

For Ian Miller the concept is more visceral, citing films like *Alien* as Lovecraftian in mood: "Things hidden in the shadows, in tight dark places, dangerous, scratching, moving, creeping, stalking, mysterious, and always at the peripheries of one's vision waiting in the shadows to spring out and bite you...Things arcane. Airless dark places with strange smells. Dark cupboards. Things that scratch and suffocate. Tight shoes and fish eyes...I suspect fear fueled by adrenalin gave rise to the notion of warp speed, though I'm sure some would disagree."

How, then, do these artists put their own personal stamp on something so strong and powerful on the page, and thus indelibly imprinted upon readers' minds?

For Eggleton it's trying to give "a kind of epic feel to [the paintings]. A sense of the familiar and then at the same time, something alien and bizarre."

Harry O. Morris approaches Lovecraft through ambiguity: "For me, the best way to express this uncomfortable aura visually is to leave portions of the picture undefined, in shadow, and influenced by chance/chaos. Also, I'm inclined to try and convey a sense of timeless antiquity which seems to be a cornerstone of Lovecraft's vision."

John Picacio also believes the best Lovecraftian art doesn't try to show everything. "It leaves something to the imagination, a few conceptual voids here and there, purposely left for the mind to fill with something personal and therefore much more potent....I think trying to literally illustrate a Lovecraftian monster usually misses the mark. It's just not as scary anymore because the terror has somehow been contained in the lines and the strokes, and therefore distilled. That's why his stuff is so difficult to effectively translate to comics and film although so many have tried."

Coulthart is one of those creators who, in addition to his Lovecraftian paintings has successfully translated the icon's vision to comics: "I wanted to take Lovecraft's fiction seriously on its own terms, something which—in the comics world especially—wasn't happening very often. When I started illustrating his work in the 1980s there was little apart from the Lovecraft special issue of *Heavy Metal* from 1979 which had attempted that. I tried to match his dense writing style with an equally dense and detailed drawing style and tried to make things look solid and historically accurate. I've always been interested in architecture, and Lovecraft's concept of alien architecture continues to fascinate."

This might make the art seem ultra-serious, but it's not all "cosmic." As Jerad Walter, the genius behind Centipede Press points out, "Some of the artwork is humorous or whimsical, and rather good-natured. There's a difference in humor between the 'Deep One' Horrora Model Kit image, which is more nostalgic, and the 'Where the Great Old Ones Are' image, which is just a send-up of Lovecraft and Maurice Sendak, and the black humor of the Gahan Wilson piece, which is just over-the-top. It is the black humor of some of the material that works best in the book, for me at any rate. I think that the humorous side comes out because all of these bleak, nihilistic visions of Lovecraft can be so dreary and depressing that a send-up of it all is just inevitable."

All of these approaches and many more are showcased in *The Art of Lovecraft*. It's a stunning love letter to a long and storied tradition.

Walter says, "I don't think any reader of weird fiction can ever look at tentacles the same way after Lovecraft. I remember boiling some squid and chopping off the heads, putting them off to one side of the cutting block, planning to save them for something, until my wife quite reasonably asked if I was out of my mind."

When we asked Walters how long it took to bring this amazing project to completion, his answer displayed a refreshingly fanatical approach to the details. "It took about two years. The hardest part was simply contacting all of the involved artists and narrowing down the range of material. It was physically demanding, too, in that hours and hours were spent color correcting all of the scans. Many images took upwards to 20 hours to get them just right."

As for his own favorites in the book, Walters told me he likes it all, but "perhaps the Lee Brown Coye section and some of the fold-outs. The thumbnails section is useful. With any project of this size, of course there are going to be small details that you wish you could change. However, I feel very fortunate in that everything I wanted to be in the book is in the book, and everything I wanted to do has been done. I do miss the presence of Wayne Douglas Barlowe, whose Old One would have been a good inclusion. However, I feel very privileged to have made a book that includes at least one work of every major fantasy and horror artist of the last 50 years. Wrightson, Frazetta, Whelan, Giger, Morris, Potter, Fabian, Coye, Rowena, Palencar, Eggleton, Bok, Finlay, Ian Miller, Tim Kirk—they are all in here."

ALFRED KUBIN AND THE TORTURED TRIUMPH OF *THE OTHER SIDE*

Omnivoracious, June 2009

Austrian Alfred Kubin (1877-1959) fits loosely within an Expressionist/Decadent/proto-Surrealist tradition. A highly praised artist, he produced only one major work of fiction, *The Other Side*, published in 1908. Although still underrated, the novel has managed to retain a cult status simply because it has long been a favorite of a variety of writers and artists. It would be hard to believe, for example, that Mervyn Peake had not read Kubin prior to writing his Gormenghast novels. (*The Other Side* is perhaps most akin in tone to Peake's *Titus Alone*.)

The details of Kubin's life relevant to his fiction are these: his mother died when he was ten, he had a sexualized relationship with an older, pregnant woman when he was eleven, and his father was a tyrant whose death in part triggered the writing of *The Other Side*. Kubin, in his nonfiction, is amazingly frank about all of these personal issues, giving us rare insight into motivation and influence.

These events, as well as unhappy romances, contributed to his uneasy, melancholic state, which manifested itself in unique visions, which then manifested in his art as the truest way of portraying the nightmares occurring in his head. Kubin had no internal editor telling him "no, this is too much." Moreover, he may not even have realized that what he was creating might startle people. Did it amuse or horrify him when gentlemen and ladies who viewed his art reportedly fainted?

There's the sense, too, in reading the praise of Kubin's contemporaries that they found him too rough, too flawed, and yet it's impossible to separate out the "good" from the "bad"—a condition common to some of the best "weird" writers and artists. As Austrian critic Richard Schaukal noted in a 1903 review, "He has not studied drawing. That is clear at a glance. But what does that tell us when confronted with this stunning oeuvre!"[1] Given these underpinnings of Kubin's inspiration, it's perhaps remarkable that *The Other Side* has as much story as it does; not merely a series of images strung together, it is a true masterpiece of rising tension and horror.

The Other Side tells the tale of a Munich draftsman asked by an old schoolmate named Patera to visit the newly established Dream Kingdom, somewhere in Central Asia. Patera rules the Dream Kingdom from the capital city of Pearl. The wealthy Patera has had a European city uprooted and brought to its new location, along with sixty-five thousand inhabitants. The narrator, after some hesitation, agrees to visit and travels with his wife through Constantinople, Batum, Batu, Krasnovodsk, and Samarkand—Samarkand being the last of any identifying landmarks on their journey.

The narrator soon finds that the Dream Kingdom is, well, a kingdom of dreams. People experience or live "only in moods" and shape all outer being at will "through the maximum possible cooperative effort." A huge wall keeps out the world and "the sun never shone, never were the moon or the stars visible at night....Here, illusions simply were reality."

Over time, strange rituals and aberrations have sprung up. Pearl also *shifts* in odd ways, and in this sense has a kinship with M. John Harrison's far-future Viriconium, which also functions from more of a metaphorical than a chronological foundation. This doesn't bother the narrator at first, but as the city's changes become more and more grotesque, it's clear that the Dream Kingdom is faltering, descending into madness.

Despite the claustrophobic atmosphere and unseen horrors that form the emotional foundation of the novel, *The Other Side* is remarkable not just for its vivid imagery, laden with surrealistic subtext, but for how the relatively modern aspects of the novel—American tourists, for example—are perfectly integrated into a timeless, festering milieu. The battle that occurs between the irrational and rational as the Dream Kingdom disintegrates takes on

---

1 *All quotes not attributed taken from the excellent and highly recommended* Alfred Kubin: Drawings 1897-1909 *(published by Neue Galerie).*

an updated Grand Guignol quality that oddly enough has the texture of modern-day war. It's almost as if the novel channels *Apocalypse Now* by way of Hieronymus Bosch.

Where did *The Other Side* come from, other than from Kubin's visionary art? Consider this tangle of influence: Kubin had been commissioned to illustrate a book of Edgar Allan Poe novellas by a Munich publisher in 1907. At roughly the same time, Kubin met with Gustav Meyrink to discuss illustrations for Meyrink's novel-in-progress *The Golem*. When Meyrink hit a snag in finishing *The Golem*, Kubin took his preliminary sketches and found ways to use some of them in *The Other Side*. Not long after publication of *The Other Side*, Franz Kafka read and enjoyed it, and then later used elements from it in the creation of his own *The Castle*. (Kubin might have been aware of Kafka's early work, as well.)

Labels like "outsider artist" aside, Kubin was definitely connected to the creative communities of his day. Indeed, when Kubin arrived in Munich, Germany, to study art as a teenager, who should he be discovered by than the iconic Franz Blei, who was also one of Kafka's friends.

Blei gives us a semi-amused description of Kubin as a "frail young boy who was always dressed in black and had a pale face that was always straining a little to grow dark and pretending to be as shy as a young world that had been dragged from a hollow into the light."

That Kubin was a creator who either "was compelled by forces that guided his hand," or trained himself to be so compelled, is clear even from his description of his reaction to an exhibition of Max Klinger's etchings in Munich in 1882:

> I grew moody...And now I was suddenly inundated with visions of pictures in black and white—it is impossible to describe what a thousand-fold treasure my imagination poured out before me. Quickly I left the theater, for the music and the mass of lights now disturbed me, and I wandered aimlessly in the dark streets, overcome and literally ravished by a dark power that conjured up before my mind strange

creatures, houses, landscapes, grotesque and frightful situations.[2]

In that context for Kubin's inspiration, there's perhaps no finer evocation of the effect Kubin achieves in his art and in *The Other Side* than this 1903 description from the *Berliner Illustrirte*: "This art always dreams of the last things in apocalyptic fantasy; its beings and forms are not of this world, and you cannot measure them by the ruler of correctness or anatomical possibility; they are complete distortion, total gruesome exaggeration; just as their landscapes dream away in the eternal twilight behind time and space. But you will always find one thing in this art, which dispenses with every depiction, every illustration of being, it has a convincing power to make things present and will grip you and sweep you away, conveying to you ideas and moods of uncanny reality that will burn themselves into your brain as if with hot iron punches...the suggestion of this foreboding art of the soul, the rare, the distant, the lustfully dreadful...is always powerful and enduring."

The Other Side still appeals to a modern reader because of these qualities, after many novels initially seen as more enduring have faded from memory.

---

[2] In counterbalance to this depiction, Andreas Geyer notes in *Alfred Kubin: Drawings 1897-1909* that although Kubin might have emphasized the raw, pure nature of his art and inspiration, "It must always be recalled that Kubin had a constant tendency to self-promotion, self-stylizing, and posing." In pure Nietzschean fashion, Kubin "initially presented himself from the perspective of a 'most faithful, most trusted friend,' who 'because of his high status had to remain [the] anonymous [artist character] Kubin.' This 'Kubin' is a genius." All of these contradictory but not irreconcilable aspects of Kubin's character presage the antics of such surrealists as Salvador Dali—creators who tap into deep subconscious impulses and desires while at the same time constructing outer personas that seem fake or contrived but in no way take away from the power of their work.

THE "BLACK BOOKS" OF DEREK RAYMOND

"I have said a lot about writing in these memoirs, with particular reference to the black novel. I could not have described my life in any depth without almost constant reference to the work that has given it meaning—the effect that being a writer has had, not only on myself as a person, but on how I have transferred my experience to others—in fact, how I regard the other. Yet, in order to be able to take a realistic view of the other, to feel him, know him and in an apparently magical way to some extent become him, it is necessary to do that difficult thing, become oneself first." —Derek Raymond, from his memoir *The Hidden Files*

1. Experiencing the Factory Novels

"I put down the book stunned. I was sitting outside and, suddenly, quite ordinary traffic along Camp Bowie Boulevard seemed fraught with meaning. Streetlamps came on, dim and trembling in early twilight. I realized that this novel on the bistro table...had carved its way into me the way relentless pain etches itself indelibly upon the body...Five or six times in a life you come across a book that sends electric shocks skittering and scorching through the whole of you and radically alters the way in which you perceive the world." —James Sallis, about *I Was Dora Suarez*

The first four Factory novels by Derek Raymond—*He Died with His Eyes Open, The Devil's Home on Leave, How the Dead Live,* and *I Was Dora Suarez*—have long been hailed as classics of noir mystery, with the new Serpent's Tail editions featuring introductions by the likes of Will Self and James Sallis. Reviewers often reference the seeming contradictions of the series, for example the *Daily Telegraph*'s observation that the novels contain "a bizarre mix of Chandleresque elegance...and naked brutality." But life gives us order and elegance in equal measure with betrayal and brutality. Some of us are lucky enough to experience only the order, but Raymond knew that most of us experience some form of disorder or upheaval during our lives, and the most extreme version of this situation exists in the form of murder and murder investigations.

In the Factory series, the nameless narrator works as a detective in the Department of Unexplained Deaths. He often clashes with his superior, Bowman, and has turned down promotion at every chance. His wife is in a lunatic asylum and is responsible for the central tragedy of the detective's life—as is an earlier relationship with a woman who remains the love of his life but who can never be brought back to him. He has a sister he wishes he were closer to, but otherwise, at the time of the cases related in the novels, the detective is utterly alone.

This isolation is key to understanding the inner psychology of the Factory novels. The detective literally lives through his work, and feels most fully engaged and connected to the world when he can inhabit the lives of the victims. Although the detective alludes to other cases, ones not related in the novels, the reader has the sense that he wasn't as invested in those victims. He can recite the details, but there's no emotional life to them.

But the cases in front of him—they're all about an inner life, of bringing back the dead in a sense. In each case, to greater and lesser extents, the detective reanimates the victims, attempts to identify with them, attempts to honor them, to memorialize them through his efforts. In *How the Dead Live*, the detective has empathy for a doctor trying, in essence, to do the same thing in a more figurative sense.

> It takes love to bugger up a life and smash it to pieces, yes, it takes love in its stranger forms to do it, good and evil being so hopelessly mixed up in all of us...So, suddenly, it was all over, and I understood yet again how everything is far more complex and serious than we suppose, as though I had ever doubted it... "You understand how passion changes us back again into what we once were, must have been" [he said]. I told him I understood, even though I wondered if I did. Perhaps the only true crime is knowing what understanding means, so that as you live for the other, you also die for him.

But it's not always clear what came first: the dissolution of the detective's life or his empathy for the victims he encounters in his job. Is the empathy fully replacing what he's lost in his personal life, or did, to some extent, his obsession with the dead push out his ability to understand and appreciate the living? Perhaps the detective's own secret guilt provides the key for why, in *He Died with His Eyes Open*, the detective identifies so fully with Charles Staniland, an alcoholic whose diaries reveal to the the detective that here was a man in existential crisis—a man of genuine passion, feeling, and empathy whose quest for experience, and for finding meaning in life, robbed him of his family and put him into a downward spiral with a woman he was obsessed with but who wasn't good for him…

> Staniland's question was *the* question I had once read on a country gravestone erected to a child of six: "Since I was so early done for, I wonder what I was begun for." Though Staniland had died at the age of fifty-one, he still had the innocence of a child of six. The naive courage, too—the desire to understand everything, whatever the cost…This fragile sweetness at the core of people—if we allowed that to be kicked, smashed and splintered, then we had no society at all of the kind I felt I had to uphold. I had committed my own sins against it, out of transcient weakness. But I hadn't deliberately murdered it for its pitiful membrane of a little borrowed money, its short-lived protective shell—and that was why, as I drank some more beer…I knew I had to nail the killers.

He Died with His Eyes Open is the first Factory novel, and perhaps the finest. Certainly, it is the most perfect of the books in intent and execution. In it, the reader finds the purest distillation of those elements that make the series so compelling: a satisfying murder mystery coupled with an extraordinary eye for the details of lower-class and villainous London, an enervating and sad personal life for the narrator, a great ear for (often darkly funny) dialogue, and a victim in the case whose life could itself have made for a great novel.

Of all of these elements, the genius for describing people and places seems the most important. It's this ability on Raymond's part that makes the novel gritty—and gritty plays perfectly against the existential angst of both the detective and Charles Staniland. The shabby, decaying quality of life recalls the best scenes in the original version of the cult classic movie *Get Carter* (not the remake). These details also work to make bearable the pervading sadness in the series, with the detective meeting any number of what you might call "colorful" characters in any number of authentically seedy places.

Put another way, it's as if someone took the characters from Paul Auster's *New York Trilogy*, or the world-worn detective from any of a number of European mystery series in which the anonymity of the setting provides a kind of luminous quality...and dragged them through the dirt, shoved their noses in the grime, made them look at it all from ground level, even to the point of the obscenity of staring directly at, for example, an arm hacked at by an ax.

Here's a good general example from *How the Dead Live*:

> What maddened me sometimes with my work at A14 was that I could not get any justice for these people until they were dead. These university dropouts, these mad barefoot beauties that had been turned away from home who staggered down the streets with plastic bags filled with old newspapers against the cold—wrongo's, drugo's, folk of every age, colour, and past, they all had that despair in common that made them gabble out their raging dreams in any shelter they could find. They screamed at each other in Battersea, moaned over their empty cider bottles in Vauxhall, not having the loot for a night in Rowton House, their faces the colour of rotten stucco under the glare of the white lights at Waterloo Bridge and wreathed in the diesel fumes of the forty-ton fruit trucks that pounded up from Kent to Nine Elms all night long. In the days you could see them, white, faded and stained after such nights in winter; I saw them at the morning round-up at the Factory, waiting in various moods to be taken for sentencing at Great Marlboro Street—the thin, crazy faces, strange noses, eyes, hands rendered noble by madness and hunger, the rusty punctures in their arms, their whiplash tongues, and then, later, the flat, sullen grief of their meaningless statements to the magistrate.

There's a hyper-real aspect to such descriptions that wouldn't be out of place in M. John Harrison's Viriconium novels. It provides a solid, roughly beautiful, context for the grimness of Raymond's plots. So, too, does the way he depicts violence, as in this scene from *I Was Dora Suarez*:

> Roatta immediately screamed Wait Wait! but his eyes were brighter than he was, and knew better. They had stopped moving before he did, because they could see there was nothing more profitable for them to look at, so instead they turned into a pair of dark, oily stones fixed on the last thing they would ever see—eternity in the barrel of a pistol. His ears were also straining with the intensity of a concert pianist for the first minute action inside the weapon as the killer's finger tightened, because they knew that was the last sound they would ever hear. So in his last seconds of life, each of them arranged for him by his senses, Roatta sat waiting for the gun to explode with the rapt attention of an opera goer during a performance of his favourite star, leaning further and further forward in his chair until his existence was filled by, narrowed down to, and finally became the gun...As age goes in the world Roatta was fifty; but as he detected the first, barely perceptible sound in the gun's mechanism he was suddenly a hundred and fifty, then a thousand and fifty, and then two hundred thousand and fifty until, when the killer fired, Roatta's face was bright yellow and he was a million years old, his face hardened in iron concentration before the bullet even struck.

Thus what might have seemed overly dramatic in the Factory novels becomes just part of the hardness of existence. For readers who wonder why some writers have to include not just the facsimile of life but the real piss-shit-sweat-cum of it in an often hopeless context...well, the Factory novels answer that question: because at the micro level, this is where we're at sometimes as intelligent animals whose passions outweigh our intellects and whose finite lives cause a formless anxiety and pain by definition.

I Was Dora Suarez is perhaps the novel that least asks for our forgiveness on this score. In fact, it's a novel that, in trying to get to the center of such questions, often jettisons the kinds of scenes and the kinds of responses we as readers expect from a "mystery" novel. For this reason, I can't call Suarez a perfect novel—it veers into moments of melodrama and it has nothing like a brilliant story arc as a mystery or noir. This makes it the most honest of the novels, however. It steadfastly refuses to give the reader the ability to escape the enervating horror and sadness evoked by the detective's investigation. It steadfastly refuses to give up on the idea that our lives are melodramatic and filled with passionate last stands and reversals and irrational attachments and all of the other creations of our minds that attain a reality of the soul regardless of how they manifest in the physical world.

But to get to that place, to be allowed that kind of self indulgence, Raymond first offers the reader perhaps the finest opening thirty pages of any novel I have ever read. It's a masterpiece of sustained narrative and tight, elliptical writing, as the detective recreates the murder scene from several perspectives, coming back again and again to the horrible details of Dora Suarez's death—and each time giving us something new, something else we can't escape. There are transitions to the past and back to the present within these passages that display a talent comparable to writers such as Vladimir Nabokov, and in Raymond's deliberately brash way, every bit as careful and precise detail. The skill and discipline and nerve required to pull off this feat is comparable to the emotional resolve it took to write the novel in the first place. I wish I could quote the opening in full, because no excerpt or summary can really convey the effectiveness and verve of those thirty pages. Here's an excerpt:

> Her sprawling limbs admitted only one image. They were what they could only be—joints of chilling, upset meat—and her bloodstained grin, the fixed, yet slack absence of her dark eyes were the worst of all sentences, the one that condemned a killer by looking past him. Yes, something had gone wrong this time. Now the place chilled him; it had acquired an intensity of its own. Since he was in no way equipped to face the appalling result of his butchery, raging, he blamed the

room. While he was out it, being sick, it must have found a subtle opportunity to plot against him, and that was why now the motionless air in there, the feeble electric light, had become thickened, slyly menacing him...He glanced into the mirror at which he had so lately smiled in triumph. He shouted: "I look pretty good!" and flexed his muscles, but any third person would have registered nothing more there but a bent and hollow shadow, a seamed, yellow face and eyes that would have made even a trained nurse turn away in horror.

But it's not just the detective examining the scene from every angle, it's also the killer defining the boundaries of his personal cage of ritual, rage, and insanity. The plot, too, circles in on itself, as the detective relates scene after scene of interrogating the same subjects over and over until they break—interspersed with recollections of Suarez also defining the limits of a cage caused by poverty and disease. Just as Standiland in *He Died with His Eyes Open* kept trying to escape.

The core of what the detective is really circling in *Suarez*, however, isn't so much the murder as the fact that in encountering the victim he has, for once and for all, in the twilight of his career, utterly alone, found the love of his life, and she is already dead, and there's nothing he can do about that. He can't bring her back. He can't do anything except find the killer, which in this context is an act of love. It's an irrational, scary, sad, terrible thought that Raymond explores, and it hardly bears contemplating.

In a truly brave part of the novel, the detective leans down to the murdered woman. Raymond has brought us again to the murder scene, this time not during the act but during the detective's exploration of the apartment, and again he brings the reader something new, as that this circling now is revealed to serve the purpose of obsession, of the narrator's obsession with the primary thing he knows about the woman he loves: her death. The passage is worth quoting at length.

> Presently I got out my flashlight and shone it over her, because the place where she had collapsed and died between the beds was so dark, and the old white

light-shade overhead, thick with dust, was wrongly placed to shed enough light on her. In the glare of the torchlight her indifferent eyes glittered coldly past me. On these eyes, the dust of our great capital was already beginning to settle. She was still a very beautiful girl for a few more hours yet as long as you looked at the untouched part of her, for she was only newly dead. Only her brow, drawn in the stiff frown of terror, spoiled her expression, and her lips were unnatural; they were slightly but slackly parted to show her teeth, as though she were finally bored with some argument...but the saddest thing to me, because it was totally incongruous, was the outflung gesture of her unhurt arm, which seemed to be waving to everyone in the world, telling them not to be afraid but follow her—and it was only when I touched her back and felt the arch of her spine impossibly bent against the side of the bed that I saw how, in her last abominable agony, the poor darling had wanted to try to stand up again to escape death for just one second more so that she could explain everything that she was so suddenly having to leave...A short way from her, three feet from the beds, stood a low table which had not been overturned in the struggle; on it lay a magazine open at a travel agent's advertisement offering cut-price charter flights to Hawaii...It was then, and only then, that I understood what it really meant, the feeling of people's rightful fury and despair, and it came together with my desire to bend over Suarez and whisper, "It's all right, don't worry, everything'll be all right, I'm here now, it'll be all right now"—and the feeling was so strong in me that I knelt and kissed her short black hair which still smelled of the apple-scented shampoo she had washed it with just last night; only now the hair was rank, matted with blood, stiff and cold.

If love is a form of madness, then the detective has one of the severest manifestations: love at first sight, in the most perverse setting possible. As once the murderer kneeled over Suarez, now the detective does as well, and if his aims are 360-degrees apart from the murderer's, then still it means he stands back-to-back with him. It's a scene of the alien, and a scene of deep characterization, and it allies our sympathies with those of derangement.

Following on this scene, Raymond opens up Suarez's character, and thus the detective's attachment to her, through the use of Suarez's personal diary. A variation of this technique occurs in three of the four novels, absent only from *The Devil's Home of Leave* (which, perhaps not coincidentally, is my least favorite of the Factory novels).

Raymond's excerpts from Suarez's diary work well enough, but they don't have the same resonance as those from Standiland in *He Died with His Eyes Open*. For some reason, I didn't have the sense that a particular excerpt came from some longer entry. Indeed, in some cases, Suarez's excerpts seem intended simply to create sympathy in the reader. This is a difficult thing to ascertain, though, especially when you deal with individual people rather than types, with specifics rather than generalities. And Raymond also saves Suarez from the maudlin by withholding detail, too. "Don't you remember how you used to invite me in to the back of the shop for tea? Don't you remember how you said to me: 'Courage, girl,' Suarez writes. She knew I had terrible problems at home; she was one of the few people I told. 'Have you ever known love?' I asked her once, 'because I never have, not yet.' 'Only once,' you said, turning away. I don't now why, but that was the moment when I thought to myself: 'Only rotten things will happen to me.'"

Self-pitying, perhaps, but Suarez does have AIDS, after all. Also, the reader never receives the specifics of those terrible problems at home that would, ironically, render Suarez banal by their inclusion. Raymond allows the character to hold onto those details as truly personal—or, rather, the detective protects Suarez by, for the most part, not entering them into his account.

More effective by far are entries by Suarez detailing her friendship with her landlady, Betty Carstairs. It's in that relationship—in which Raymond is able to imagine a closeness between two women that requires no controlling male influence or aegis—that Suarez truly comes alive as a person, and the detective seems to acknowledge this in how he also provides the dignity of the specific to Carstairs in relating details of her life and death. Carstairs was important to Suarez, so she's important to the detective.

Standiland's journal entries by contrast have the luxury of being by a writer, and thus fall more naturally into the form of anecdote and story. For example:

> I dreamed I was walking through the door of a cathedral. Someone I couldn't distinguish warned me: "Don't go in there, it's haunted." However, I went straight in and glided up the nave to the altar. The roof of the building was too high to see; the quoins were lost in a dark fog through which the votive lamps glowed orange. The only light came through the diamond-shaped clear panes in the windows; it was faint and cold. This neglected mass was attached to a sprawl of vaulted ruins; I had been in them all night; I had wandered through them for centuries. They had once been my home; burned-out rafters jutted like human ribs above empty, freezing galleries, and great doors gave onto suites soaked by pitiless rain.

Standiland's purpose, too, is getting to the heart of the tragedy of his jettisoning superficial happiness for a fool's chance at some greater truth. He's in all ways a "beautiful loser" who's never going to get back to the right side of anything. But he keeps trying, just like Dora Suarez keeps trying—and as the doctor in *How the Dead Live* keeps trying.

In *How the Dead Live*, the confessionals take the form of tape-recorded conversations between the doctor and his sick wife. It's part of their ritual for staving off death, here manifesting in a literal rather than figurative form—their hubris leading to tragedy. The effect, then, is much different than in the other two novels that use this technique. The detective ghosts their voices into the narrative in the appropriate places, the reader at first wondering how the detective can possibly have eavesdropped on such intimate discussions. At times, they even seem to be echoing the detective's very thoughts. At other times, the transcripts document a descent into madness—yet another decaying orbit entered into through love-induced insanity. If so, Raymond through the detective tells us madness is preferable to sanity at times; some forms of madness are more lucid, more real, than the alternative.

Part of the madness that informs all four novels also involves how the detective puts himself in harm's way during the climax. It's not required by the plots, but by the detective's very nature. As he confronts the absolute darkness of the soul, he must confront the eventuality of his own negation, and in regaining dignity for the victims, he must make himself a victim—in a sense relive what they could not survive. Each time, then, he offers himself up to death, and it's often the sheer verve of this act—the fact he doesn't care if he lives or dies—that saves him...because the killer lacks that particular brand of insanity (or bravery, depending on your perspective) and can neither understand nor replicate it. In a very real way, the killers are confused by the detective's actions, because they see in the detective a servant of order, when he is actually no such animal.

In conversation with another officer in *I Was Dora Suarez*, the concept of objectivity comes up: "It seems to me that the worst of a serious police enquiry—by which I mean enquiry into a murder—is that too often the investigating officer, and he can be the best you like, can't stop unconsciously thinking about how he is getting on with his enquiry in relation to his superiors—he will always tend to commit the error of thinking of himself. The result of this is that it blinds the officer to the dead person, and since he is generally unaware that he is committing it, it is a very hard fault for that officer to correct."

For the nameless detective, the fault is caring too much, and he'll never be cured of it except by death. He'll anger, even enrage, his superiors at every turn if it means he can get to some truth about the victims and their killers. He'll tempt death because, quite simply, there's nothing else in the world that engages his passion or his humanity. It may be a form of madness, it may mean that he's past redemption, that he's a creature imbued with life only through the lives of others, and that, in a sense, he's avoiding engagement with the world by not allowing the living to impact upon him. But in a world we create in part with our memories and our passions, it's a form of madness that might not be any worse than any other.

After *I Was Dora Suarez*, Raymond didn't write another novel for quite some time. It's easy to see why. Truly great writers live inside their narrator's heads, and while working on *Suarez*, Raymond had to inhabit a place that must have been devastating. Words on a page are at one remove from the true reality of any novel—a barrier of translation that the reader has, protecting him or her from the storm of rage or grief encountered there. But the writer has no such barrier, nor even the ability to put down the book, because the story is in your head, even the deleted scenes. In the theater of the mind, there's a resonance and immediacy that can drain you, burn you out, even, potentially, destroy your life if you dig too deep.

I can't tell you that reading Derek Raymond is uplifting or joyful, but I can tell you that it's a hard-won victory to come out the other side, and that along the way you'll experience extremes of horror and strange beauty, of humanity and passion, that are often revelatory. Raymond's not a perfect novelist, but I'm not sure I want perfect in the context of his Factory novels. I'll "settle" for honest and brave.

2. The Pathology of Dead Man Upright

> "Killers are like mushrooms; the deadly ones look like the ones you have for breakfast, unless you happen to have the sense to turn them over and look at the funny underneath."

Dead Man Upright, the fifth and final volume of Derek Raymond's Factory series is altogether a different beast than its predecessors. It inverts the structure and intent of most of the prior volumes by focusing more on the killer than the victims; in this respect, it most closely resembles *The Devil's Home on Leave*, but with more variation and more interesting situations. *Dead Man Upright* also presumes a lot. There's not much of our nameless detective's personal life, mined to such effect in the other four novels, and as a result the killer assumes even more significance, especially for readers who haven't encountered the other cases related by our Unexplained Deaths detective.

Several reviews of Raymond's fiction indicate that *Dead Man Upright* is a dying fall after the fourth Factory novel, *I Was Dora Suarez*; in fact, it is a continuation with the preoccupations of that novel, *sans* the emotional involvement of the detective with the victim. In some ways, with Our Anti-Hero beyond love and absolved of the sorrow of his past if only by dint of its remoteness, *Dead Man Upright* is the most sober and sobering of the Factory novels. Although the change in emphasis may throw some readers, all of the Raymond strengths manifest herein: the great ear for dialogue and local color, the ability to animate the minds of victims and killer, and the edginess and conflict of the detective's relationship with his superior.

There's no getting around the fact that serial killers are mostly men and that their victims are mostly women, and that Derek Raymond is a male writer, and yet within that constraint Raymond manages in the novel to create astonishingly precise and individual portraits of the three or four victims he profiles. We don't feel their victimhood so much as their fierce individuality, which feeds into the sense of the killer being a consummate actor. (That said, there is a need within noir to provide some antidote for this paradigm, much as Achebe's *Things Fall Apart* provides the antidote to Conrad's *Heart of Darkness*.)

Softening the harshness, the detective for once has actual friends in the novel, from his colleague Stevenson to the retired cops Ballard and Firth (who, in this case, serve as able replacements for the gutter-speak and flash of the rogues and villains that serve as bit actors in the other books). In this sense alone, then, *Dead Man Upright* seems more comfortable than intense: the detective has relaxed into his role within the Department of Unexplained Deaths; he seems at peace with the idea of living out his days there.

Once again, though, Raymond refuses to deal in TV cop hyperbole, as the mystery itself isn't much of one—just like most real cases. Firth suspects his upstairs neighbor of being a serial killer, given a high turn-over among female visitors: six in eighteen months, each abruptly disappearing from the life of Ronald Jidney. The mystery is more in the many aliases Jidney uses, and the search for evidence to force his arrest, than in any ambiguity as to the identity of the killer. As in *I Was Dora Suarez* and *The Devil's Home on Leave*, the police work mostly takes the form of mind-numbing (for the detectives) repetition of interrogation and research.

Where *Dead Man Upright* veers from the prior Factory novels is in its altered use of confessional, personal materials. Gone are the diaries and journals of the victims. Gone, too, as mentioned, is much insight into the detective's personal life. Instead, the reader gets the prolonged letters of Jidney and re-creations of his life. In a sense, the detective offers up his account of the case as a profile of Jidney, and in cataloguing the strange appeal of evil, banal or otherwise, manages to provide just as unique an experience as Thomas Harris' *The Silence of the Lambs*. Here's a representative selection from Jidney's letters:

> People never really go into the killer's state of mind. They only think they do—I reckon it's because they're too frightened of what they might find buried in themselves if they really got in there. Frightened they couldn't get out again. So they do it the easy way, waste their time trying to assess a killer by their own standards, it's just childish, you can't catch the moon in a butterfly net. They're up against interchangeable man, the gregarious loner, the man with another man to go with him who's got to be disguised as a normal man, because he's not that abnormal that he wants to get caught. All those old prats you see at a safe distance on the box putting the moral point of view about murder, priests and so on, they ought to spend a night with me alone in a room. There'd be no violence—old men and bores don't turn me on—but we could have a talk, and they'd be singing a very different tune in the morning…People ought to see a killer when he's in between times—he's as safe as a parked car! You could drink a pint with him, you could share a room with him!

Even in Harris' novel, there's an element of performance, of being on a stage, in Lecter's grand escapes and flamboyant gestures. On some level, through both the novels and the movies, we're made as observers find something to *admire* in Lecter, something we wish we had, almost as if he's a rock star. There's none of that in *Dead Man Upright*. There's something more insidious and subversive: an attempt to make us understand Jidney, and by understanding Jidney see something common in his experience—something we all share, in some part of our reptile brains, but not something we want or admire. Raymond also makes no attempt to sugarcoat or dramatize the women's deaths. Instead, the reader receives matter-of-fact depictions that seem so perfectly out of an actual case file that we both accept the details too readily and are repulsed by the sheer tired-sofa, worn kitchen-counter aspect of them ("…and when the blood's dried on you go and lie down on the bed and pick the little crusts off"). The planning and execution of these slaughters also takes place in a conveniently familiar context, and thus attain a comfortable aspect even as they horrify us.

> A killer wouldn't mind being normal—he's a hyena that would rather be just a man in an armchair, and he can give a good imitation of one, too. If he's living with others he does his share of the housework and washing-up. Nine days out of ten he's just someone walking up to the off-license for beer and cigarettes—people can't seem to get it through their heads that even if a man's a killer he's still got to find a place to live, pay the rent, get a job, buy clothes, go out and get pissed; he feels up, he feels down the same as a normal john.

It's hard to call a novel "mesmerizing" when the reader knows the answer to the mystery within a few chapters, but *Dead Man Upright* is indeed mesmerizing. The pathology of its characters brings us through to the end, and if it's a dying fall, it's one of great and piercing insight—and in no way a disappointment. The novel also gives the reader the satisfaction of seeing a much-loved character—a hard-won love for a detective whose means have often been suspect—reach at least a provisional truce with himself, a kind of self-acceptance that removes the image of agitation and anguish that marked him at the end of *I Was Dora Suarez*.

Still, by the denouement of *Dead Man Upright*, Raymond gives readers of the complete series the understanding that the past isn't dead, that it still haunts and changes the person who has experienced it, as the detective writes: "All at once I am speeding after [my daughter], who is wobbling down our front path on her bike. Next week, she'll be nine. I am rushing after her with my arms open and calling out: 'I love you! I love you!' But she is always just out of reach."

This is how the dead live, and this is how Raymond—through a fierce, sad love—animates words on a page so that they bring us out and into the world, no matter how merciless or ultimately unknowable.

A GIANT OF LITERATURE, J.G. BALLARD
Omnivoracious, April 2009

J.G. Ballard (November 15, 1930 - April 19, 2009) rewired the brains of generations of readers and writers. A member of the largely British New Wave movement of the 1960s, Ballard wrote mind-bending stories that changed reader perceptions of space and time, along with novels that dealt with every conceivable major theme of the twentieth century. His fictionalized memoir of his childhood, *Empire of the Sun* (1984), was made into a movie that brought him more readers than ever before. Ballard's devastating satires of American politics, in particular his notorious jab at Ronald Reagan, went right to the edge of fictional possibility. But controversy and pushing boundaries were never problems for Ballard, as proved by books like *Crash* (1973), with its examination of vehicle-based auto-eroticism. Such books also proved the lasting value of both literature and experimentation, being irreproducible in other media.

Another giant of post-World War II literature, Michael Moorcock, said, "Ballard and I, together with the late Barry Bayley, 'plotted' what became the New Wave revolution in the late 50s and early 60s. A regular and frequent contributor to *New Worlds*, he was a hugely inspiring and generous friend, if a little reclusive. Raised his three children single-handed after his wife died suddenly in Spain while on holiday and wrote a moving, exceptionally warm memoir, *Miracles of Life*, which was published in 2007, when he knew he was dying. His influence on a generation of writers in all fields, including Martin Amis and Will Self, was enormous and he remains perhaps the finest imaginative writer of his generation. He refused a CBE from the Queen in protest at the United Kingdom's involvement in Iraq, and because he thought the title of Commander of the British Empire a ludicrous title for a modern Briton. He leaves a partner, Claire Walsh, who was his companion for over forty years and nursed him through his long illness."

Born and raised in an American-controlled part of Shanghai, China, Ballard went on to study medicine at King's College at Cambridge, intending to become a psychiatrist. However, realizing that this career would not allow him time to write, he left King's College in 1952 to study English literature at the University of London. Stints in the Royal Air Force and as the editor of a chemistry magazine were contiguous with writing short stories, and he soon found a home for many of them in the now-iconic *New Worlds* magazine. *New Worlds* would eventually become the flagship of the New Wave, which included writers like Michael Moorcock, James Sallis, and M. J. Harrison. In 1962, Ballard published his first novel, *The Wind From Nowhere*, and quit his day job to become a full-time writer.

Ballard came out of science fiction but, like other iconic figures, transcended the limitations of any particular genre. He dealt with issues like colonialism, worldwide disaster, sex, and, yes, such classic themes as love and death. Because of this, his influence was writ large. In terms of pop culture, Ballard also influenced bands like Radiohead, The Sisters of Mercy, and Joy Division.

Novelist Elizabeth Hand recalls "reading him when I was young in the 1960s, in some New Wave anthology or other…and then when I was older I sought him out wherever I could, and reviewed several of his later books. There was something so exhilarating about his vision of the world's decline, this combination of a very cold-eyed observation of humanity's greed and failings, and then a sort of glee in reporting it. His earlier work, things like *The Drowned World* (1962) and *The Crystal World* (1966), was so sensual in its detail; and then you ran head-on into stuff like *The Atrocity Exhibition* (1969)…fueled by that completely in-your-face rage and more of that inhuman glee, and so furiously intelligent—it was very heady stuff. My four dystopic SF novels and much of my earlier short fiction were inspired by Ballard."

Ballard was unflinching in examining humankind's ecological effect upon the world. But in placing most of his fiction, until recently, in projected futures or other speculative settings he ensured that it would largely remain timeless and undated.

Writer and reviewer Paul Di Filippo began reading Ballard in U.S. science fiction magazines around 1967, when he was thirteen years old. "He stretched my adolescent mind to new permanent fractal dimensions, an effect he had on many of my generation, and on plenty of adults as well, both 40 years ago and for the next several decades of unfaltering artistic accomplishment. He was the truest prophet and journalist of everything we saw going down around us during those tumultuous days. His astringent yet joyous take on all our self-inflicted dooms, technological, sexual, and cultural, assured us that the future would be much weirder than any Arthur C. Clarke prediction, even if we never left the surface of the planet, but only delved deeper into his patented realm of 'inner space.' The world is now deprived of a vital voice we still need, possibly more than ever."

On a personal note, I came to Ballard through his short stories while still a teenager, through collections like *Terminal Beach* (1964) and *Vermillion Sands* (1971). I first encountered Ballard on the back shelves of used bookstores, and thought he was one of the best treasures I ever discovered there. I always felt, reading his work, that I didn't process a Ballardian piece of fiction; instead, it processed me. I saw the world differently after reading Ballard. Often, while in the middle of one of his stories, I would literally feel as if the spatial dimensions around me were shifting and that I was adrift. Somehow, as Martin Amis has said, Ballard got to a different part of your brain than other writers. This sense of enveloping the reader in the unknown and alien had a huge influence on my own fiction, and gave me permission to experiment in a way I don't think I would've done otherwise.

"I think it's safe to say there are very few writers of speculative fiction who came of age after the 1960s who were not influenced by him in one way or another," Hand told Amazon. "He captured the zeitgeist of a world in crisis and wrote about it fearlessly, and while his work was often cruel, it was never cold. He was an iconoclast who seemed to revel in the sound of our world shattering."

The depth of that influence became apparent as messages on Facebook and Twitter from all types of writers flooded the Internet Sunday afternoon. Reviewer and critic Ed Champion wrote: "Ballard was one of the greats: an imaginative giant, a profoundly erudite iconoclast, one of those rare talents who came up with a warped concept if it was wild and provided the speculative heft needed to keep a thought experiment going." Experimental novelist Lance Olsen commented, "We're all poorer for the loss. It doesn't get much better, much more unhinged, than *Crash* or *The Atrocity Exhibition*. Ballard taught us worlds." And, as Czech editor Martin Šust said, "He was one of my favorite authors, especially for his short stories. He was a writer with international influence. His works are still unforgettable, and he is now immortal for all of us."

Ballard commented in his own autobiography that the imagination transcends death. In the eyes of the readers he challenged and the writers he inspired, this statement is by no means hyperbole. He will be missed. In addition to his devoted partner Claire Walsh, Ballard leaves behind three children: James, Fay, and Beatrice.

The Cosmology of Jeffrey Ford
Introduction to Jeffrey Ford's *The Cosmology of the Wider World*, 2006

Jeffrey Ford is the kind of guy you can sit down with and have a beer and shoot the breeze about sports—or have a long, intricate conversation about some aspect of literary theory, or talk about the foibles of some long-dead eccentric. His comments are as likely to be pithy and unrepeatable as they are to be rather wise and lengthy.

I mention this fact because it pertains to his fiction. Ford's short stories, novellas, and novels often seem to have a comfortable and laid back aspect to them. The characters are ordinary guys who readers can easily and quickly identify with and follow during the course of the story.

And yet... there's also a surreal, serious, dreamlike, and eccentric quality to Ford's fiction. In the quintessential Ford tale, we start somewhere strange but unthreatening and it becomes stranger, or we start with the familiar only to have our comfort level undermined in some way. The reader almost always comes to realize that the strangeness was there all along.

I find the effect close to the process by which divers avoid getting the bends by descending and ascending slowly, by degrees. (And yet, worth the wait—for when they reach the ocean floor, what marvelous oddities they find there.) What I love about Ford's fiction is that, despite this facade of comfort, it rarely seeks, in the end, to *be* comforting. The comfort comes at the beginning, in the effortless voice, and the skill Ford has in finding a way into the story that allows the reader full access as well.

In his latest work, *The Cosmology of the Wider World*, Ford presents the reader with the tale of the minotaur Belius. The minotaur, of course, has a long and storied past. In Greek myth, Theseus, aided by Ariadne, slew the minotaur to stop King Minos' yearly taking of tribute in the form of human lives. The minotaur lived in a maze called the Labyrinth on the island of Crete. As a creature that had citizenship in neither the animal nor human world, the minotaur came to be seen as a symbol of that which exists outside the conventional bounds of society.

In the twentieth century, the Surrealists embraced the minotaur as representative of the West's dual nature; one of the principal surrealist magazines, Albert Skeer's review, *Minotaure*, which appeared from 1933 to 1939, used the minotaur as its central motif.

Ford's Belius borrows from both the classic minotaur of Greek myth and the more surreal modern representations. Belius doesn't live inside a physical labyrinth, but a mental one—haunted by his past and trapped in a maze of his own thoughts. He is his own monster.

As Ford takes us into and out of Belius' past, the character, who seems mythic and strange, becomes more and more recognizable as one of us. The alienation and angst are just more extreme versions of what most of us go through at some point in our lives. Even the events that bring Belius to the Wider World are not so far removed from our own experience—certainly, each of us at some point has realized that but for fate or chance, our lives could have taken a very different turn. Belius' quest to understand himself and the world he lives in is the same quest we all embark upon, taken to an extreme.

The core of the maze that is *The Cosmology of the Wider World* might be Belius, but that surreal Wider World is itself the maze, and part of the genius of the book. Ford's striking depiction of talking animals such as Pezimote the tortoise and Vashti the owl are as adroit in their quick brushstrokes as is his more lingering characterization of Belius. I took much delight in the details of these depictions.

But, again, that delight becomes counterbalanced by the unsettling. The more we learn about this world of talking animals, and the ways in which its inhabitants try to help Belius, the more we realize we're not in a Disney movie. The machinations of the old ape Shebeb and Belius' relationship with a flea are the kinds of elements more usually found in the interstices of existential noir fiction. The animals' final solution to Belius' problems is odd and yet logical, but could have come right out of a Decadent-era novel. The ultimate fate of Belius' half-finished manuscript "The Cosmology of the Wider World"—his attempt to find meaning—could not be more fitting, or strange.

In short, it's unlikely that you will have read anything quite like *The Cosmology of the Wider World*, with its mix of the familiar and the odd, the slapstick and the serious. Where else but in the mind of Jeffrey Ford could you find a suffering minotaur, a philandering tortoise, bestiality, a love story, multiple references to Dante *and* multiple references to drug culture, the real world, and the Wider World? And where else would it all make sense?

Five Years of Sfar and Trondheim's Dungeon Series
Omnivoracious, May 2009

One of my great reading pleasures this decade has been the discovery of Dungeon in the lovely little volumes from NBM Publishing, which provides English translations of this near-iconic series originally released in France. This month, you could do worse than check out the whole series, as NBM is celebrating five years of Dungeon with the tenth volume, *Zenith: Back in Style*.

Dungeon is the brainchild of French geniuses Joann Sfar and Lewis Trondheim. Part of their brilliance in creating these books is to both send-up the heroic fantasy genre and provide one of the most compelling arguments for its relevance. The Dungeon books chronicle the adventures, trials (sometimes literally), and tribulations of the inhabitants of the titular dungeon, which is run by the Dungeon Keeper, an old bird with a thousand stories under his wing. Recurring characters include the heroic battle veteran Marvin the Dragon King, the sometimes foolish but always feisty Herbert the Timorous Duck—perpetually in love with the cat-like Princess Isis—and Marvin the Red, a crazy rabbit named after the dragon king, and clothed in what sometimes looks like atomic armor.

Each of these characters, and many supporting players, are fleshed out over the course of the series to an astounding degree. One masterstroke by Sfar and Trondheim in mapping out the narrative was to create different story "threads." Thus, readers can enjoy three main series—the dungeon's Early Years, Zenith, and Twilight—with minor stories that still support the main narrative collected in the parallel series Monstres and Parade. Not only does this allow the creators, and a series of guest artists, to work on whatever parts of the narrative interest them at any particular time, it makes the effect truly three-dimensional. Further, you can, more or less, begin with any particular thread you want, and then read through the others—every point of entry creates a different experience of situation and character.

For example, if you start with the Dungeon Zenith series, you may have a view of the Keeper as a somewhat cold, jaded character. But, if you then backtrack to volume one of The Early Years, *The Night Shift*, you find a riveting, often tragic tale of how the Keeper came to run the dungeon, and your view of the character becomes much more charitable.

Another example? Marvin the Dragon King, also known as the Dust King. Throughout the series, he's the bed-rock of everything that's noble and reasonable and heroic in a recurring character, even with a few lapses. Marvin projects those qualities no matter where readers first encounter him. However, the Dungeon Twilight volumes one and two deepen and provide nuance to Marvin's character.

The "twilight" of the dungeon also refers to the twilight of the world of Terra. In this series, Terra has stopped turning, creating a perpetual world of light and a perpetual world of darkness. A now-blind Marvin must undertake a harrowing quest to the graveyard of the dragons, accompanied by his namesake Marvin the Red. This volume is fairly dark, and among the most affecting in the series.

After his experiences in the dragon cemetery, Marvin, renamed the Dust King, has become invincible, although it's not a power he much wants. Setting out to discover the whereabouts of his son, he and Marvin the Red embark on a journey both apocalyptic and at times hilarious, while the planet of Terra disintegrates around them. Along with volume one of Twilight, Armageddon showcases the apparently limitless powers of Sfar and Trondheim. Indeed, the Twilight volumes in particular contain some of the finest artwork, characterization, and storylines of any comic I've ever read. It's rather remarkable that embedded within some excellent humor (and some of it slapstick, at that) readers will feel a real emotional connection to the characters.

Other highlights include the aforementioned Early Years volume, *The Night Shift*, and the first of the Zenith volumes, *Duck Heart*. In *The Night Shift*, The Keeper's idealistic formative years are explored in a story of Machiavellian intrigue and betrayal. The Keeper becomes a kind of would-be super hero, defending justice in the city, only to come up against hard truths, have his heart broken, and almost get killed. This is one of the most complex tales in the series, morally ambiguous and at times heart-breaking.

Duck Heart, meanwhile, is the first book to properly introduce the main characters of the series. This wonderful mix of adventure and humor also has a truly awe-inspiring full-page panel of a summoned monster rumbling, "I am absolute evil, and I hope you didn't bother me for nothing." As with all of the Sfar-Trondheim volumes, the panels are uncluttered yet full of precise detail. Marvin and Herbert take center stage.

Another worthy volume, *A Dungeon Too Many*, occurs between the first and second Zenith volumes. This story of a rival dungeon setting up next door to the Keeper's dungeon has some side-splitting laugh-out-loud humor in it. Although it doesn't strive for the emotional depth of some of the other volumes, it more than holds its own in terms of exquisite pacing and complexity of situation. As the two dungeons compete to attract adventurers, the stakes get higher and higher. Guest artist Manu Larcenet's light, fluid style emulates the story in a pleasant way.

I've mentioned story and character, but not the art. Especially in the volumes created by Sfar and Trondheim alone, Dungeon features some of the most imaginative and beautiful art in fantasy comics. There's a clarity and sharpness—an ability to create diversity and complexity within panels without crowding or cluttering things—that reflects a mastery of composition. The art often recalls Bosch or Brueghel in its proliferation of cleverly drawn monsters. Some sequences are little short of miraculous. *Twilight: Armageddon* serves as a particularly outstanding example, especially when an entire planet splits into chunks. The audacious storytelling is matched by the art. Several times, I'd turn a page and just stare at the art before even continuing with the story.

The original French editions are in a much larger format, but I'm not convinced bigger is better. The NBM reproductions are excellent, and very readable. The series itself appears to still be growing in strength and scope. Sfar and Trondheim have threatened to produce over three hundred volumes by the time they're done, but I'd be content just to have the next ten translated in, oh, I don't know, the next six months.

HOW TO RAISE AND KEEP AN IMAGINATION:
JOSEPH NIGG AND THE POWER OF FANTASY

Realms of Fantasy, 2008

Once upon a time, in a world in which Harry Potter and the Spiderwick Chronicles had primed children's imaginations to expect the extraordinary, a rather remarkable book called *How to Raise and Keep a Dragon* appeared in bookstores. This lavishly illustrated tome—supposedly written by a descendent of the 17th-century British naturalist Edward Topsell, author of the *Historie of Serpents* (1608)—presented an array of fantastical serpents, including such delightful eccentricities as the Joppa Dragon, with its walrus-like nose and "blazing eyes." Each entry came complete with a map locator for each species, skin swatch, egg description, and height/size details. Topsell also claimed to provide all of the information needed to acquire and take care of a dragon, up to and including the addresses of supposed dragon sellers. The would-be dragon owner could also learn more prosaic details, such as housing basics, training tips, and showing dragons in competition. Practical advice included such wisdom as: "the larger the dragon, the more expensive it will be" and to "Be honest [about wanting a dragon] because if you're not, you—and your dragon—might be in for much grief." As might be expected, then, this rare and fanciful book became an international bestseller—although not without certain consequences for the true author.

Perhaps some collisions between fantasy and reality are inevitable. Noted author Joseph Nigg, who wrote *How to Raise and Keep a Dragon* under the fanciful pseudonym "John Topsell," found that out in 2006, soon after publication.

Nigg began to get fan mail from kids who wanted their own "Standard Western Dragon" or "Multi-headed Dragon." Typical questions were a testament to the effortless level of detail Nigg had brought to his creation. "How big should a miniature dragon's room be, at the smallest?" one child asked. Another wanted more information on common dragon diseases: "I saw the thing about mouth-rot but how do you see it and [cure] it?"

One of the world's foremost experts on imaginary beasts, Nigg was no stranger to the spotlight—he had been the subject of frequent interviews, been reviewed in *USA Today,* and appeared on the "Dragons" episode of A&E's "Ancient Mysteries" TV series. Nigg's 1999 Oxford University Press anthology, *The Book of Fabulous Beasts: A Treasury of Writings from Ancient Times to the Present,* which traces the literary evolution of a host of mythical beasts, from the Babylonians to Tolkien, had established him as perhaps the Joseph Campbell of his field. Respected experts like David Leeming had called *The Book of Fabulous Beasts* "the definitive work."

None of this prior experience prepared Nigg for the tidal wave of reaction to *How to Raise and Keep a Dragon*—in part because, as he noted in an *Edmonton Journal* interview, "I wrote it as an adult book, as a parody of animal-raising books. I figured bookstores would put it next to the books on how to train dogs."

But by the time the book was published, it had morphed into a fake but serious dragon guide aimed at children, with convincing two-page spreads by the somewhat less mythical artist Dan Malone. Previous books and awards had put Nigg on the map, but via Topsell's creation it now appeared his fans were drawing him into uncharted territory. He'd never experienced "anything like the enthusiastic readership that *How to Raise and Keep a Dragon* enjoys."

"Enthusiastic" might be an understatement. Two years later, Nigg continues to receive fan mail from young readers and some parents; he even received a new one on the day I interviewed him for this article: "I would like to find the actual address and phone number for Dragon House Inc. because I think it would be awesome to have a miniature Standard Western Dragon. By the way, please don't order me a dragon."

Nigg's approach to writing the book—not winking, not giving in to the temptation to reveal the fabrication—is not without its dangers, as his fan mail reveals. Some who have written to Nigg express this cautiously, as exemplified by the reader who told him, "I am an eleven-year-old fan of dragons, and I am wondering what you think about them. I must ask, do you truly believe dragons are/were real? Please answer truthfully, I do not like being misguided."

However, others have clearly taken the "deception" more personally, with one child writing: "Why did you lie to me? I was so upset when I asked my mom where Babylon was, because I wanted to train a Mushussu dragon. She told me about how it was now Iraq and that it no longer exists. I hate you!"

Another interesting dynamic soon emerged as well. While some parents had clearly told their children the truth about dragons, others had found ingenious ways to support their kid's imagination, without exactly lying. One anonymous commenter wrote, "My dad believes, but he believes they are in a different world, and that you have to get there through a portal. He knows a dragon summoning spell, but he said it's too hard for me."

Nigg used to try to gauge from the tone of correspondence whether a child or parent was "playing or serious." Depending on the context, he would give a whimsical or realistic response. But now, because it's often difficult to determine context, "unless I can tell if a young fan is playing (already has a dragon that sleeps on the couch, goes to the store, etc.), I give my standard response about mythical creatures and lizards called 'dragons,' and that I recommend imagining a dragon friend and raising it while reading the book."

More publicly, an often heated debate over the existence of dragons still rages in the comments thread to an Amazon.com feature on Nigg's book. On this thread, any statements that dragons are imaginary have been met with contempt by the kids invested in responding.

Some dragon enthusiasts on the Amazon.com thread also lament their lack of a dragon, like a boy named Tian, who wrote, "I am a student dragonologist and it would be really helpful if I actually HAD a dragon! That way I could ask it so many questions, like 'How do you breathe fire?' The phosphorus method doesn't work. I tested it myself. Please post back to the question how to get a dragon!"

Others actually have a dragon, like Ashly: "I just got the drakon dragon and it's a boy. He is so cute. Has very hard scales that are orange-ish-yellowish, has three rows of teeth and has a three-forked tongue. He's a miniature, and he ate his egg when he was born. His egg was golden and shiny."

Still others have used the Amazon debate to spin tall tales about dragon creation. An entry by a boy named Indago related how he came across a spell that helped him find a dragon. After "going through the inconvenience of getting thirty banana slugs, I did the spell." A week later, says Indago, he bought a Dragon of India figurine in a pet store, as an adornment for an aquarium. The next day it was gone, "and so were the fish." Later, he found the live dragon, which he has named Gold Fire, while walking on his family's two-acre lot. So far as anyone knows, Indago and Gold Fire are still inseparable companions to this day.

Among the hundreds of emails and letters Nigg has received, he has a couple of clear favorites.

"The most touching was a kid who cut the Worldwide Dragon Club registration application out of his book, completed it, and with his grandmother's help, sent it to me. Even though I made it clear to him that this was a fantasy, I returned the form to him, approved, along with a Certificate of Merit that the application promises. His grandmother sent me a photograph of him with a dragon he made of baking clay body and coffee filter wings, and told me that in his school play that night he was a dragon that escaped from a dungeon and became a hero. The grandmother thanked me effusively for a wonderful experience for her grandson and wrote me later that he had bought another copy of the book—which remained intact.

"I was also delighted by the postal letter of a young girl in New Zealand. Along with her questions about dragons was a colored drawing she made of a Mushussu and a hand-drawn map of her country, containing a dot labeled, 'This is Where I Live.' She requested a picture of a Mushussu to hang on the wall of her room, so I sent her one." As might be expected, Nigg finds this level of commitment healthy: "It's natural. Separating the [real and the unreal] is the process of maturation, socialization, but to live fully is to balance the two.... Whether they believe in dragons or joyfully participate in the fantasy, young dragon fans have vibrant imaginations that one can only hope they retain in later life."

Supporting a child's imagination is often an important part of becoming a healthy adult. As Nigg puts it, "The richer their youthful imaginations are, and the longer they can nourish them, the fuller and happier their lives are likely to be thereafter."

The classic fantasist Lloyd Alexander is famously known for quoting another icon on this subject: "When asked how to develop intelligence in young people, Einstein answered: 'Read fairy tales. Then read more fairy tales.' Fairytales and fantasies nourish the imagination and imagination supports our whole intellectual and psychological economy."

But why have *dragons* so captured and fascinated *so many* young imaginations? Nigg has some theories.

"Dragons are the most ancient and universal of all imaginary animals—and the most difficult to write about, because they are so fluid. People of virtually every culture since the Babylonians have needed dragons so much that they created their own—perhaps, at least in part, to control fears of cosmic forces they did not understand. Even after 17th-century science discredited most imaginary animals, such creatures eventually returned in art, literature, and all commercial forms. We—and not just kids—wanted them back. We needed them for our inner lives. In the case of children, there is also the fixation with dinosaurs, extinct relatives of imaginary dragons."

Nigg also points out that, "it's not just kids and dragons. A life-long geologist friend of mine, a serious scientist, was disappointed when he realized that the documentary he was watching on the discovery of fossilized dragon bones in an ice cave in Romania was a fanciful dramatization. And what about our perennial interest in Bigfoot, the Loch Ness Monster, the Abominable Snowman, and all? Hamlet says, 'There are more things in heaven and earth, Horatio, than you have dreamt of in your philosophy,' and we all translate that in our own way. We want there to be more than what we see around us. It's our way of nourishing the inner life, balancing it against the outside world. That's just the way we are."

Nigg's inner life has long included the fantastic, starting with a fascination with "an image of a winged lion with a fish tail, on an old brass oil lamp from my parents' antique shop. Intrigued by the creature's hybrid nature, I began researching imaginary animals, which led me to the eagle-lion griffin. Years later, when my young boys were playing on the living room floor and a friend's daughter was showing me a unicorn book she'd gotten for Christmas, a grand griffin figure surprisingly materialized in my imagination. Soon after that, my wife Esther told me about a griffin she knew of in a storeroom at the local art museum. When we went down there, the staff allowed me to see—*and actually hold in my hand!*—an ancient Persian silver cup embossed with a griffin image. Time melted for me. I was hooked."

For this reason, the eagle-lion griffin is perhaps Nigg's favorite. "It was the first that showed me the rich cultural histories of imaginary creatures. Also, the combined King of Beasts and Monarch of the Air, personifying both the real world and the transforming imagination, is, for me, the ideal writer's emblem. I dedicated the book to my sons, Joey and Mike, and Joey still collects griffins. My grandkids have grown up with a three-foot-high griffin in their living room.

"I'm also enthralled by the mythical phoenix, which dies in its nest and rises, reborn, from its own ashes. The wondrous bird's transformations in literature and art through the ages mirror its simple fable. We all relive its story every day by sleeping through the dark and rising with the sun. I've been working for years on a phoenix book, 'Bird of Wonder,' balancing it with commissioned books on dragons—and answering emails from young dragon fans. My work hours these days are divided between these two animals, variations of the two that are so often depicted together in Asian art."

The fascination children have shown toward *How to Raise and Keep a Dragon* may have something to do with the dedication Nigg has demonstrated in documenting his love of the fantastic. Certainly the instant-classic quality of the book reflects Nigg's level of comfort with the material—it's unlikely anyone else could have made it so playful yet assured.

Nigg's wife Esther, who has helped him on many projects, and to whom he has dedicated several books, has been in a unique position to observe the progression of Nigg's career and passions.

"I got to watch the books about fabulous animals take off: *The Book of Gryphons*, the Oxford University Press book, and all the others," she says. "The latest book—and his availability through his website—has been crazy. The professor who's deeply grounded in mythology is now in daily communication with fans, especially dragon-fanciers, who want to play the game, to raise their own dragons. He finds a way to answer them all, even as he works on a major new project…Amazing."

Nigg points out that all the books have been enriched by the ideas of family and friends—the current tome most of all. "Everybody who knew I was working on the book enthusiastically offered fanciful tips about how to raise a dragon," he says.

This learned and even-tempered man with multiple degrees to his credit, and a stint at the famed Iowa Writers' Workshop, seems today as engaged and energized about these "imaginary" animals as when he published that first book, *The Book of Gryphons*, back in 1982. Since then, in addition to *The Book of Fabulous Beasts* and his current volume, he has also published *A Guide to the Imaginary Birds of the World*, *The Book of Dragons & Other Mythical Beasts*, and *Wonder Beasts: Tales and Lore of the Phoenix, the Griffin, the Unicorn, and the Dragon*, a collection for middle-school students.

"The more I delve into the cultural histories of 'mythical' creatures, the more fascinated I am by the transformation of ideas and images across time. It was nearly five hundred years between Herodotus's seminal account of the phoenix and the next major telling of the tale. That second passage, in Ovid's *Metamorphoses*, did much to generate the first flourishing of the phoenix story, in Greco-Roman writings. A phoenix illumination in a medieval bestiary rises again in D.H. Lawrence's famous phoenix emblem. And so it goes, with literary archeology multiplying the dots and connections between them."

Nigg's passion extends to enthusiasm for the words of others on his favorite subject: "When Goethe's Faust sees mythical creatures on the Pharsalian Plain, he says: 'Fresh spirit fills me, face to face with these / —Grand are the Forms, and Grand the Memories!' and then, in Shakespeare's *Tempest*, one of the astonished travelers watching spirits dance in Prospero's court, exclaims: '[A] living drollery. Now I will believe / That there are unicorns; that in Arabia / There is one tree, the phoenix' throne; one phoenix / At this hour reigning there.' It is to be noted that this is an ironic passage. I also like Milton describing the phoenix as having 'ages of lives.'"

Perhaps only in an area as universal as myth and fantasy could you find such a spectrum of responses, from Milton to a ten-year-old kid who writes, "I do have a dragon pipling (baby) that no one knows about except for a few of my friends. He is a green and red Standard Western Dragon named Briton (Br-it-on). He looks just like the one displayed in the dragon breed section of the book. He is so cute and loveable, and yes he is real but he turns invisible and unhearable when strangers come around. He also shrinks for fun, and when strangers are around. He is very protective of me and everybody I know that is nice to me. If your parents tell you that dragons do not exist, they're wrong, they probably think that because they lost their kidlike mind and plus, it is very hard to purchase a dragon."

Nigg's own fantasy life, too, began early. "My father supervised the building of power plants, so I grew up in a house trailer all over the Midwest. My only constant friends were Huck, Tom, Jim Hawkins, Mowgli, and the host of characters in my treasured stack of Classic Comic Books."

Now, much as those classics nourished him, his latest book is nourishing a new generation of readers. As for that fan mail, it isn't likely to level off any time soon. *How to Raise and Keep a Dragon* has been published in more than 20 countries to date.

Authors in Praise of Beer

Omnivoracious, April 2008

For a long time, I've wondered why wine and food should have all the fun. Here at Omnivoracious, we also believe in the complementary pairing of *books* with... *beer*. Now, please note that we're not advocating irresponsible reading, but with the current popularity of micro-breweries and the role of beer in the writing of books over the centuries, it seems somehow irresponsible *not* to pair the two. We're frankly a little surprised no one's done it before.

Thus, I took it upon myself to explore the connection between hops and writing chops, going far afield to ask a diverse group of writers what beer or beers would go best with their latest work.

1. Light Beers, Lambics, Arrogant Bastard, and More!

Naturally, everyone approached the question in a slightly different way. Eastern European surrealist Zoran Zivkovic appeared to have already sampled a brew or three, sending in the rhyming verse, "Drink Bud West, drink Bud East,/Drink Bud reading *Steps through the Mist*." Elizabeth Hand echoed Zivkovic, even while confessing she hasn't drunk beer in thirty years: "But the last time I did have one, it was almost certainly a glass of Bud with a shot-glass of Jack Daniels in it. A boilermaker, which is what Cass Neary in [the dark thriller] *Generation Loss* would drink—24/7, and minus the beer."

Arianna Huffington, author of *Right Is Wrong*, decided on a more political (and surprisingly conservative) approach, writing, "Busch, of course! Besides the homonymic convergence, distribution of this beer helped make Cindy McCain rich and funded John McCain's political career."

Other books that apparently take a lighter approach include Karen Joy

Fowler's *Wit's End*, paired with Sierra Nevada Pale Ale: "The company describes it as a new take on a classic theme; it's light, but complex. This is a North Californian company, which fits me and my book. But what I like best is the slogan—'the beer that made Chico famous.' The *where?*"

Similarly, new writer Jo Graham says of her wonderful fantasy novel *Black Ships*, "I think [it] needs a nice lightweight beer for hot days—I recommend Corona with lime!," while Ekaterina Sedia (*The Secret History of Moscow*) suggests "Flying Fish Indian Pale Ale. It looks so golden and welcoming and safe, but you take a sip and it assaults you with its unexpected hoppy bitterness." Francie Lin also named several relatively light beers for *The Foreigner*, a great mystery set in Taiwan: "The literal-minded might go for a can of Boddington's or Taiwan Draft" to evoke Taipei's seedy back alleys. "Taiwan Draft is also the drink of choice among expats in Taiwan, so there's that connection too." She also suggests "a pint of the People's Pint's Provider Pale Ale...Fast and hoppy, it's a summer drink, but one with enough bitter undertones to remind you that autumn is near."

Of course, some writers have more invested in the beer-book question than others. Rising star Lauren Groff, author of the Orange Prize-nominated *The Monsters of Templeton*, has first-hand experience, having worked as an intern "one very fuzzy summer in college" for "the country's best brewery (in my humble opinion) in Cooperstown, New York, which is where my novel is based—Brewery Ommegang. They make Belgian-style beers. Though all of their beers are absolutely stellar, I'd say their Three Philosophers goes best with *Monsters*—they call it a "luscious blend of rich malty ale and cherry lambic." Like MOT, it's fruity on the surface with a dark, rich texture beneath."

Soft Skull Press's Richard Nash also suggests a cherry lambic for another "monster" book, Martin Millar's *Lonely Werewolf Girl*: "There's an earthiness to the role of the werewolf, a carnality, that's the lambic for me, and then the cherry is the fruity feminine, but not so purely feminine as a raspberry lambic…[Besides,] it looks gorgeous, and I think our book does too, if I do say so myself."

Peaches and badgers, not cherries and monsters, enter the beer discussion for Tim Lebbon's gritty heroic fantasy novel *Fallen*. Lebbon rates highly Badger's

Golden Glory, a Hall & Woodhouse ale: "It's a bitter but subtly flavoured beer with a hint—some would say a forbidden breath—of peach. It's long been said that a gift of peach blossom bring good fortune and happiness to the recipient, and such a gift would be well-received by the two yoyagers in *Fallen*....Golden Glory would light their [forbidden journeys] with its eager freshness, but it's definitely an ale with a hint of danger ... and it's not afraid of a fight."

Fanciful pairings or not, Groff's, Nash's, and Lebbon's suggestions are rooted in reality—whereas Michael Chabon and Daniel Grandbois seemed to have been drinking from the same strange, otherworldly brew when they responded. Chabon rightly pointed out that "the proper pairing with *The Yiddish Policemen's Union* would of course be a nice cold bottle of Bruner Adler lager, brewed right in the Federal District of Sitka by Shoymer Brewing, Inc."

Grandbois, meanwhile, went off on this riff for a very rare beer that seems like it might appeal to Flann O'Brien: "The peculiar pallor of Feathered Hat Lager from rightfully obscure upstarts Three Men on a Bike Brewery, whose marketing plan consists solely of the three founders donning feathered caps and riding a single bicycle together through any town that will sell their products, should yield enough warning about the taste and possible health risks to come from ingesting it, but to those who little heed such counsel, my tales of *Unlucky Lucky Days* offer the perfect complement (or, should we say, antidote) to the beer. The absurd 'fritzing-bulb' punch lines throughout these stories should prod even the most obtuse cerebellum into convincing its maverick mouth to eject the lager before it's too late."

Beer lovers with less "maverick" mouths may prefer the more sensible choices of nonfiction writers Peter Zheutlin and John Grant.

For Zheutlin's *Around the World on Two Wheels: Annie Londonderry's Extraordinary Ride*, the author suggested a brand I like a lot: "Fat Tire Amber Ale, a Belgian-style beer with picture of a retro bike on the label. It's a U.S brew named in honor of the founder's bike trip through Belgium. Though the bike on the label is more of a 1950s-style bike, it's just sitting against a tree without a rider. Annie would have hopped on and never looked back."

I would also enthusiastically second Grant's choice for his brilliant *Corrupted Science*: "For the later chapters—where I'm talking about the political, theological and ideological crimes—I'd certainly suggest as most appropriate the Californian brew called Arrogant Bastard. This also has the advantage of being a fairly strong beer, as strong as some of the less potent wines, and thus one that efficiently delivers the necessary soothing effect." (For those looking for more information on beer, Grant, under the name Paul Barnett, has written a great book on the subject called simply *Beer: Facts, Figures & Fun*.)

Sometimes, too, the beer chosen has a distinctly personal relevance related to the emotion surrounding a certain place and time, as with the vastly underrated Tanyo Ravicz's new and excellent short story collection called *Alaskans*. "Don't get me wrong, I'll drink a boutique beer as easily as a Rainier...but not as happily. Alaska [to me] is sitting on a gravel bar in the summer sunshine in the middle of nowhere without my shirt on drinking cheap beer with a friend while the sunlight plays on the water and the river rustles by. The beer must be Rainier. Up through my 30s that's all I would've ever bought is a cheap, watery beer like Rainier. Nowadays in the Palm Springs Albertson's I can't find a Rainier, not even in the warm beer section, and I get a dry feeling in my throat and have to remember there is no recovering the past. But even so, the beer that goes with Alaskans, like a caper with its caviar, is Rainier, not because I put down a fair number of them back when, which I did, but because that's where my heart is."

2. Continuing a Good Thought with Pale Ale, Guinness, and More

Much has happened since posting Part I of the book-beer pairings feature. First, I tested out Three Philosophers with Lauren Groff's *The Monsters of Templeton* and found that (1) it is indeed a great Belgian-style beer, with some very subtle yet strong flavors, and (2) it goes very well with Groff's book.

Then, I decided to check in with Gavin Grant of Small Beer Press because... well, how can you do this kind of feature and not talk to a publisher called Small Beer Press? Gavin has a lot of respect for both books and beer—and access to both locally. "We have a fantastic brewery (ok, we have a few) in the Happy Valley in Massachusetts: the Berkshire Brewing Company. Their Traditional Pale Ale is a summer time treat and all winter we survive on their Drayman's Porter.

Which is what we were drinking when the UPS guy delivered galleys of our next collection, Ben Rosenbaum's *The Ant King*." (You can now download John Kessel's excellent new collection *The Baum Plan for Financial Independence* and Maureen F. McHugh's powerful *Mothers & Other Monsters* from the Small Beer website.)

Although most participants in the second half of this feature preferred matching a dark beer with their books, a few hold-outs for lighter imbibification include Thomas Disch, Nick Mamatas, and Chip Kidd—Kidd mostly because, as a purist, he deferred to his novel: "In *The Learners*, Happy and Himillsy down Rolling Rocks at Modern Apizz in New Haven, so that would be appropriate. Otherwise, everyone drinks martinis."

Mamatas probably wouldn't typify his pick as a light beer, although it is: "The official beer of Weinbergia, the country in *Under My Roof*, is Red Stripe. Short and hip, sweet and a bit more dangerous than you might at first suspect. Plus, hipsters dig it like they dig uncombed hair and T-shirts from 1985."

Similarly, Disch, author of the forthcoming *The Word of God: Or, Holy Writ Rewritten*, selected either Rhinegold or Lowenbrau for his forthcoming farcical "memoir": "In the New York of my youth (I was 17 when I got here in '57, and Miss Rhinegold was then an annual tradition. The contestants had their pictures posted in the subways. There was also a Miss Subways. They have both disappeared in our new, unsexed era, but there is another good reason to serve Rhinegold at the book party. It is the beer Wagner made famous. Not much of a beer in itself, as I recall, which is why it may have become extinct, and not the best opera in the Ring either, but no one has ever dared to bring out a beer called Gotterdammerung....I was actually in Lowenbrau Hofbrauhaus in Munich (in 1966). There were tiers of drinking halls where roisterers bellowed out drinking songs. A kind of Valhalla."

T.C. Boyle suggested a great American beer I can personally recommend, to go with his novel *The Women*: "[The novel] deals with Frank Lloyd Wright and the women in his life. It is set in rural Wisconsin, at Taliesin, just outside Spring Green. That is, in beer central. So my pick for sipping—or guzzling or even gargling—while reading this scintillating, tragic and very funny book, is Spotted Cow." A worthy brew, indeed, as I recall from a wonderful night in Madison, Wisconsin, a few years back.

Graham Joyce's choice involved his time living in Derby "in the dark heart of England," where "there was this shadowy street in an interstitial zone of the city. At the road junction there were three pubs, one on each corner and one across the road. It was called the Derby Triangle because people seen going into these pubs would often disappear for days or sometimes months. One sold draught Guinness, one dispensed Pedigree Ales and the third and most cobwebby of the three pushed something called Theakston's Old Peculiar—usually a bottled beer, but here they had it on tap. Black as night, with a mushroom and nut savour to it, it had an alarming, syrupy body. But it slipped down well. This beer is most like my book *The Limits Of Enchantment*. Theakston's Old Peculier. I don't know where but it took me there." (Old Peculier, Americanized sometimes to Old Peculiar, even has a crime writing contest.)

Clare Dudman also had memories of peculiar brews: "There is only one beer that I can associate with *One Day the Ice Will Reveal All Its Dead* and that is the one that the grandson of Alfred Wegener (the real-life character who inspired my novel) gave me—the product of his own brewery in a grand old Schloss in Bavaria. Like his grandfather, he showed himself to be multi-talented; after treating me to a classical recital of a string quartet in the hall of his castle (he played the violin) we had a typical German meal with the beer as the essential accompaniment. His brewery produced three sorts, but the one I liked the best was uncharacteristically dark and strongly flavoured for a German ale. In fact it was very much like Old Speckled Hen—golden rather than brown, pleasantly sweet without tasting of treacle, and a bitterness that reminds you to drink long and slow...and relish each mouthful." She added, "I wish I hadn't written that—the memory is too good and there's only wine in the house."

Michael Swanwick (*The Dragons of Babel*) and Daniel Abraham (*A Betrayal in Winter*) both recommended Guinness, Wise Old Man of Beers, Swanwick "because it's the favored draught of storytellers" and Abraham as the perfect ending for the book, after "starting off with a dark ale." Swanwick's selection of Guinness, he said, must include the reader picturing "me standing with an elbow on the bar and the glass in my hand, saying, 'Listen. There once was a boy who loved dragons, and suffered because of it, but learned better...'" Abraham was also emphatic on beer purity: "nothing with funny flavors in it. No blackberries or raisins or any of that."

Hal Duncan, author of *Ink,* agreed: "It has to be Guinness—dark, black and rich. It's a scientifically proven fact, you know, that Guinness is forty-five percent fortitude."

Coming in with a variation on the Guinness theme, James Morrow wrote of the happy collegial bond between book and beer combination: "*The Philosopher's Apprentice* traces directly to an informal society, devoted to freewheeling philosophical discourse and studious beer consumption, that thrived for many years at a Penn State agora known as Café 210 West. The novel is best consumed in tandem with the libation that gave it birth: the Irish cooler, created by our Plato scholar, now an instructor at George Washington University. Fill a pitcher to the midpoint with a reliable lager. Top it off with Guinness stout. Add a flotilla of lime wedges. Stir. Pour yourself a glass. Read the first chapter of *The Philosopher's Apprentice*, sipping as you turn the pages...A novel is a long work of fiction that has something wrong with it. Pour and consume a second Irish cooler. Read chapter two. Repeat the process until the novel's flaws no longer matter."

Yet, truly, the award for Mother of All Beer Responses must go to Australian Margo Lanagan, who primes our hearts, heads, and palates for the release of her novel this fall with this Ode to beer, food, books, and everything luxurious to our senses (and which I cannot bear to truncate): "My upcoming novel *Tender Morsels* (Knopf/Allen & Unwin/David Fickling, October 2008) goes perfectly with a schooner of Toohey's Old Black Ale, 'a great Australian dark ale' to go with a great Australian dark tale. Not knock-you-over in the alcohol stakes (4.4% alc/vol), this is probably a good thing, because there's a lot to keep track of in this book: bears, babes, treasure, dwarves, giant eagles and a spot of time slippage. The story is lightly hopped, giving the reader/drinker a few underhand laughs during the smooth transition from malty, dead-sexy beginning to bitter, none-too-clean finish. The black malt enhances the forested gloom of much of the book, as well as its nicknames, '*Black Juice* revisited' and the Doylesque Tender Morsels Bwa-Ha-Ha. Many readers/drinkers are timid when it comes to dark (t) ales. If you are curious about the dark side of beer/bears, Toohey's Old/ *Tender*

Morsels is a great place to begin your exploration. Broad-hipped childbearing flavour gives way to the berry nice esters, which blend well with hoppiness and a hint of raw ptarmigan to finish with a bitter blend crescendo that will leave you wondering WTF? Why haven't you been a dark ale drinker all your life? Do you dare to turn off your bedside lamp tonight? Try *Tender Morsels* and Tooheys Old Black Ale with a juicy, still-slightly-bloody roast, with game pies and slow cooked meats. Old is also a great flavour to go with strong cheeses such as gorgonzola, blue vein and Wensleydale. But pretty much anything fart-producing will do. Just don't expect a comfy night's sleep after you've stomached this lot."

Still, not everyone advocates beer with their book, although ironically it's the mind-expanding, techno-surrealist Rudy Rucker (*Postsingular*) who urges a more commonsense approach: "I prefer to see my readers drinking a fragrant, stimulating oolong tea."

Lydia Millet agrees with the no-beer idea, making an even more revolutionary proposition: "To be honest, *How the Dead Dream* is probably best read with water. Water or coffee. Or something fresh and sour like lemonade. But if you really wanted to be drunk while you read it, and you rejected hard liquor and wine, I'd say a light-tasting beer from Europe."

As for my own books, including *City of Saints & Madmen* and *Shriek*, I always recommend the marvelous Belgian dark beers Delirium Nocturnum and Leffe Brun, the Bavarian Aventinus (a wheat doppelbock), Arrogant Bastard, and several others.

The next step in this literary experiment, of course, is to acquire all of the aforementioned beers and books, and report back on just how appropriate these pairings are. Whether this will result in another Amazon blog entry or a rather ridiculously befuddled weekend remains to be seen.

Conversation #2:

Eaten by Bears — Margo Lanagan's Tender Morsels

Clarkesworld, October 2008

Despite having already published several novels, Australian writer Margo Lanagan first came into focus in most readers' minds with the publication of World Fantasy Award-winning collection *Black Juice* (2004) and its signature story, "Singing My Sister Down." Since then, she has published another collection, *Red Spikes*, which was named a *Publishers Weekly* book of the year and a *Horn Book* Fanfare. Her latest novel, *Tender Morsels* (Knopf, October), is a tour de force of sustained narrative, weaving folktale with brutal reality. Teenage mother Liga, abused by her father and others, escapes to her own alternate world, only to be followed by wild bears and other dangers that threaten her safety. From there, the reader is drawn into a rich, original story that sometimes cloaks itself in the familiar but is at its heart deeply strange in the best possible way. *Tender Morsels* recalls such masters as Angela Carter and Rikki Ducornet, while being intensely Lanagan's own. I interviewed Lanagan about *Tender Morsels* via email.

Who is the tender morsel?

The most obvious tender morsels are the daughters, Branza and Urdda, and the dwarf Collaby Dought indicates this when he's just about to be eaten by a bear, pushing the girls forward and saying "There is nothing of me but a scrap of leather! Please, my lord, have these! So plump, so tender! Full of juice and fat! They will make a fine meal for you!"

Less obviously, Lisa is a tender morsel too, devoured by her beastly father and by the town boys. Even less obviously, all the women are tender morsels, at the mercy of the men's beastlier instincts as well as being protected and prized by them.

Joining them in their vulnerability to abuse are the children of the town, Vivius Strap's donkey, the wild bears when a party of hunters is after them, and every horse, dog, sheep and goat that comes under the control of a human being.

The novel is told in very distinctive voices. How difficult was that to maintain throughout?

Easy-peasy, once I got it going. The trouble was *not* writing in it when I moved on to other things!

No, the narrative voice was there pretty much from the first scene I wrote (which remains as the first scene of chapter 1, the first miscarriage scene). And then, just when I thought it was all getting a bit smoothly flowing and pleasant, Collaby Dought introduced himself, and he was so rude and greedy and blunt and funny, he refreshed the whole story. [Then] I had Bullock take over that role of the ungrammatical but very straightforward speaker, and Muddy Annie's dialogue was also in that vein.

But I always wanted the story to feel like a fairytale, and the main third-person narration I wanted to have the weird combination of privileged knowledge and slight distance, slight hovering-over the subjects' lives and stories, slight objectivity, that traditional oral-based stories often have.

Right from the opening lines, this is a very "adult" YA novel. Do you think about audience when you write a book like this?

I try to think less about audience than I used to. With this one, though, I was conscious, mostly as I wrote the first couple of chapters where all the awful sexual stuff happens (oh, and the good sex of the prologue), that it was likely to be marketed *somewhere* as YA, so I was careful (a) to warn people straight up with the first sentence ("There are plenty would call her a slut for it.") and (b) to glide without description over the very worst parts of the assaults on Liga. You never see the details of her being raped by her father, and there is a big jump-cut past her rape by the town boys. This way, readers who want to preserve something of their innocence can glide right with me; they know that something awful happened, but they don't have to watch either event as Muddy Annie says, "from first fumble to last thrust and drizzle." Less innocent readers will have to endure the images their imaginations throw up at them, and may not even realise that I only suggested them, didn't actually draw them on the page.

You deal with issues in your fiction that some people find controversial, like sex, abuse, etc. But I don't get the sense that you set out to be controversial. Are you surprised when people find something controversial in your fiction?

Not really; I know the parts of life that I like to explore in fiction are often the parts that many people don't like to even look at, let alone spend time wondering about, so I have to expect the occasional knee-jerk reaction.

But really, compared to the movies and just your normal day's worth of free-to-air television, my stories are quite tame. I sometimes think it's just easier to attack a book, because it isn't backed up by so much money and celebrity power, than it is to complain about a movie or TV show you think is showing sex or violence too graphically. The movie/TV powers-that-be tend to shrug and say, 'Well, no one's forcing you to watch,' but the same rule rarely seems to be quoted in relation to books—their simple presence, their availability, say, in a school library, is enough to have some people *cough* Ms Palin *cough* foaming at the mouth.

To what extent does living in Australia influence your fiction? Some would claim that when you write fantasy the place in which you live is at best expressed in your fiction indirectly...

This is a big, rich question. In terms of *Tender Morsels*...Well, I was just about to say, this is not Australia, this is some kind of fairytale Eastern Europe, but in fact you don't have to look very hard at this book to find the kind of boofhead male behaviour Australia has something of a reputation for, so maybe my homeland is making itself felt that way.

Then you could start drawing all sorts of parallels about St Olafred's being the centre of commerce and politics and power and Liga's cottage being all isolated and remote down there in the valley—but then you'd be getting silly.

I don't know that this is a question that can be answered from the inside. There are some US readers who say they can see a characteristic "Australian-ness" in my stories, but I don't really know what they're talking about. People tend to fixate a little on this, and spot Australianisms where they don't exist; for example, assuming that any strange turn of phrase they encounter is something characteristically Australian, when in fact, you know, I'm a writer, I make things up. Or that any dark-skinned person in a story is Aboriginal; generally my dark-skinned people are just dark-skinned people.

Why do you write? And what would happen if you stopped writing?

I write because, when I was pushing thirty, I decided that, as I had no burning ambition to do anything in particular, I needed to choose an activity to focus on that I could possibly develop into a career, but that was also rewarding in itself. I think perhaps I concentrated too hard on the career-development aspect for a while; these days it's primarily the reward-in-itself that I try to keep foremost in my mind as I write.

If I stopped writing, I'd have to find some other outlet for this vast backlog of ideas I've accumulated. I'd probably collage, and maybe take the WD-40 to my drawing skills.

What about the world do you most love?

The fact that I'm not here by myself.

INTERROGATING OTHER PEOPLE'S MONSTERS

Prague Reimagined:
Michal Ajvaz's *The Other City*
Omnivoracious, June 2009

The Other City by Czech writer Michal Ajvaz repopulates the city of Kafka with ghosts, eccentrics, talking animals, and impossible statues. As the jacket copy reads, the novel serves as a kind of "guidebook to this invisible 'other Prague,' overlapping the workaday world: a place where libraries can turn into jungles, secret passages yawn beneath our feet, and waves lap at our bedspreads." Clearly, the publisher, Dalkey Archive Press, is trying to evoke echoes of Italo Calvino and Jorges Luis Borges. However, *The Other City* tells a more conventional story than Borges and it is too much Ajvaz's own creation and style to be called "Calvino-esque"—especially since Ajvaz's prose in translation is meatier, less dry in its humor, more generous in its descriptions.

A book, naturally, triggers the adventure embarked upon by our nameless narrator, a book that shows that "the frontier of our world is not far away; it doesn't run along the horizon or in the depths. It glimmers faintly close by, in the twilight of our nearest surroundings; out of the corner of our eye we can always glimpse another world, without realizing it."

There's a definite whimsical streak in *The Other City*, and at first I thought it might overwhelm the solid foundation of reality needed to make most fantasies work. However, the whimsy becomes encrusted with the absurd and the grotesque until it begins to make the reality look almost ephemeral by comparison. Strange scenes involving bizarre fish and other monstrosities evoke the great Czech filmmaker Svankmajer, with a hint of Dali in their nimbleness.

Then there are overheard conversations, as when the narrator eavesdrops on a surreal discussion between a teacher and a girl, with the teacher bombastically making various claims only for the girl to give this remarkable speach: "The girl moved closer to the teacher. 'Don't fool yourself,' she said harshly. 'The artillery will never return. They will study in a decaying, incredible Oxford of garbage tips. The candied books will be confiscated and, for the glory of shiny and cruel machines, they will be tossed into saurians from the reviewing stand. (Saurians in those days will still parade obediently four abreast, but soon afterwards they will conspire with us little girls and declare aloud what has been hushed up for centuries, namely, that dogs have no objective existence).'" When the teacher protests that he has solved this problem by purging "geometry of polar animals. Are you saying that was all in vain?" the girl replies, "Of course it was all in vain… You purged geometry of polar animals…You've forgotten the first axiom of Euclid states that there will always be one or two penguins in geometrical space?"

And so it goes. There's a tension in *The Other City* between the fanciful and the baroque, the cleverly odd and the deeply odd, that makes the novel work. It's the kind of book you let wash over you in waves—episodic, funny but not too silly, and marked by a first-class imagination. It deserves a longer review than I've given it here, but full marks to Dalkey Archive Press for introducing readers in English to the talented Michal Ajvaz.

The Perils and Triumphs of Transformation: China Miéville's *Un Lun Dun*
Previously unpublished

Commonsense tells us that fantastical cities must contain echoes of real cities—from architecture to culture, from the cadence of street speech to the heel-extinguished cigarette in the gutter. Usually the foundation of the imaginary creation comes from the general *feel* of one or two familiar cities, onto which the writer grafts the more speculative elements. Like all grafts, some fantastical cities are more successful or "authentic" than others. For each reader the point of failure to make a place believable may be quite different. It might be as simple as a sloppy detail or as complex as a false note in the way a city's government deals with its citizens. (Historical novelists face some of the same technical issues, because, in a sense, they are creating phantom cities.)

The writer of contemporary fiction has an arguably different burden of proof. Portraying a city as if through a window is a kind of creative journalism. Consult your favorite travel guide series, excise some interesting facts, and sprinkle them throughout your narrative at your peril. Actually traveling to or living in the city in question gives you a much better shot at getting it right. You know how the place sounds, feels, and tastes. You know its cafes, its bars, its attractions, and its rhythms. Still, you may get it wrong. No matter how these rhythms may seem the same, every city has its own surprises. At a train stop at a city in Germany last summer, my wife and I walked through a bustling station and up to our platform. Two minutes later, I wandered back down to get some snacks. Every shop was closed and there wasn't a soul in the station. I'd chanced upon an unfamiliar, very specific urban pattern, but to me it was like entering an eerie fantasy land.

When a writer provides a *deliberate* reflection or shadow of a real city, the situation changes somewhat. Many readers will be familiar with the reality and judge the extrapolation or transformation in the fantasy more sternly because of it. Authenticity, even when it comes to shadows and reflections, matters to readers. So does playfulness, however, and a deliberate reinterpretation provides a myriad of possibilities for play.

China Miéville's *Un Lun Dun* follows this third route, taking London's urban grime and fashioning an UnLondon from it in which the real city's problems are literalized, sometimes in unexpected ways. The novel follows the misadventures of Zanna and her friend Deeba. After Zanna receives a series of hints in the real London that she is "the chosen one," the two girls find their way to the mirror UnLondon. In UnLondon, honest—if strange—folk are fighting against evil smog that threatens to kill them all. After a series of encounters and a return to London, Deeba embarks on what amounts to a tour of UnLondon while dealing with traitors, trash can ninjas, bloodthirsty giraffes, and many other odd things, before, as might be predicted, everything returns more or less to normal.

As a fantasy for children, *Un Lun Dun* contains many delights, including Miéville's plentiful illustrations, which may remind the reader of work by the famous German illustrator Walter Moers. Adults may have difficulty enjoying the novel, however, as the characters are flat and interchangeable, their dialogue often seeming like a placeholder for something more authentic. A kind of faux moxie seems to be Deeba and Zanna's main attribute, which becomes grating, especially when the novel comes to a clattering halt for lengthy conversations in which helpful eccentrics explain various aspects of UnLondon to them.

However, Miéville largely saves *Un Lun Dun* by virtue of his transformative imagination, as he turns Real into UnReal. In doing so, he tends to make his fantasy city universal by default: an ur-urban place of waste and decay and pollution in which those elements become perversely charming for the most part, rather than threatening or depressing. In short, this is not UnLondon, but UnCity.

For Londonphiles, this may seem like a wasted opportunity or a failure of nerve. To which I say, if you want a good dose of gritty young adult urban fantasy set around London, read the *Borribles* trilogy by Michael de Larrabeiti. If you want the literalization of extended metaphor at the service of universal urban elements, you'll enjoy Miéville's vision.

Miéville's principle means of urban transformation is anthropomorphic in nature. This is evident from the first scenes in UnLondon, in which the two girls wind up with a pet milk carton after being followed by a "trash pack," a pile of living refuse:

> The rubbish was close. It had slowed, and was creeping towards them. The stinking heap came with motions as careful and catlike as its odd shapes would allow. The stench of old dustbins was strong. Ragged black plastic reached out with its rip-arms, trailing rubbish juice like a slug's slime.

In this visceral way, Miéville reminds us of what a city leaves behind—and that what it leaves behind doesn't disappear. It has to be dealt with by someone.

Buildings receive various random treatments throughout the novel, depending, I would imagine, on Miéville's mood at the time of conception. Some are "like London terraces, but considerably more ramshackle, spindly and convoluted." Others are comfortingly domestic/rustic, basically trees with "open-fronted bedrooms, bathrooms, and kitchen" perched in their branches, people visible "brushing their teeth or kicking back their covers." Still others defy real-world parallels, such as "a house-sized fist...with windows in its knuckles" or "the shell of a huge turtle, with a door in the neck hole"—although certain architectural experiments of the 1960s and 70s come to mind.

Houses in Miéville's imagination, as often in ours, can also "leer," they can look like "skyscraper-high chests of drawers," with "spires like melting candles" or "like enormous hats." Except, in UnLondon you can never be sure just how figuratively to take such descriptions. Sometimes while reading the novel, I imagined Miéville walking through the streets of London, transforming the city. Such descriptions, while often just eye candy, are still wonderful to read.

In terms of an urban ecosystem, Miéville creates tie-ins to the architecture that make a rough biological sense. Perhaps the most dramatic of these is the grossbottle, a kind of fly that feeds on dead buildings and also serves as transportation for rogues. A giant fly feasting on urban remains is a potent symbol of the cycle of decay.

But the most ubiquitous urban element in *Un Lun Dun* is smog. Disappointingly, given the blissful lack of explanation about his other literalizations, Miéville decides to explain how smog became alive in UnLondon:

> There were so many chemicals swelling around in it that they reacted together. The gases, and liquid vapor and brick dust and home dust and acids and alkalis, fired through by lightning, heated up and cooled down, tickled by electric wires and stirred up by the wind—they reacted together and made an enormous, diffuse cloud-brain.

Because of the Frankenstein explanation, the smog is one of the few imaginative elements that at first seems trite. However, out of smog and smog brains comes a wonderful assortment of smog underlings and byproducts, including smog zombies, stink junkies, smog zones, and smoglodytes. All of these creations bring a smile when first encountered, being horribly delightful, but then a frown. That these images are escapist is an inescapable conclusion—they make tolerable, even cute, something that in reality is far worse than any manifestation of it in UnLondon.

The smog subculture isn't the only stroke of inspiration in the novel. Another relates to our inability to accept the consequences of our consumption: the concept of "moily technology," derived from the acronym MOIL, for Mildly Obsolete in London. A bus driver points out "a building made from typewriters and dead televisions" and explains:

> You've seen an old computer, or a broken radio or whatever, left on the streets? It's there for a few days and then it's just gone. Sometimes rubbish collectors have taken it, but often as not it ends up here, where people find other uses for it. It seeps into UnLondon.

In other areas of invention, Miéville does, admittedly, miss opportunities or come up short. For example, there's a definitely underwhelming shock of the new when Deeba and Zanna first arrive in UnLondon and are confronted by a sloppily-described market: "It was big, full of stalls, and scores of people, movement, the bustle of a market." A bus the two girls ride in, even when it functions like a hot air balloon or grows arms, cannot match such classic public transportation transformations as the cat bus in Miyazaki's *My Neighbor Totoro* and seems like a second-rate invention.

More importantly, while reading *Un Lun Dun,* I never got a sense that the author knew his creation that well. Character descriptions and literalizations like the gross bottles or the smog zombies aside, there is a sense missing of how the streets come together, of where one place is in relation to another, and even the basics of where characters are standing in certain scenes. After awhile, you feel as if you're on a stage or production set—that if you push too hard against a wall, it will fall down and reveal a parking lot and the corner fast food restaurant. The sense of place is rooted less in the *place* than in the literalizations that inhabit the *spaces* used for scenes in the novel. In a sense, the grossbottle, the trashcan ninjas, the trash pack, the smog zombies—these characters are the setting and there's no *there* there anymore.

For this reason, *Un Lun Dun* is a sometimes maddening mix of first-class imagination and an odd inability, on one level, to visualize the City Transformed. Characters, likewise, are colorful and brash, but no more so than, say, the grossbottle. Is Miéville saying that urban landscapes devour people? That people in a city exist at the same level of relief as the material things around them? I don't think so. I think these are just flaws in an interesting, often fun, but never perfect novel.

TWO NEW ANTHOLOGY SERIES, TWO VIEWS OF COMICS
Bookslut, November 2006

The Best American Comics guest edited by Harvey Pekar

Clearly a lot of thought and love went into the creation of *The Best American Comics*, this first volume in a new series from Houghton Mifflin. The gold highlights and lovely subdued mystery of the cover match a commitment inside the book to a layout that effectively showcases the content. (Some readers may note a similarity to the McSweeney's comics volume, a great model.)

Guest editor Harvey Pekar and series editor Anne Elizabeth Moore have assembled an equally attractive collection of thirty-one comics, including work from Kim Deitch, Chris Ware, Alex Robinson, Lynda Berry, Robert Crumb, Ben Katchor, and Rebecca Dart.

Moore says in her preface, that "The collection of work you now hold in your hands is a small army of... examples of insolence. Many of the works are political in nature, disdainful of war, corporate culture, the death penalty, labor rights, and rampant right-wing politics." This may be true, but there are several apolitical pieces, and the style of illustration varies from simple to complex, from the pseudo-primitive to fine-art sophistication. Sources are as various as *McSweeney's*, *The Guardian*, and *World War III Illustrated*, among others.

Moore also admits to a preference for "inventive yet accessible graphic storytelling," but her definition of "accessible" demonstrates great range.

For example, I can't think of anything I've seen in comics or fiction recently (well, maybe Mark Danielewski's latest novel) as wonderfully odd, as formally experimental, and yet as satisfying as Rebecca Dart's *RabbitHead*. This mind-blowing sequence of surreal adventures begins as one narrative thread and branches out into seven threads before collapsing back in on itself. *RabbitHead* demonstrates a twinned playfulness and seriousness that hooks into your thoughts for days after reading it.

I asked Dart about her inspiration for the comic, and she wrote back:

> It was the summer of 2004 and I was watching a Polish Movie from 1965 called the *Saragossa Manuscript*. It's a great movie, a little long and slow in some parts, where a couple of characters start to tell a story and the narrative switched to that story and this continues until you have all these stories that have to wait their turn to be told. I thought this was a really neat structure, but it was easy to get lost and forget who was whom. I thought it would work better as a comic [because] you could have the stories running simultaneously on the same page. So I worked out a structure in thumbnail form and just sort of made up the story as I went along. I had also just seen [Jodorowsky's] *El Topo* on the big screen, and fell in love with the symbolic messages being painted with a western brush…I did a thumbnail first to work out the structure and the basic story, so I drew the narratives simultaneously. A lot changed as I drew out the finishes and re-worked some things. When the narratives ended, I worked backwards for a few panels to make sure they ended where they were supposed to.

In contrast, a comic like Justin Hall's "True Traveled Tales" draws as little attention to its structure as possible in telling the very human and sad story of the narrator's encounter with a disturbed woman during a bus tour of Mexico. A realistic yet stylized approach with effective use of black for contrast reflects the weight of the tale being told. Jonathan Bennett's "Dance with the Ventures" from *Mome* uses the simple structure of following a man as he walks around the block near his apartment and yet manages to include childhood memories and a series of commonplace neuroses that somehow take on a mysterious rather than annoying quality.

Lynda Barry's full- and half-page comic "Two Questions" is about what it means to be a creative person. The style is deceptively simple and yet each frame is so alive with image and motion that you can study a panel for a long time and not exhaust its richness. The honesty of the questions posed by the narrative capture the reader, while grace notes like a recurring octopus delight for their own sake.

Other highlights include the stark desperation of Anders Nilsen's "The Gift," the deeply silly adventure riffs of Joel Priddy's "The Amazing Life of Onion Jack," the bold, unapologetic "Nakedness and Power" by Seth Tobocman, Terisa Turner, and Leigh Brownhill, and the sobering realism of Joe Sacco's "Complacency Kills," to name just a handful.

A few entries do phone it in. Alex Robinson's *Tricked* had a really bad pay-off and was mediocre compared to his amazing *Box Office Poison*, so I was a little surprised to see *Tricked* excerpted in this volume. There are also no surprises in R. Crumb's entry and some readers will wonder if his inclusion is for iconic reasons alone. But, in general, this book is alive, vibrant, and engages the world in a variety of ways, from the overtly political to the surreal and the subtle.

I also like what Pekar has to say in his introduction. There's a kind of absolutist mentality displayed by many year's best editors that isn't present in his approach: "Now listen, I'm not claiming these are the absolute best comics issued in a given twelve-month period. I haven't seen all of the comics published in that time and neither have the hard-working, painstaking people I'm working with. But there's good, often original stuff in this collection that I hope will open readers' eyes to the breadth of subject matter that comics can deal with effectively."

Any year's best is going to reflect a mere sampling of quality, especially in a field as crowded as comics and graphic novels. However, I think Pekar and Moore have done an excellent job of presenting a variety of voices and approaches. It's an auspicious, raucous, multi-faceted debut.

***An Anthology of Graphic Fiction, Cartoons, & True Stories*, edited by Ivan Brunetti**

First, the good and most important news: editor Ivan Brunetti has created a lively, rambunctious overview of the North American comics scene with this four-hundred-page tome covering the past several years, along with several classics. Some of my favorite comics of all time are in *An Anthology of Graphic Fiction, Cartoons, & True Stories*, including R. Sikoryak's "Good Ol' Gregor

Brown" and work from the amazing Lynda Barry, Jim Woodring, Richard Sala, Adrian Tomine, Tony Millionaire, and Bill Griffith, among dozens of others. The best work I hadn't encountered before—I overlooked his contribution to *McSweeney's*—was the creepy and insanely stippled "Agony" by Mark Beyer, which in part riffs off of the style of Munch's "The Scream."

Brunetti tries to be comprehensive within certain parameters, and succeeds, but I would have liked to have seen more surreal and fantastical work. And where are Matt Groening, Will Eisner, and Charles Burns, to name but a few? However, an editor should play to his passions and Brunetti tries very hard to be diverse and inclusive within his own set of likes and dislikes. (Although Brunetti should have resisted the impulse to include his own work in the volume.)

The other good news is that, graphically, *Anthology*, like *Best American Comics*, refers back to the *McSweeney's* comics volume, which, it appears, has become the design touchstone for these kinds of books. (Someday, someone in a laboratory somewhere may come up with something more original that works better, but in the meantime...)

Now for the bad news.

Almost all of the essay-article text in the book is mediocre, starting with Brunetti's introduction. It seems as if it is there mostly to take up space. Anyone who "behooves to articulate" or who reduces comics down to banal statements like "...when we begin to read [comics], we enter their world so to speak, and suddenly characters, situations, and emotions are seemingly animated in our mind's eye" is aching to be put out of the reader's misery. An ill-fated extended analogy comparing comics to "the inexorable march of life" reminded me of the English papers of countless first-year college students trying, in excruciating fashion, to reach a minimum word count. There's really no other way to explain something like this: "Of course there's also the eventual calcification and decay of old age, not to mention the inevitability of death, so it may be best not to further belabor this fragile, shaky metaphor, wholly unfounded as it is."

The rest of the nonfiction is a mixed bag, with Charles Schulz's essay the most grossly repetitive and simplistic. The placement also seems unbalanced, given that most of the nonfiction appears in the first fourth of the anthology, after which it disappears until the very end.

Like the editors of *McSweeney's*, Brunetti eschews using a table of contents (other than a useless whimsical illustrated one) so you can't find anything easily, especially the nonfiction, and the reader has no clear idea of when most of these comics were first published or where, or which might be originals, if any such exist in the book. Some of the excerpts include copyright dates, some don't.

Part of the point of an overview is to provide anchors to time and place, and Brunetti's only concession to this is to end with thumbnail creator notes, which are marginally helpful. Take, for example, "Good Ol' Gregor Brown," mentioned above. I vaguely recall seeing it in a volume of *RAW*. There's no way of telling from *Anthology* whether I'm right or not.

In this sense, and a few others (like having an ungainly subtitle as a title), Brunetti has created an inspired *sprawl* rather than a focused anthology. Why does this matter? It matters if you care about things like the difference between being an editor and a caretaker of an anthology. It matters if you think the details are important. And it matters if you think, like I do, that comics are maturing (not in Brunetti's simplistic chronological sense) and that therefore not just their history but the facts of that history are important.

Now, do I still think you should run right out and buy *Anthology*? Yes, absolutely. No single volume can really do the comics scene justice. You have to cross-triangulate if you want completeness. Acquire the *McSweeney's* comics volume for some insightful essays and excellent excerpts. Buy *Best American Comics* for material published in a particular year. Get *Anthology* for a richer sense of American comics and for its sheer exuberance. And then go out and buy *Flights* for a cross-section of more fantastical fare that includes American creators.

Tove Jansson's Moomin Comics
Bookslut, Omnivoracious, July 2009, February 2008

Among the many pleasures of visiting Helsinki, Finland, last year—sauna, island restaurants, choppy boat rides, great people—was discovering the multi-faceted work of the late Tove Jansson. You couldn't go anywhere without tripping over Moomin books, picture books, cartoon collections, stuffed toys, erasers, stationery, and a thousand other things. At first, before we knew the context, Moomin was a mysterious creature. We even thought that perhaps Moomin was a cartoon character created by the Finland tourism board to facilitate communication with visitors. But slowly, as we walked through Helsinki, everything became clear...

Utterly delightful for children and adults, Moomin is a hippopotamus-looking creature who, along with cohorts like giant rats, white finger-looking creatures, and others, has strange and wonderful adventures. Moomin and the other creatures Jansson drew are rendered in an appropriately simple style, while the backgrounds are often nuanced and complex.

The Moomins form a strong family unit, accompanied by a cast of revolving secondary characters including, erm, Snorkmaiden. The sense of family is strong in these comic strips, even when they argue. Also strong is the sense of humor, which varies from slapstick to a more subtle undercurrent of wry amusement about the world. Absurdity also plays a part, as when Moominpapa tries to reassemble two broken household appliances and winds up building a time machine instead. What makes the whole world of the Moomins work, however, is something kind of old-fashioned and yet sincere: love and affection not only for each other but for the world. Although conflict and plot complication based on conflict exist in Jansson's universe, she also manages to make the stories work because of themes like friendship and working together to solve problems.

In less skillful hands, this would be fodder for sticking one's finger down one's throat in revulsion at the treacly whimsy of it all. However, Tove Jansson was a pragmatist and also, if her work is any indication, a wise person. Beneath the gentle surface of *Moomin* there is a sly, wicked wit and much non-didactic commentary about the world and people's place in it.

Moomin: The Complete Tove Jansson Comic Strip from Drawn & Quarterly finally collects the Moomin comics for U.S. readers. First run in the 1950s in the *London Evening News* and syndicated around the world, *Moomin* has a timeless quality. The fantasy element and the emphasis on universal themes like love and friendship—combined with eccentric quests (sometimes with a slapstick quality to them)—allow modern readers to appreciate these classics all over again. A typical storyline might include Moominpapa having to house unexpected relatives and thus seek out extra money to cover the expense, leading to a series of misadventures from which he emerges unscathed but none the richer.

Something also must be said about the effortlessness of these comic strips. There isn't a word or image out of place. I cannot think of another comic strip that gives me as much pleasure as this one.

Because of these qualities, there's a pleasure in reading Moomin that's somewhat unique. We're battered all day by various types of white noise and by all kinds of blaring media, from television to video games. Moomin has a restorative, calming effect while never being maudlin, sentimental, or boring. (Indeed, Jansson's eye for satire can be sharp and unforgiving, within the context of her beloved characters.)

In her native Finland, Jansson's creation is the equivalent of Mickey Mouse here or Bugs Bunny in the United States—beloved and a national institution. It's wonderful that English-language readers can now collect the entire comic strip in such attractive editions. Jansson also wrote books for adults, and I highly recommend her *The Summer Book*, a funny, sometimes sad, and always wise series of vignettes about a grandmother and granddaughter living on one of Finland's outlying islands.

Bittersweet Fantasy: Kazu Kibuishi's *Amulet, Book One: The Stonekeeper*

Realms of Fantasy, 2007

The history of Fantasy is littered with the scattered remains of books that took their magic seriously but not their characters—or, more accurately, didn't take life seriously. True fantasy classics, in any medium, reflect what we know about the real world: that it is a bittersweet place in which terrible things sometimes happen for no apparent reason. Further, imagination and creativity must be wedded to the personal, with actions having real consequences. Otherwise, we're left with diaphanous eye candy that may hold up on a first read but doesn't remain in the reader's memory any longer than the weather report on the evening news.

Which brings me to Kazu Kibuishi. As the editor of the groundbreaking *Flight* series, a very good yearly anthology of fantasy comics, Kibuishi has introduced readers to great fantasy storytelling from a wide variety of creators. Now, in *The Stonekeeper*, book one of his Amulet series, Kibuishi unveils the beginning of a truly imaginative yet grounded story that may well become a classic.

In the opening scene of *The Stonekeeper*, Emily and Navin's father, David, dies in front of their eyes during a car accident. Two years later, the children and their mother, Kathy, move to an ancestral home because they can't afford to live in their old house anymore. Silas Charnon, the children's great-grandfather, purportedly locked himself away in the house after the death of his wife and was never heard from again. Now, years later, Kathy is spirited away into a tunnel by a tentacled creature. The children race after her, only to find themselves in a strange underground land. In their attempts to find their mother, they encounter all manner of peculiar creatures and people. Elves, robots, and mysterious cloaked strangers make appearances, without these disparate elements seeming to clash.

In terms of the larger story arc, the children have stumbled into a larger battle, the outlines of which they can only vaguely see, but which, in part, revolves around an amulet Emily found in the house. By the end of book one, a few mysteries have been resolved—like, what happened to Silas Charnon—but new mysteries have replaced them.

The art in *The Stonekeeper* is fully up to the task of illuminating the complex and multilayered plot. As a counterpoint to the intense nature of the action, Kibuishi finds joy and delight in ingenious portrayals of monsters and of the underground land through which Emily and Navin travel during most of *The Stonekeeper*. Giant mushrooms used as parachutes, stampeding herds of huge tick-like creatures, land-dwelling squid embedded in the walls of a corridor, a marvelous flying ship—these are only a few of the wonders that await readers. The color palate throughout is burgundy-rich without being garish, Kibuishi's drawing style expressive and deft without being facile. The detail work on backgrounds is complex but not overwhelming.

In interviews, Kibuishi has cited Jeff Smith's *Bone* and Hayao Miyazaki films as influences. If so, the influence is subsumed enough that *The Stonekeeper* doesn't feel like pastiche. Unlike *Bone*, Kibuishi doesn't indulge as much in slapstick—given the serious subject matter, it would be difficult to incorporate too much humor. The book also lacks Miyazaki's environmental concerns, which tend to affect the overall tone and individual set pieces in his movies.

In fact, there's a great old-fashioned feel to *The Stonekeeper*, in that there's little irony and no winking at the audience. This helps to reinforce suspension of the reader's disbelief even during the most outrageous events. For example, could a giant mushroom really work as a way for a child to glide from the top of a cliff to safety? Probably not. But, under the spell of Kibuishi's magic, we believe it for as long as we need to. This old-fashioned quality is mirrored in the design of the robots in the book, which harkens back to the 1950s. It's a charming effect.

The Stonekeeper is being marketed to children and young adults, but it contains plenty of marvels for all readers. I highly recommend it.

Dream Worlds: David B.'s *Nocturnal Conspiracies*
Omnivoracious, June 2009

The inspired grotesqueries of dreams haunt or delight those who experience them, become ready-made anecdotes to tell to friends and family at least in part to dilute their power, sometimes even to reassure the dreamer that there's no reality to them. Opportunists like writers and artists go a step further and use dreams as the fodder for inspiration. Sometimes the final drawing or story, painting or novel, strays far from the original sleeping vision, with the less organic but often necessary accoutrements of plot or of a larger context added to give the spark a greater or more complex or just more logical life. But at other times, the temperament of the creator—for example, an Alfred Kubin or a Franz Kafka, an Angela Carter or a Rikki Ducornet—is perfectly suited for taking dream and making it powerful for an audience without adding much. Simply by reporting back from the realm of the subconscious, their voice, their style, their view of the world, creates a satisfactory reaction from the reader or audience.

For this type of art to work, it must be composed primarily of what I call "charged" images. On a basic level, an image in a book or a painting can either be inert or charged, with other descriptions of this latter state ranging from "luminous" to the banal and simplistic "symbolic" (because the term inevitably reduces image to one thing or another, and evokes the word "Freudian," which imposes strict purpose on imagery in a way I find distasteful). An inert image is one that more or less *is* what it represents, without any further life inhabiting it. A charged image is also what it represents, but contains some other quality that animates it in the reader's mind. It has a *resonance* that connects with something universal, or perhaps even something personal.

In addition, because a dream-story or dream-art tends to bring the stylized, the ritualized, to the foreground—in a sense making subtext physical—there's a kind of intensity of detail that must occur to make the surface of the story or art work.

Let's say a bear in a dream has some psychological or other significance beyond being simply a bear. Placed into a story or piece of art in a dreamlike way, that bear must still function at some level other than symbol—although its actions may be symbolic or in some way use *other-logic*, the physicality of the bear provides the surface or skin of the story or art. This is why so many surreal paintings, for example, require a realistic approach on the micro level of detail to make the macro level of grotesquery seem convincing.

This is a somewhat roundabout way of saying that David B.'s *Nocturnal Conspiracies*, a graphic novel of nineteen dreams dreamt by the creator, works because these illustrated vignettes get the details right, and David B. knows when to add just enough causality to allow his images to remain charged and dreamlike without diluting their effect. It's irrelevant whether this is because he's true to dreams in which he is a passive observer to active events or because he's added this element of suspense. The press release in this case is quite right that "there is nothing deeply Freudian here," but the images *are* charged, they are powerful, they are not inert.

For this reason—because David B. doesn't edit the ferocity or insanity of the images that form the nuclei of his dreams—*Nocturnal Conspiracies* can be deeply disturbing in places. People on spits. A corpse being devoured by monsters. A creature in the form of a gun. Sometimes these elements have a political, contemporary element, and sometimes they do not, but the block print quality of David B.'s art lends them all the same detailed-yet-surreal imprimatur of dream. It brings cohesion through strength of style to what might otherwise seem random—it makes the book more a continuing journey than a series of episodes, with images feeding off of each other in interesting ways.

There's a sense, too, of the jolly grotesquery of, well, Grotesques, which were often amusing drawings of fantastical beasts created by gold- and silversmiths, even if we are most familiar with them in the context of Bosch's more apocalyptic work. A cat-squid creature resembles a spirit-world cat bus from Miyazaki's delightful movie My Neighbor Totoro. A panel of covers from "books by Roland

Topor which I didn't know about" includes a boy-headed dog looking at a dog-headed person. A book of documented dreams can encompass both the horrifying and the absurdly funny in part because the wellspring for both impulses is the same.

Finally, there's the further frisson while reading *Nocturnal Conspiracies* of recognizing that because David B. is working in a non-realistic although detailed style we are only getting an approximation of an approximation of his actual dreams, many of which you'd really have to call nightmares. In recognizing the distance between what's disturbing on the page and what's disturbing in someone's mind—where realism comes with no pricetag, no matter how expensive a dream-scene might be to stage in a movie—then you could also say there might have been some necessity on the part of David B. to set these images down on paper. The block print style creates intimacy for the reader but distance for the creator. I know when I write a dream out into part of a story, whatever I write—which invariably cannot match the incredible sensory (sometimes terrifying) detail of the experience—replaces the dream in my head, and if it's particularly nightmarish, this has a cathartic effect. In a sense, it's therapeutic, even if this has no bearing on how my readers view the story.

This line of inquiry, however, begins to make claims for David B.'s purpose that cross into the highly speculative. The main point here is: David B. has created a graphic novel that manages to be playful, wildly revelatory, darkly imaginative, and outright creepy by finding a medium through which to make his dreams interesting to a reader. It's a great book, and if I've meandered here it's in part because it evoked a complex reaction from me.

Silence and Aversion: J. Robert Lennon's *Castle*

Barnes & Noble Review, April 2009

Intense psychological profiles dominate the literature of unease, sometimes known as "neo-gothic" and typified by such modern masters as Brian Evenson. In these tales, the suggestion of something *not quite right* about the narrator or the protagonist is followed by the dread that we will learn unsettling information not only about the character but about ourselves. In *Castle,* an often brilliant new novel by J. Robert Lennon, this classic paradigm is updated for a new century and a new context. *Castle* continues Lennon's fascination with offbeat and alienated characters, explored in a different voice and meter in his prior novel, the black comedy *Mailman.* Terrible events from the past anchor *Castle.* Their psychic weight presses down in unexpected ways on the present and in particular on Lennon's narrator, Eric Loesch. Loesch returns to his childhood town of Gerrysburg, New York (pop. 2,310), intending to make a fresh start after experiencing severe trauma. A financial settlement received as a result of his discharge from military service has provided him with enough money to buy an old house sitting in hundreds of acres of nearly impenetrable forest.

The details of Loesch's temperament and history aggregate to produce a subtly off-kilter portrait. A loner, Loesch keeps people at arm's length out of an impulse to do no harm. He regularly practices relaxation techniques to keep himself calm. The circumstances of his parents' death are sketchy at best, and he doesn't keep photo albums because he isn't "prone to reflection at all." As Loesch puts it, "I make my most important decisions according to the facts on the ground, and do not allow the past or some sentimental interpretation of it, to interfere with my present actions." The tragic absurdity behind these somewhat bloodless words becomes apparent later, but at the time the statement makes Loesch appear somewhat grounded and practical.

Have circumstances forced Loesch to come home, or is he searching for something? He asserts that "the world was my enemy; it had driven me here, to this sanctuary," but can we trust him?

The "sanctuary" of Loesch's house has a cellar that terrifies him. Invoking a traditional gothic feel, Lennon describes the paint on the walls as actually "peeling, although from an underlying dampness and rot." He also finds, among other peculiar things left by the former owners, a child's drawing of a "kind of castle, made of stone and turreted, with crenellated parapets, cannon ports, and a broad keep with round-arched windows."

The house may be odd and creepy, but it's the huge rock jutting out of the forest that proves downright perplexing. For starters, his realtor confirms that it doesn't belong to him, despite being surrounded by his property. However, the monolith's physical presence disturbs Loesch more than the question of ownership: "...the way it interrupted the gentle curve of the land seemed like some kind of challenge or rebuke. It appeared much the way I imagined a great whale might break the surface of a calm sea to draw a mighty breath." Throughout the novel Loesch hides many things beneath the "surface of a calm sea," revealing them only in his nervousness or unease. Lennon's symbolism here may seem too overt, but it's only from such clues that we can begin to piece together Loesch's story.

After renovating the house, Loesch sets out to discover the owner of the rock. In doing so he sets in motion a series of events that force him to confront his past, and each encounter jars loose more memories. First, his sister Jill visits, and he drives her away because of a past grievance involving their family. Then he becomes fixated on an ethereal white deer that appears at odd moments. He tries to penetrate the woods to reach the rock, only to become disoriented despite his military training. This disorientation causes him to tumble into a pit clearly dug to trap human beings. While he is stuck in the pit, stress brings the memory of his parents' death to the surface.

For awhile, the world *does* seem to be Loesch's "enemy," or at least somewhat threatening and mysterious. When Loesch finally makes it to the rock, he receives a further jolt to his psyche: "There was not one such outcropping, it now appeared; there were three, plus a fourth that was shaped like a box. They were all connected by a high stone wall, and were not natural formations at all." In short, the rock is the castle in the drawing Loesch found on the wall in his new house.

Loesch's discoveries at the rock—and a subsequent nightmarish retreat from the forest after someone steals his backpack of supplies—are the scenes on which *Castle* pivots and where the novel begins to subvert reader expectations. Lennon's claustrophobic style and mood, which could support a classic supernatural approach, begin to veer instead toward the mundane. Meanwhile, the novel's trajectory wormholes deeper into the past, opening up even more memories that Loesch has tried to keep hidden through his tricks of non-reflection. The primary revelation concerns the details of his parents' involvement with a psychologist named Dr. Avery Stiles. Stiles' methods were unsound, his research experimental, his results controversial. The man has also been missing for quite some time.

Pushing up against this discovery of Stiles' role in Loesch's past are other mysteries. What was the castle's purpose? What happened to Loesch in the military? Who is stalking him through the forest? The answers often shock both Loesch and the reader, leading to a conclusion that is satisfying, appropriate, and oddly hopeful.

But plot doesn't carry *Castle*—that burden falls to Loesch, the true castle under siege. He captures our attention by the bewildering number of defenses he builds to shut out what he doesn't want to remember. In his silences and his aversions, we begin to see the outline of his burden, and we come to care about him because he chooses to try to shield others from the weight of that burden by locking it all inside.

This tale of alienation and unease, of a war both internal and external, serves as one of the best arguments I've read for the potency of neo-gothic literature in the 21st century. Lennon has mobilized all the elements of the classic horror tale—including the descent of a character into dark places—to speak to modern issues. *Castle* proves that in skillful hands these elements retain their power, relevance, and surprising ability to humanize, even in our jaded and surreal times.

STAIRS TO NOWHERE: *HOUSE OF LEAVES*, MARK Z. DANIELEWSKI

A house that's bigger on the inside than on the outside.¹ A family filmed falling apart and coming back together again, horror mixed with a love story, the love story intertwined with a metaphysical/metafictional mystery—and all of that hidden by frames within frames and doors within doors. Is *House of Leaves* a document related to a horror movie of events that never happened, or is it a record relating the events behind a documentary?² This is just one of the compelling questions set up by Danielewski in his ever-moving kaleidoscope of a novel.

But I am so taken with *House of Leaves* not because it represents an updating of techniques first canonized by Vladimir Nabokov, Jorge Luis Borges, and, later, the first postmodernists. Nor do I admire it primarily because, in its copious use of visuals, footnotes,³ annotated texts, appendix-type material,⁴ color-coding, and odd typography,⁵ it represents one of the

---

1 Danielewski is exacting about *just how much* the house subverts reality. When the novel's protagonists move into the house, it has an extra six feet of corridor inside that should not exist. Not four feet. Not seven. Not some undisclosed amount. No, the husband actually measures it, based on the house's outside dimensions, and comes up with six feet. Somehow, the precise nature of this measurement adds to the horror.

2 Danielewski sprinkles his story with quotes about this film from famous artists, filmmakers, etc., but in such a context that the novel absorbs them. Seventy years from now, even if no one knows who Dr. Joyce Brothers is, her quote will still resonate in *House of Leaves*. In a sense, the novel devours and recycles the real world whenever, through use of specific detail, it comes into contact with it.

3 It may be true that some of the novel's copious footnotes stumble through the text like wayward explorers caught in the bowels of a house bigger on the inside than the outside—sometimes a little closer to home, sometimes completely lost, and losing the reader at times, too.

4 It may be true that the additional text in the novel's coda provides lovely epistolary entertainment while not always justifying its presence in the narrative.

5 However, all of this can be forgiven as a necessary subterfuge—a kind of self-conscious camouflage that helps *House of Leaves* achieve greater depth and breadth. Sometimes a book has to be bigger on the inside so it can be bigger on the outside too.

first novels that could be considered a creature of the Internet.[6]

No, I love *House of Leaves* because the author deploys its myriad effects in the service of scaring you half to death and making you care about its characters. Will Navidson, award-winning photojournalist and his (sometimes estranged) wife Karen Green, achieve a remarkable reality in Danielewski's mirror-fractured narratives. Their struggles with life, their attempts to love each other, their attempts to deal with the horrors of their house—all of this has a raw yet sometimes delicate poignancy.

That may seem like a simple response to a novel composed of complex parts, but, really, the duality of love and horror forms the heart of *House of Leaves*. To dismiss or ignore these elements in favor of focusing on the pyrotechnics of Danielewski's approach is to ignore the reason why this novel has lingered in so many readers' imaginations like some strange, dark, half-remembered song. It also ignores the reason why *House of Leaves*, already a cult novel, will someday be considered a classic horror novel.

I love *House of Leaves* for moments like this one about a Raleigh colony-era hunting expedition caught in winter blizzards, conveyed in a footnote that, when I first read it, had me shivering with the delight-in-shock that speaks to the so-called "primitive" part of the reading experience:

20 Janiuere, 1610
More fnow. Bitter cold. This is a terrible Place we have stumbled on. It has been a Week fince we haue fspied one living thing. Were it not for the ftorm we would have abandoned it. Verm was plagued by many bad Dreames last night.
 …

---

6 That *House of Leaves* is at least a familiar of the Internet is echoed by the story that the novel was first published in various editions on the Internet. Is this true? It doesn't matter; given the ephemeral nature of electronic publication, the rumor has a kind of mythical truth to it

22 Janiuere, 1610

We are dying. No food. No fhelter. Tiggs dreamt he faw all fnow about us turn Red with blood.

And then the last entry:

23 Janiuere, 1610

Ftaires! We have found ftaires![7]

This digression provides a miniature example of how the author has managed to channel the marvelous sense of expanding-contracting space and time J.G. Ballard perfected in his early short fiction—almost as if Ballard had taken a sudden right turn into the horror field. Throughout *House of Leaves*, Danielewski plays with the reader's sense of scale, meshing more cerebral mind-bending with the emotional struggle at the heart of the book. In what other novel can the reader find the more disturbing elements of the *Blair Witch Project* cross-pollinated with a Kierkegaardian existential quest?

In the end, the novel achieves its greatest effect through its exploration of Karen Green and Will Navidson's wounded relationship—and through Will's obsession with discovering the mystery behind the house and Karen's willingness to risk everything to try to save him. These two elements could be lifted from the oldest of horror novels. Because, if you slough away the various tricks and special effects, *House of Leaves* is a tangled and knotted narrative rope leading down into a formless abyss. We care about the characters clinging to that rope, and do not want to see them fall.[8]

---

[7] At the time, I was in a small plane that was making a difficult landing in a thunderstorm, but nothing could tear my attention away from *House of Leaves*. Despite the sometimes maddening digressions, the novel held me as rapt as any airport thriller, making it hard for me to decide whether to read fast to find out what would happen next, or to read slow to savor the heady sense of unease. The hint of the house's influence extending into the past, conveyed through that one short footnote, created the same shudder of recognition as more visceral shocks I'd had reading more direct horror novels.

[8] "But what about Johnny Truant? What about Zampano? How can you ignore two whole layers of the novel?" you may ask. To which I reply, I haven't ignored them at all, if you examine this record closely.

Future Past: Brian Francis Slattery's Liberation
The Believer, February 2009

Central Question: What's the difference between a criminal and a liberator?

Representative Sentence/Line: "Write your anger on the surface of world in letters of fire, and let them rage until the words have destroyed everything."

In Brian Francis Slattery's second novel, *Liberation: Being the Adventures of the Slick Six After the Collapse of the United States of America,* the collapse of the dollar has led to a slavery-based society run by the new boss of Manhattan, a man known as the Aardvark. Facing off against the Aardvark is Marco Angelo Oliviera, a kind of killer's killer whose stealthy-fast methods seem superhuman. Marco is a member of the Slick Six, a scattered and diminished gang of international criminals. Escaping a prison ship, Marco decides to re-form the Slick Six, resulting in a trek from New York to North Carolina, then to Louisiana and on through to California. In addition to tracking down his fellow Slick Sixers, Marco encounters, among others, the New Sioux (a group of Native Americans hell-bent on avenging injustices) and the Americoids (a group of hippie nomads led by Doctor San Diego). He and his cohorts also march deep into his own past, and the country's past, aided by a psychic emanation called "the Vibe."

If this sounds like Thomas Pynchon or John Calvin Batchelor territory, you would be correct. Slattery's approach walks a tightrope between absurdism and a kind of accentuated Byzantine realism. Marco's portrayal, for example, lies somewhere between outrageous comic book anti-hero and true three-dimensional characterization. Surprisingly, it soon becomes clear that Marco's need to bring the Slick Six back together is as much about a nascent sense of family—and proving that he's still human—as it is about liberating the country.

Still, it's not the characters so much as the novelist's roving, restless eye as Marco travels west that gives the novel its true sense of poetry and purpose. Through a series of brilliant descriptions, Slattery writes a love-song to a poor, multi-cultural America that survives on the debris of the past. Kids play with "a soccer ball skinned of its color, patched with duct tape, denim, and glue" (109). A "colony of dogs lives inside the rusting body of an armored troop carrier" (116).

These depictions of America transformed are often long, and, in another kind of novel, might have become unwelcome digressions. However, in *Liberation* most of these sections give the reader a crucial understanding of Slattery's vision of the future *and* further illuminate Marco's own complex past. They also provide the anchor for the reader's belief in the new slavery that forms the heart of Slattery's post-collapse economic system. As Slattery writes, "The places that used to sell stirrups, spurs, and license plates to tourists are now flophouses, whorehouses, stands selling heroin and whiskey in tiny increments. Men and women in dirty clothes, tattered cuffs, ragged hems, stand in a jagged line and wait for their fix, to call up their courage, blunt their terror at selling themselves into slavery." True to the spirit of America, there are "men in sandwich boards selling binoculars, the woman festooned in colored foils yelling lollipops, cotton candy, tin toys for the children." The dollar may be dead, but a severely warped brand of capitalism is still going strong.

As the Slick Six begins to get back together and Marco is stalked by the Aardvark's enigmatic assassin, the novel's pace quickens, gaining momentum at the expense of Slattery's vision of a twisted American Dream. The satisfying if inevitable final clash between the Aardvark and Marco is pulled off with skill, but the truly amazing moments come from Slattery's vision of America, past, present, and future.

Not Good at Dying: *The Many Deaths of the Firefly Brothers* by Thomas Mullen

Los Angeles Times, February 2010

"We…we just can't die."
"No, we seem to be pretty good at dying. But something's not letting us stay dead."

Set in the Depression-era Midwest, Thomas Mullen's second novel, "The Many Deaths of the Firefly Brothers" (Random House) tells a rip-roaring yarn that manages to be both phantasmagorical and historically accurate. In its labyrinthine, luminous narrative, reminiscent of Michael Chabon's best fiction, readers will find powerful parallels to the present-day.

The Firefly Brothers, bank robbers Jason and Whit Fireson, wake in a police station morgue after having been shot dead. They do not remember the events leading to their demise. Confused but undeterred, they escape and embark on a crime spree intended to bring in enough cash to disappear for good. Complicating their plans, Jason's girlfriend Darcy Windham has been kidnapped by rogues unknown. Will the Firefly Brothers find her in time? Will their law-abiding but jobless brother Weston turn them in for the reward money? More importantly, what happens if the police shoot them dead again?

The elements a jaded reader might expect are all present: the plucky main squeeze, stumble-bum cops, accomplices with names like Brickbat or Chance McGill, greedy bankers, an intrepid federal agent, and the sometimes glib but darkly glamorous outlaws themselves. But Mullen avoids cliché by digging deep into the past lives of his characters, exploring not only the bond between brothers, but their relationship with their uncompromising yet deeply flawed father, Patrick Fireson—a man who conjures "invisible advantages from the darkness, had taken emptiness and poverty and turned them into the raw materials of a life's adventure..."

The novel also features brilliant set pieces, like a shoot-out in an old house and a harrowing car chase, while even incidental descriptions are appropriate to the time period. "The old man's face was unreadable," Mullen writes, "like a pile of discarded typesetting keys in a junkyard." The sound of bullets hitting a metal harness is "almost musical, like coins plinking a pond's surface as they're transformed into wishes."

Mullen's careful observations of the brothers, post-resurrection, help ground the novel as well. After their second miraculous return following a shoot-out, Whit finds that he's covered in purple welts where "the cop had riddled him good." His fingers are "tacky with blood." After awhile, Jason not yet conscious, "[Whit] needed to escape his brother's presence for a moment, needed to be spared the horrible and unknowable responsibility of being a living person in the company of the dead."

The novel also keeps circling back to creation of the myths surrounding the Firefly Brothers. A populace desperate for hope has turned them into folk heroes while, in stark and damning contrast, ordinary people are disappearing: "They vanished from the factories and warehouses and workshops…the doors padlocked, the buildings like tombs." The desolation of such passages comes not so much from an appreciation of hardships suffered in the past as from the overlay in readers' minds of similar scenes from the present-day.

The longer the Firefly Brothers remain on the lam—the more times they die only to return—the greater the power of their mythology: "That was the thing about death: it could leave the old mysteries unsolved. The stories could go on telling themselves with the passage of time."

But which stories, and which versions? Some stories contain a hint of the truth, while in others the brothers are "impregnating ex-lovers, coaxing kittens from flimsy branches, delivering impromptu sermons at Congregationalist services." Federal agent Cary Delaney sees the Firefly Brothers as "men who couldn't handle the pressures everyone else is facing, so they decided to just take from decent people, even if it means killing along the way." Darcy, as Jason's lover, tries to turn the bank robber into a superhero, telling one of her kidnappers, "[Jason] walks through walls. He can change faces, slip through stakeouts... Bullets pass through him."

Sometimes, though, the *participants* don't want to be part of the myth. In a flashback conversation, Jason tells Darcy about a time he saved Whit's life, saying with disgust, "I let them put a bunch of other sick folks in my car, too, so the story gets twisted that I'm this saint ferrying the poor to the hospital, like I run my own ambulance service for the needy." Part of Jason's disgust stems from the way the stories have outgrown his ability to control them or their message.

By novel's end, reality and myth are entangled forever, and finding one single version of the truth seems unimportant. Mullen provides enough traditional resolution—Darcy's fate, the facts behind Patrick Fireson's involvement in a murder—that any ambiguity to the secret behind the brothers' resurrection seems less a tease than essential to the novel. The brothers live within a ongoing and unsolvable story: "Whit asked Jason if he thought this would keep happening, or if maybe this was the last time. How much longer would they haunt each other like this. Or would they both vanish, to each other and the world."

Mullen's first novel, *The Last Town on Earth* (2006), garnered significant praise. It's easy to see why. In *The Many Deaths of the Firefly Brothers* Mullen has created a stunning work of fiction that is intense, deeply satisfying, and always uniquely American.

Re-Envisioning the West: Emma Bull's *Territory*
Science Fiction Weekly, 2006

Emma Bull's *Territory* is a rich blend of fantasy, ambiguity, sheer pleasure-inducing entertainment, and retold American myth. When a stagecoach is robbed, suspicion falls on supposed lawmen such as Wyatt Earp and Doc Holliday. Simultaneously, a strange man named Jesse Fox enters Tombstone, odd events following in his wake. Fox's confidant is a somewhat mysterious Chinese man named Lung. In this novel, historical and made-up characters freely mingle, each equally fascinating.

Take, for instance, Mrs. Mildred Benjamin, secret writer of suspense tales for *Gallagher's Illustrated Weekly*, who spends her days setting type for Tombstone's daily newspaper, *The Nugget*. When the Earps and Holliday catch one of the supposed stage coach robbers and put him in jail, Mildred quickly becomes involved in a jail break. At the urging of her boss, Mr. Henry, Mildred gets the mysterious Fox to help free the man before either Earp or Holliday can stop him from talking.

However, things take a turn for the worse the next day when the man's severed arm shows up outside of the newspaper's office, much to the horror of both Mildred and Fox. In the man's hand is a strange silver wire. When Fox takes it to Lung, Lung tells him it's "a warning sent from one knowledgeable man to another." A sorceror's warning—and anyone who has knowledge of it will be unable to hide that fact if they touch it. Despite Lung telling him to throw it out, Fox keeps it and goes looking for trouble, in the form of a local poker game. He throws the wire in the pot, hoping to get a reaction from the players, but gets only a measured stare from Earp upon seeing it. Does Earp know what it is? Just what kind of shadow war is being fought behind the scenes here?

Curly Bill Brocius doesn't make things less tense by pretending to shoot at Doc Holliday as an April Fool's joke. Drunk, he accuses Holliday of being involved in the stagecoach hold-up. Meanwhile, the Guilded Age Mining Company is trying to buy up everybody's land, using a heavy-handed approach. Something odd is going on in Tombstone, and it's not quite of this world. As Mildred and Fox get more and more entangled in what is, as the title suggests, a deadly battle for territory, more bodies turn up and things only get stranger.

Emma Bull has conjured up a truly unique American novel from the reality and myth of the Old West. From romance to gunplay, political intrigue to betrayal, Bull writes in a seamless, muscular style that will captivate any reader. Some scenes, like Fox's taming of a skittish colt for one of the Earp brothers, are masterpieces of attention to detail while others, especially a confrontation between Wyatt Earp and Doc Holliday, are nothing short of incandescent. Many passages deserve to be quoted at length, but I'll restrain myself to this one section where Holliday learns Earp has used his Kate as a ploy in an interrogation connected to the stage coach robbery:

> Anger was like a wildfire in him, the kind that skimmed through the dry grass unnoticed until it met the trees, to explode up the trunks and leap from bough to bough.... Outside the moon was up, full and bright and low in the east. Wyatt was untying his horse from the porch rail. Doc took hold of the reins just below the bit.
>
> "Do I bandy your wife's name about?" Doc said. The fire in his chest had grown until he could barely speak above a whisper.
>
> Wyatt's back was to the moonlight; Doc couldn't see his face. "I don't know. Do you?"
>
> "If I did, what would I get from you?"
>
> "I think you know." From his voice, Wyatt was smiling.
>
> "Then tell me what you deserve for lying about Kate."
>
> A gust of cold wind rattled the scrub around them.
>
> "You're not angry because I made use of Kate," Wyatt said calmly. "Besides, I did her no harm." He took hold of the reins below Doc's hand. Doc didn't let go.
>
> "I don't believe you gave a damn about that."

Wyatt stepped forward. He occluded the moon, so that the black shape of him was rimmed in silver. The night wind whistled through brush and boards and every opening that might hum with it. There was a knife hidden in Doc's sleeve…But he felt helpless even so.

"I didn't give a damn," Wyatt answered, cold as snow. "If I have to hurt everyone in the world to protect what's mine, I will do it like a shot…" Wyatt drew his reins out of Doc's fingers, backed his horse, and led him off toward the corral.

Doc clutched the porch rail and stared out at the silver-and-black landscape. The air felt thin in his lungs, searing as he dragged it in. He'd thought he was the wildfire. Now he knew he was only the tree.

I have to admit that historical characters fleshed out in historical novels often seem stilted to me. I am also not the biggest fan of Westerns, perhaps because some of them are formulaic. However, in reading *Territory*, I found that Bull overcame most of my reservations about both Westerns and historical characters. In fact, perhaps the most astonishing thing about Bull's accomplishment in *Territory* has nothing to do with the fantasy element. She has managed to portray Doc Holliday, Wyatt Earp, and the rest of her historical figures as deadly, funny, laconic, real, and yet also larger-than-life. These men have a sense of their own place in history. That she has managed to do this while placing them in such an imaginative and lively context, with the made-up characters fully as fascinating is even more impressive.

HOLLYWOOD PUNK: STEVE ERICKSON'S *ZEROVILLE*
Washington Post Book World, November 2007

My first encounter with Steve Erickson was *Arc d'X*, which I devoured in 1993 while fatigued and feverish and bedridden. In that context, it became one of the great reading experiences of my life, virtually phantasmagoric. But I don't know if *Arc d'X* would have seemed any less hallucinogenic under normal conditions. Over his entire career Erickson has challenged readers with a fiercely intelligent and surprisingly sensual brand of American surrealism that can, at times, seem impenetrable.

For this reason, it surprised me that almost everything in Erickson's new novel *Zeroville* entertains so readily without seeming watered down or slight. Zeroville is funny, sad and darkly beautiful, built around short chapters that allow the author to capture the essential moment and move effortlessly through time.

Set primarily in the 1970s and '80s in Los Angeles, *Zeroville* features an ex-divinity student named Vikar, a punk in the age of hippies who on his shaved head has a tattoo of Montgomery Clift and Elizabeth Taylor from the movie *A Place in the Sun*. Damaged, violent and probably slightly autistic, Vikar arrives in Hollywood to pursue his devotion to the movies. He soon finds work building sets on a studio lot, meets a renowned editor and gets a few editing jobs. He becomes famous when he re-cuts a movie in New York City that has a controversial debut at the Cannes Film Festival.

As with everything that happens to Vikar, he stumbles into the good and the bad with equal indifference. He is always looking ahead to some glowing theater screen in the distance, and nothing in his immediate field of vision carries any weight.

That single-minded devotion, the way it creates a counterpoint in Vikar's interactions with other characters, is often hilarious. I can't recall having laughed out loud so much reading a novel. Vikar is a bit like Chance from Jerzy Kosinski's *Being There*, with touches of Voltaire's *Candide*, which leads to some outstanding set pieces. After Vikar surprises a thief in his apartment, knocks him out and ties him to a chair, they wind up having a long conversation about film while watching bad movies on TV. When Vikar goes to Madrid for an editing gig, he is kidnapped by revolutionaries and forced to splice together porn scenes and other footage to create a propaganda film. When he visits France for the release of his experimental film, he attends a press conference that goes hideously wrong.

These scenes aren't just funny—they exhibit a curious combination of satire and depth, in part because Vikar, despite his limited emotional range (or because of it?), may be Erickson's most likable character. Whether he is calmly ranting at the Cannes reporters, having a private conversation with a prostitute or reliving childhood memories that suggest the movies might literally have saved him, Vikar's devotion to film lends him an integrity that puts him above the fray, making him untouchable.

The novel is just as steeped in films and film lore as its main character. Subtle cameos by a young Robert De Niro and other stars are skillfully handled, while Erickson does a nuanced job of depicting both genuine artistic impulse and all that corrupts it. Best of all, Erickson mixes high art and low pulp throughout *Zeroville*. "Emmanuelle 7," for example, is as likely to be mentioned as "The Long Goodbye," which are equals in Vikar's eyes.

However, Erickson isn't content with this wonderful exploration of character and place. The hyper-surreal elements of his prior novels gradually infiltrate *Zeroville*. Vikar's random encounters with a woman named Soledad, who may be the daughter of Spanish filmmaker Luis Buñuel, take on a cryptic significance. A search for a lost film suddenly becomes important, evoking comparisons to Theodore Roszak's cult-classic novel *Flicker*. Ghosts appear, real or imaginary. A recurring refrain throughout the novel, "God hates children," takes on more than symbolic weight. Finally, a shift in perspective occurs, with Erickson intentionally violating the internal logic of his own structure.

By the end of *Zeroville*, then, I was back in bed in 1993, reading *Arc d'X* and not "getting" all of it—my heart more convinced than my head—but blissfully happy nonetheless. *Zeroville* is that kind of novel. You want Vikar to have his peace, and you want Erickson to have his ending, because Vikar always acts according to his nature, regardless of the hand of God or author.

Exchange Students Plot to Take Over America: Chuck Palahniuk's *Pygmy*

Washington Post, Arts & Living, May 2009

Sloppy yet smart, simultaneously structured yet staggering around like a drunk living in a strip mall parking lot, Chuck Palahniuk's *Pygmy* gets a lot of things right and an equal number wrong. Within a page, sometimes a paragraph, the novel veers from the sublimely ridiculous or deadly to just plain ridiculous or dead.

A infiltrating agent from a nameless authoritarian country, the narrator, nicknamed "Pygmy," joins the Mid-western family of Donald Cedar. "Host father," as Pygmy calls him, works for the Radiological Institute of Medicine, and has access to bio-toxins. Pygmy is just one of several undersized operatives masquerading as high school exchange students so they can unleash Operation Chaos on an unsuspecting American populace.

Much of the novel's demented genius derives from Palahniuk wisely eschewing either broken or perfect English for Pygmy. Instead, Pygmy writes using a clipped, precise syntax. "Host mother claws keep shut inside mother talon" describes the hand of Cedar's wife, for example. This economy extends to speech, as when Pygmy says to an aging Wal-mart greeter: "Revered soon dying mother distribute you ammunitions correct for Croatia-made forty-five-caliber long-piston-stroke APS assault rifle?"

It's a gut-busting line in a novel filled with them, but I can't figure out what it has to do with running a covert operation—and this is part of the problem with *Pygmy*. Palahniuk has such a lust for a good or a profane joke that he's willing to sacrifice consistency of tone, even logic, to get to a situational absurdity.

Brutal flashbacks to Pygmy's rigid indoctrination also sit uneasily next to later sections that, one could argue, consist mainly of extended vibrator jokes— nearly, you might say, vibrator *mise en scene*—which turn *Pygmy* into broad farce.

Even worse, just about every adult in the novel acts like an idiot, from the boob of a host father to the priest who (*que surprise!*) sleeps with under-age girls, from the vapid host mother to the teacher-judges of the high school science fair. Most of this stupidity by adults occurs so that Palahniuk can advance his plot.

That's a shame, because Palahniuk is brilliant in sharing Pygmy's background, and juxtaposing its horrible madness with the equally horrible madness of contemporary American society. Pygmy, for example, has a preternatural sense of smell, and describing Donald's breath as "In talk, breath of Viagra, reek of Propesia, and... chewing gum" tells us volumes about his character and his status as a twenty-first-century American white male. A scene in which the high school stages a model United Nations summit may be some of the finest comedy the author has ever written, with descriptions like "Operative Chernok as delegate Italy sucking the earlobes of Lady delegate Venezuela." Pygmy's speech as the United States' delegate is hilarious and pointed, including the unforgettable "make available cherished American children, ship overseas as lifelong chattel slaves, gesture shown of goodwill."

Still, it's another great scene sacrificed to the novelist's lack of discipline. A climax at the national science fair that seems right out of a made-for-TV movie rushes to a sentimental ending in which Palahniuk seems so in love with Pygmy that he won't let him behave as to his true nature; this is, after all, an agent so indoctrinated he brutally raped a boy who bullied him. Maybe Palahniuk's not capable of doing more with Pygmy's great voice than to use it to strike a series of poses comparable to the narrator's Striking Cobra Quick Kill or Lashing Lynx kung-fu, not caring about consistency or clashing effects, or maybe I am just immune to the holistic pleasures of a novel that features more slang terms for breasts than the Inuit have for snow. Either way, *Pygmy* could've done with fewer vibrator jokes and more ripping out of jugulars.

Looking for Love: Alexander Theroux's *Laura Warholic: Or, The Sexual Intellectual*

Washington Post Book World, January 2008

Can a novel about love and the illusions of love be created out of almost 900 satire-laced pages devoted to obscene invective, hatred, pettiness, ignorance, pity, pride and hubris? This is the question raised by Alexander Theroux's first novel in 20 years, *Laura Warholic: Or, The Sexual Intellectual*. If the answer is "maybe," the blame lies less with Theroux's prodigious natural talent than with how he has chosen to structure his narrative and the repetitive nature of his characterizations.

Eugene Eyestones writes a sex column for Quink, a Boston magazine edited by the slobbish Minote Warholic and staffed by an eccentric band of misanthropes with names like Duxbak, Ratnaster, Clucker and Discknickers. Eyestones has been seeing—with the intermittent frequency and heat of a sputtering light bulb—Warholic's estranged wife, Laura, while obsessing over the unobtainable bakery employee Rapunzel Wisht. Although apparently a Vietnam veteran, Eyestones acts like a teenager, idealizing Rapunzel while cataloguing Laura's every fault. The intensity of this scrutiny is magnified by the torrent of insults offered by Minote Warholic, most of Quink's staff and several others. They present Laura's defects in eloquent and lengthy detail, "slacker and total skullcase" being perhaps the most understated of these comments. Eyestones becomes complicit in this character assassination by his silence, a passivity also exemplified by his unwillingness to either ditch Laura or commit to her.

Theroux's use of metaphor in these sections remains as startling and daring in its brilliance as in his masterpiece, *Darconville's Cat* (1981). Through the early pages of this new novel, Theroux's genius appears to reflect a generosity of spirit toward character akin to that of 19th-century influences like Dickens and Trollope. However, it soon becomes clear that Theroux is using his amazing powers of grotesquery and caricature to make almost everyone look morally, ethically and intellectually ugly. As a result, the reader's delight at Theroux's descriptive powers quickly changes to disgust at the unrelenting brutishness of these characters, and that disgust, finally, is transformed into boredom as the barrage of details and constant repetitions begins to seem not only gratuitous but insulting to the reader.

Theroux does try to vary the tone and form of *Laura Warholic*. In addition to insults that have the wit and bawdiness of Shakespearean monologues, he includes pages of Eyestones's sex columns, notes for columns, a fairy tale and often scandalous monologues on Jews, religion and lust. In the middle of a lengthy road trip during which Laura and Eyestones argue their way across the United States, Theroux even offers up chapters on sex and democracy, hodge-podge collections of facts and observations with no particular organization. *Darconville's Cat* also contained digressions, but they served to intensify that novel's effect. Here, where the main characters practice indecision, digressions merely intensify the lack of movement.

Near the end of *Laura Warholic*, after the mismatched couple has broken up, Eyestones has a change of heart. He wonders: "Had not he blundered by looking at Laura far too closely, just as he had looked at Rapunzel from far too great a distance? Would not his attempt at solving both riddles have been avoided in a state of proper balance?" This epiphany is offered up around Christmas, that most sentimental of holidays, and it is so jejune—creates a portrait of a character unaware through so many hundreds of pages—that I began to wonder if Theroux meant for his novel to be satire, and satire only. But surely not. Surely he means to be sincere on some level because otherwise we have read his mammoth undertaking only to be told that life is a pointless farce, and that is not an answer worth enduring all these pages.

It seems only appropriate that *Laura Warholic* ends with a two-paragraph lecture from the author after the main characters have exited the stage. A little more space for the reader, a little less for the author, and this fiercely intelligent, frustrating, disturbing, wonderful, dawdling, horrible and ultimately didactic novel might have been a masterpiece.

THE LOST GIRLS OF ALAN MOORE AND MELINDA GEBBIE
Bookslut, October 2006

For me, Alan Moore's *The Watchmen*, *V for Vendetta*, and *From Hell* form a visceral trilogy of masterpieces created with an uncompromising intelligence and vision. Moore has, over the years, made it seem as if anything were possible in the graphic novel form.

In his latest endeavor, *Lost Girls*, Moore and his collaborator Melinda Gebbie create a pornographic cornucopia that attempts to be salacious but moral, inquisitive yet responsible. In a way, Moore is like the director in Terry Southern's novel *Blue Movie* who sets out to make "an artful erotic motion picture, with studio support and mass-distribution" (terrysouthern.com).

Moore has chosen a very simple plot (perhaps too simple): Three women staying at a hotel in Austria on the eve of World War I become friends and then lovers. They share the secrets of their dark sexual histories against a backdrop of repression and liberation. Almost every possible form of sexuality is explored, all in the colored pencil textures and pastel hues of Gebbie's artwork.

The women are meant to be (the real-life?) Wendy, Dorothy, and Alice from *Peter Pan*, *The Wizard of Oz*, and *Alice in Wonderland*. The bizarre coincidence that brought these three (fictional?) women to this particular hotel at the same time is left to the imagination.

In *Lost Girls*, all three have been stripped of their fantastical context. There's a suggestion that Alice's mirror talks to her (or she talks to it) and that Lewis Carroll, making an appearance as a pedophile, is inspired by Alice to write his books. But in general Moore presents the pasts of the three women as realistic explanations for the fantasy elements in those works. For example, Dorothy lives through a twister during which she experiences a sexual awakening. When she walks out into the ruined landscape, a damaged road sign now reads "OZ," but she's still in Kansas. Peter Pan is just an androgynous male prostitute and there is no Never Never Land other than the mental one in which Peter leads Wendy and her brothers into a sexual initiation. I often wondered while reading *Lost Girls* if Moore had so unhinged some characters from their fictional origins that they could no longer function as those characters in any meaningful way. I don't think this is a niggling point.

More perplexing, given the already static structure of a frame mixed with memories of the past, is the relative lack of characterization in *Lost Girls*. Moore has chosen to let the women's sexual histories serve as their entire background. Is Moore saying that for victims of sexual abuse, the whole world becomes about sex from then on? I don't think so, but the practical effect of focusing solely on sex is to rob us of three-dimensional portraits of these women. (That Moore seems to recognize the possibilities of integration is evident from this *Onion* interview excerpt: "I think in the future, I'd prefer to take what I've learned from *Lost Girls* and follow that back into my other work. To include sex scenes alongside the adventure scenes and everyday-life scenes, as if they were all part of the same thing. Which of course they are.")

But what about *Lost Girls* as pornography?

Gebbie's art is supple and ever-changing, whether in the main sequences or parodying Victorian-era pornography. The softness of the colors makes the sex scenes more human and less mechanistic or harsh. The level of detail in backdrops is precise but not cluttered, with Gebbie able to modulate her effects to convey scenes of unease and horror. Her drawing technique proves better than I would have thought for conveying motion, so that her rendition of an orgy scene during a showing of *The Rites of Spring* might as well *be* in motion.

Often, too, the distance between her color choices and the events in *Lost Girls* proves effective—for example, the flatter, less grainy style chosen for Wendy's memories. As a work of art, *Lost Girls* is as flexible, inventive, and heartfelt as a good lover.

As for Moore's story, the erotic set pieces demonstrate once again his mastery of the graphic novel form. At the beginning of book two, for example, Dorothy's repressed husband writes to a colleague, his banal, blind-to-debauchery letter juxtaposed with riotous sex scenes that mischeviously undermine his account of events. Several of these set pieces work as erotica while being structurally innovative.

However, *Lost Girls* is as much a commentary on sexuality and pornography as an artifact of pornography. For this reason, readers will be simultaneously turned on and disturbed by the book. Many times the erotic act is stimulating, while the context provokes a "I shouldn't be reacting this way" response. This technique allows Moore to engage both heart and head, and it does give all three women more depth than they would have had otherwise. (Otherwise, they're just delivery systems for nontraditional sex.) As the women tell their stories, *Lost Girls* gradually becomes a tale about the price of sex, the price of coercion, and the attraction of abusing power in personal relationships. (Although a case can be made that *Lost Girls* is about this subject from the very beginning, given the interplay between the three women.)

At one point, in the middle of an orgy, while examining a book of pornography, the hotel manager says:

> You see? Incest, *c'est vrai,* it is a crime, but this? This is the idea of incest, no? And then these children: how outrageous! How old can they be? Eleven? Twelve? It is quite monstrous… except that they are fictions, as old as the page they appear upon, no less, no more. Fiction and fact: only madmen and magistrates cannot discriminate between them… You see, if this were real, it would be horrible. Children raped by their trusted parents. Horrible. But they are fictions. They are uncontaminated by effect and consequence. Why, they are almost innocent. I, of course, am real and since Helena, who I just fucked, is only thirteen, I am very guilty. Ah well, it cannot be helped.

There's a lot going on in this speech. The hotel manager isn't real, either, so any outrage or pleasure is also a construct. But Moore provides just that extra level or layer so for a second we're thinking: *The manager's blasé about committing a crime.* And then the cycle of thought (or, rather, one possible cycle of thought):

Is thinking about such things a crime? Maybe not, but can't someone hurt another person just at the level of the imagination? Isn't that part of what inequality, sexual or otherwise, is all about? And is Moore telling us we might as well disregard the pain of his protagonists and just revel in the sex? (But isn't it just the manager talking?) To what extent is he letting the reader off the hook by stating this? Or is it more of a kind of taunt, Nabokov-style: We all know this is a fiction, but if I do my job you'll still be horrified at what happens to these characters?

Lost Girls is a vehicle for sex and ideas about sex that overflows with intelligence and feeling but didn't always work for me. Toward the end of book two, I began to be bored by the sex scenes, especially the lesbian scenes between the three women. I found my attention drifting in part because of the stilted dialogue in some of these scenes, but mostly because they become narrative and artistic time-wasters between gradually revealed backstory. At times the backstory couldn't hold my attention, either. And the denouement, tying into World War I, just seemed an end rather than an end*ing*.

However, despite these reservations, *Lost Girls* is always *alive*, it deals with subject matter that isn't always given this kind of emphasis, and it takes chances. Ultimately, *Lost Girls* rewards a serious (and not so serious) read, but I'm conflicted as to whether it or not it belongs beside Moore's best work.

London's Last Stand: Jonathan Barnes' *The Domino Men*
The Washington Post Book World, January 2009

The premise of Jonathan Barnes's frenetic, uneven, sometimes bleak *Domino Men*, a sequel to his first novel, *The Somnambulist*, sounds like a combination of spy novel and Lovecraft pastiche: From 1857 to the present day, the mysterious Directorate and the English monarchy's House of Windsor have waged a secret war against each other because of a pact between Queen Victoria and a supernatural monster known as Leviathan. Long ago, the queen accepted Leviathan's offer to "guide us, keep us, protect us [and] render us inviolate against invasion." In return, the queen promised to eventually hand over London to the monster.

Leviathan has been kept at bay due to the efforts of a missing Directorate agent named Estella, who must be found to end a stalemate in the conflict. The key to finding her lies with the Domino Men, two diabolical killers imprisoned within an infernal circle beneath 10 Downing Street.

The Somnambulist, set in 1901 (also in London), featured a wonderful freak show of magicians, time travelers and the undead. Barnes made this grotesquerie reader-friendly through brilliant narration and a dark sense of humor familiar to fans of Douglas Adams and Terry Pratchett. With very different results, *The Domino Men* uses a similar mixture of the grotesque and humorous.

The narrator, Henry Lamb, works at a thankless job for the Civil Service Archive Unit. His father dead and his mother indifferent to him, Lamb is a loner who has a charming crush on his landlady. The only distinction he has achieved to date was as a child star on a BBC sitcom, "Worse Things Happen at Sea."

But Lamb comes from stock with higher ambitions, as he discovers when approached by sinister men after his grandfather collapses into a coma. The men tell him that his grandfather was a Directorate agent, and they want Lamb to take the old man's place. In a secret part of the London Eye Ferris Wheel, he meets the head of the

Directorate, Dedlock. "Wrinkled and puckered, wattled, creased and liver spotted," Dedlock, defender of the city, is almost as strange as Leviathan: He lives in water, has what appear to be gills and can inhabit the bodies of his employees.

When Lamb asks questions—understandable given the circumstances—Dedlock tells him, "Comprehension is unnecessary. From now on you simply have to follow orders." Those orders include talking to the dangerous Domino Men about Estella, something Lamb dreads but does without much complaint.

Unfortunately, as the extent of Leviathan's evil plans becomes clear, I began to wish Lamb would question orders more. Instead, he obeys and obeys, despite operating in a miasma of ignorance. The result is a kind of narrative impotence. When a former agent pleads with Lamb to take action after a Domino Men jailbreak, Lamb merely replies, "What can I do?" Barnes eventually provides a good reason for Lamb's inaction, but that doesn't make his role as a chess piece any less problematic for the reader. Confusing matters further, another voice begins to hijack the narrative. Identified only at the novel's end, this narrator provides background on the queen's deal with Leviathan and briefly re-invigorates the story with its sarcastic counterpoint to Lamb's account. But soon the second narrator just seems repetitious, because there's no reason Lamb couldn't have related the same information himself.

However, nothing—not the promise of its opening nor the lurching complications of its middle—can prepare the reader for the shock of *The Domino Men's* resolution. It's one of the most perplexing endings in recent memory. Characters are brutally tortured while London suffers cataclysmic upheaval. A final, extremely odd science fiction twist brings the reader back to the realm of dark humor.

Perhaps the key to making sense of all this is to forget Lamb entirely and remember the book's title, which turns the spotlight on the Domino Men, those "creatures of fire and sulphur." Introduced in *The Somnambulist*, this leering pair, otherwise known as Hawker and Boon, are terrifying in a jovial, vaudevillian way: a demented, supernatural Tweedledum and Tweedledee who take pleasure in pain. They are Barnes's greatest achievement in this novel, and he gives them unmatched life and verve.

The jaded reader may doubt that Barnes intended this fusion of hysterical hilarity and frenetic nihilism, suspecting, instead, that the author simply surrendered to his material. Does he really mean to combine gonzo science fiction with detailed sadism? If he does, it's because he let the Domino Men—more than Dedlock, Lamb or even Leviathan—take control of this novel.

Otherwise, all is chaos.

THE NEWT SPEAKS VOLUMES: JACK O'CONNELL'S THE RESURRECTIONIST

The Washington Post Book World, June 2008

You would think that a conversation between a mad scientist and his prized newt might not stand out in a novel dominated by sociopathic bikers, a father's unbearable guilt and a sad quest by a group of sideshow freaks.

You would be wrong. In the strange crucible of reality and imagination that is *The Resurrectionist*, by Jack O'Connell, their one-sided exchange exemplifies the author's sheer chutzpah: from its meticulous attention to detail to the parallels between Dr. Peck, founder of a coma clinic, and his blue-spotted newt, Rene. "Both [man and animal] were naturally nocturnal," O'Connell writes. "Both were deaf to conventional wisdom. Both were regenerators, magicians who could raise up that which had been lost or damaged or cut away." Despite its static qualities, the scene is a classic of recent modern fiction, revealing worlds about a pivotal character.

The Resurrectionist is full of such surprising scenes. An emotionally damaged man named Sweeney has brought his son, Danny, to Dr. Peck's clinic. He's trying to get away from Cleveland, the site of the accident that led to Danny's condition and killed Sweeney's wife. Though the boy is comatose, we see his dreams about a band of freaks from his favorite comic book, "Limbo." O'Connell threads these freaks' purgatorial adventures throughout the novel. Meanwhile, in the real world, a biker gang led by a thuggish visionary intends to enter the comic book world of "Limbo" by means that might either harm or save Danny. When Sweeney discovers that Dr. Peck has been subjecting his coma patients to horrible experiments, he must navigate through this funhouse landscape to try to save his son and himself.

Much of this unholy amalgamation, set in the same contemporary "rustbelt" city as O'Connell's prior novels, shouldn't work—and some of it doesn't. At times the layering of levels and symbolism doesn't quite cohere. And faced with an overabundance of plot complications, O'Connell allows certain characters to disappear for too long.

Yet these flaws seem minor in the context of the novel—nullified by brilliant writing, original concepts, emotional resonance and O'Connell's fearlessness. I've read *The Resurrectionist* twice now, and both times it came as something of a revelation. It seems odd we should care so much about the freaks, for example, when we know they're merely characters in a boy's comic book. Nor should the dream-life of a coma patient be so resonant, and yet it is.

The newt may be mute, but it speaks volumes.

Not Enough Bite: Victor Pelevin's *The Sacred Book of the Werewolf*

The Washington Post, Arts & Living, October 2008

Rough werewolf-on-werefox sex. Were-creature philosophy that doubles as satirical content. Plucky underage Russian prostitutes who are actually millennia-old supernatural beings. Nonstop references to iconic authors, philosophers and pop culture.

If you enjoy having all these elements in your fiction, you'll love Victor Pelevin's *The Sacred Book of the Werewolf*. The rest of us, though, might come away from this novel feeling bitten. There's something distinctly unholy going on here, something Vladimir Nabokov might have labeled "poshlost," or "philistine vulgarity," for all the times Pelevin tries to use the old butterfly collector to prop up his own words, citing everything from *Lolita* to *Ada*.

This fitful, phantasmagorical tale—a bestseller in Russia—is told by A Hu-Li, a werefox posing as a 15-year-old hooker in Moscow. She bewitches her johns using the magic properties of her tail so she can feed off of their sexual energy. While her victims believe they're having sex with her, she sits in a corner reading magazines. But after a couple of missteps, including killing a customer when he sees her true form, A Hu-Li runs into trouble with the Russian secret service. Col. Mikhalich apprehends her for his mysterious boss, known as Alexander.

In a masterly sequence—one of the few times Pelevin sits still long enough to really develop a scene—Mikhalich decides he wants to sample A Hu-Li's services before turning her over to Alexander. But that requires Mikhalich to reveal that he's a werewolf, too, by injecting a powerful psychedelic into his own arm. Among A Hu-Li's special skills is the ability to see into people's minds. Her description of Mikhalich's drug trip is a wonderful example of making the abstract and personal into something concrete: "There was a flash, with pulsating stars and stripes of flame receding all the way to the horizon like the markings on an infinitely long runway. It was blindingly beautiful and reminiscent of a news report I saw in the 1960s of a trimaran speed-boat that crashed: the speedboat lifted up off the water, performed a slow, thoughtful loop-the-loop and shattered into small fragments against the surface of the lake."

Every scene involving the menacing, terse and sometimes comic Mikhalich takes on a satisfying weight. Unfortunately, however, he is relegated to a minor role. It is Alexander who plays the male lead here, becoming entranced with A Hu-Li. This attraction drives the plot for the rest of the book. The two have rough werewolf sex, followed by long, obvious conversations about, among other things, the Little Red Riding Hood folktale. A Hu-Li's growing attraction to Alexander eventually leads to an irreversible, possibly tragic transformation, and the novel ends in a fizzle of nebulous Eastern philosophy and unearned redemption.

Suspended over this plot like a bomb that's never dropped looms the myth of the super-werewolf, who, it is foretold, will soon walk the Earth, delivering something special to the were-peoples. The nature of that special something only becomes clear late in the novel, in a bit of farcical anticlimax. By that point, the reader has been asked to invest too much time and effort in an existential joke that really doesn't matter.

In an interview in *The Paris Review*, Nabokov defined his made-up word "poshlost" as, among other things, "Corny trash, vulgar clichés…imitations of imitations, bogus profundities, crude, moronic, and dishonest pseudoliterature." Pelevin is neither crude nor moronic, but his personal Rubicon is a seeming inability to stop using others to shoulder the burden of writing his novel. Thus the reader must endure Bulgakov sightings, silly doubled-up references ("I suddenly understood that Pushkin was killed by a homonimic shadow of Dante"), and stultifying snippets of dialogue in question-answer form about various movies. Many readers will realize they are bearing witness to an odd kind of abdication of responsibility on the part of the author.

Pelevin doesn't seem to understand how his borrowing creates "bogus profundities." Or that his philosophical points would be more interesting in essay form. Or that his pacing is too slow to make the humor sparkle. Yet on the rare occasions that Pelevin dispenses with all the clutter, he demonstrates a remarkable talent that makes me want to read more of his fiction. For example, an undeniably eerie yet funny scene in which Alexander and Mikhalich, in werewolf form, conjure oil out of the earth compares favorably to the work of the best Russian absurdists.

Near the end of the novel, Alexander and A Hu-Li hole up in a bomb shelter, in a scene that displays much-needed tenderness. A Hu-Li says to Alexander, language is "the root from which infinite human stupidity grows. And we were-creatures suffer from it too, because we're always talking."

Ultimately *The Sacred Book of the Werewolf* fails because Pelevin just can't shut up long enough to tell his story.

Hot Ice: Marcel Theroux's *Far North*
New York Times Book Review, August 2009

In Marcel Theroux's post-Collapse novel *Far North*, global warming has reduced civilization to largely pre-industrial levels of technology, and made sparsely populated areas like the Siberian tundra safer than lawless cities. There's a satisfying sadness and finality to Theroux's vision, but the true power of the story comes from the hard-won victories of Makepeace, Theroux's remarkable narrator. *Far North*'s enduring achievement is to feature a character that lives up to Makepeace's own claim that "a person is always better than a book."

Face scarred by past violence, Makepeace patrols the streets of deserted Evangeline, a Siberian town founded by Quakers. After mistakenly shooting a Chinese boy named Ping and then nursing him back to health, Makepeace learns that Ping, like her, has a secret—and it's the same secret. Ping is a woman, disguised as a man to fool a violent world. In Ping's case, she's also trying to disguise her pregnancy.

Theroux is never shy about subverting reader expectations. Soon after Ping recovers, Makepeace writes with typical yet heart-breaking understatement, "I can't dwell on what happened next...but in June, Ping died, and the baby died with her." Ping's death serves as a kind of turning point for Makepeace: it will kill her or it will force her to engage the world.

Witnessing a plane crash saves Makepeace from suicide by replacing despair with a question: Is the plane a sign of returning civilization? During Makepeace's quest for the answer, members of a strange cult take her prisoner and sell her to slavers. The line that destroys the reader is the same one that destroys her: "Sometimes, when you've suffered a lot, it turns out to be the small thing that breaks you. That chain almost finished me."

In contrast, the harrowing account of the journey to the work camp has the full weight and context of twentieth-century history behind it. But when

Makepeace reaches the camp, personal revelations again dominate *Far North*. Transferred from hard labor to working in a garden, Makepeace is unable to bear "the ghost of what might have been" and is "mired in the shame of what I'd become." If being shackled can break you when you've already suffered so much, then small pleasures, like gardening, can also break you by making you foolishly believe that you have a chance for a normal life.

Next to such moments, even desperate scenes in a contaminated city—where workers are forced to search for technological marvels—seem oddly unimportant. Theroux can do little more in this wider context than echo dozens of disaster fiction predecessors, from J.G. Ballard to Cormac McCarthy.

But echoes have their own integrity and resonance. The true flaws in *Far North* are coincidences that betray Makepeace or seek to artificially tie her past to the novel's present. Would Makepeace, having escaped once from religious fanatics, really return to the same settlement without the author's prodding? Is it believable that the person responsible for Makepeace's disfigurement runs the work camp? The reader doesn't need banal explanations, and Makepeace doesn't need the closure.

Makepeace also doesn't need the rebirth motif at the end of *Far North*—it borders on the sentimental and is far-fetched in conception. It's easy to forgive Theroux, though, for succumbing to the temptation. So much has been taken from Makepeace that she's earned some form of kindness.

Deep into this unbearably sad yet often sublime novel, Makepeace writes, "Everyone expects to be at the end of something. What no one expects is to be at the end of *everything*." There's nothing left to say after that—and yet Makepeace keeps going, and the reader follows her if not hopefully than in the hope that she will win out, and that her life will have meaning to someone, somewhere.

Philosophy in Fiction's Clothing: Neal Stephenson's *Anathem*

Barnes & Noble Review, September 2008

1

Anathem:...an aut by which an incorrigible fraa or suur is ejected from the math and his or her work sequestered (hence the Fluccish word Anathema meaning intolerable statements or ideas).

Any writer who wants to create a sense of verisimilitude about an imaginary setting must wrestle with how to convey both the similarities and differences between the created milieu and the real world. In his previous novels, Neal Stephenson has faced this test while attempting to convey an amazingly deep array of ideas and situations. From the hip nearish future of *Snow Crash* to the nanotech-encrusted *The Diamond Age*, and even in such "historical" novels as *Cryptonomicon* and the three volumes of the Baroque Cycle, Stephenson's challenge has been making the alien *real* enough so that he can then explore the implications of various philosophical or technological issues, providing entertainment to the reader at the same time as he engages in a complex dialog about our present and our future. In Stephenson's new book, *Anathem*, a stunning sprawl of a novel set on the planet Arbre, clever new solutions to the problem spring up in every paragraph, on every page—without which not a single line of dialogue, a single character study, would convince the reader one iota.

Among the most impressive of Stephenson's accomplishments in this area is how quickly the reader adjusts to terms like *aut* and *fraa* and *suur* from the quote above. An *aut* is a ritual. A *fraa* is a male "avout," a *suur* a female avout, and *avout* roughly means "monk." For example, *Anathem*'s narrator is the 19-year-old fraa avout Erasmas, and he lives in a "math" that is thousands of years old. The *maths* are more or less monasteries for scientists and philosophers, protecting accumulated knowledge from the rise and fall of civilizations outside their walls. A *Saunt*, or saint, is not a religious martyr but rather a "great thinker," a lovely inversion. In another brilliant tactical move by Stephenson, the Sæcular world outside of Erasmus' math during the events related in *Anathem* is as sophisticated as our own today. This creates important opportunities for contrast between the two cultures.

The mystery that emerges from Stephenson's meticulous world building involves nothing less than a threat to the planet. It's a truth that slowly comes into focus as Erasmas shares seemingly surface details about his life, his surroundings, and his mentor, Fraa Orolo. These early sections of *Anathem* are mesmerizing, the discussions among the avout both mind-blowing and hilarious. Some of the finest scenes in the novel occur as Stephenson expertly takes the reader through the rituals of Erasmas' math. (It is difficult to think of another writer who could make a long description of a clock-winding ceremony so fascinating.)

Soon, though, Stephenson expands the scope of *Anathem* to include the rest of Arbre—indeed, the rest of the cosmos. Erasmas, Fraa Orolo, and others notice disturbing deviations during routine observations of the night sky. Their subsequent investigation puts them in grave danger as they acquire forbidden knowledge. As a result, Fraa Orolo and Erasmas in turn are expelled into the Sæcular World; however, while Orolo's departure is the result of an anathem, Erasmas' expulsion may well be part of a plan to aim a weapon at the heart of a mysterious enemy.

2

Ita: In late Praxic Orth, an acronym...whose precise etymology is a casualty of the loss of shoddily preserved information that will forever enshroud the time of the Harbingers and the Terrible Events. Almost all scholars agree that the first two letters come from the words Information Technology, which is late Praxic Age commercial bulshytt for syntactic devices. The third letter is disputed; hypotheses include Authority, Associate, Arm, Archive, Aggregator, Amalgamated, Analyst, Agency, and Assistant.

Stephenson's ability to create and deploy convincing terminology makes Erasmus' story possible. But it's his playful sense of invention in fleshing out his world, bringing to mind his youthful exuberance in *Snow Crash*, that gives *Anathem* most of its energy and makes it largely a joy to read. Calling a truck a "fetch" is merely clever, but elements like an extended discussion between students and instructor about Sæcular perceptions or the avout—"iconographies"—are in a different class altogether.

In the Muncostran Iconography, for example, a scientist is thought of as "eccentric, lovable, disheveled theorician, absent-minded, means well." The Pendarthaan Iconography, by contrast, portrays scientists as "high-strung, nervous, meddling know-it-alls who simply don't understand the realities; lacking physical courage, they always lose out to more masculine Sæculars." The undeniable satirical quality of these iconographies is wedded to a practical purpose: avout who come into contact with the outside world need to understand which stereotypes, which belief systems, represent a threat to them or their maths. This initial discussion of perception and belief recurs repeatedly, a continual probing of the nature of reality and the power of the mind to construct its own version of it.

Throughout *Anathem*, Stephenson displays a genius for creating details that multi-task by being clever and funny *and* functional. This is particularly important during the middle of the novel, in which Erasmas travels across a continent to reach a rendezvous point for an expedition that may lead to answers about the threat from the heavens. The pacing that worked so well in the math seems somewhat slower during Erasmas' journey, the theoretical conversations more ponderous. The insertion of oddly absurd yet believable elements, like "Everything Killer" weapon systems and an internet that runs on "bulshytt" and "bulshytt elimination," helps make this slower pace more palatable.

3

Bulshytt: In Fluccish of the late Praxic Age and early Reconstitution, a derogatory term for false speech in general, esp. knowing and deliberate falsehood or obfuscation...

The overall level of bulshytt in *Anathem* is relatively low. In one sense, of course, the entire novel is bulshytt of the kind expected from professional liars: game playing at a level so high that in some places the author's imagination alone keeps the whole audacious contraption spinning in the air long after it should have cracked to pieces against the floor.

But what negative bulshytt does exist occurs because Erasmas is a deliberate, detail-oriented narrator with a somewhat understated approach. The reader is given the sense that this is part of his training, and in the context of his math this restraint works well. However, when Erasmas is out in the wider world this quality lends Stephenson's prose an "and-then-this-happened-and-then-that-happened" quality. Erasmas maintains the same tone, whether he is describing being buried in the snow while traveling over the north pole of Arbre or narrating his narrow escape from an angry mob with the help of some truly butt-kicking "ninja" monks.

The liveliness of the ideas surrounding Erasmas' adventures often masks this defect but cannot, for example, disguise the increasingly superficial nature of his romantic relationship with Ala, a suur avout with a pivotal role in the plans being made against the enemy. His reactions to their separation, and to the dangerous prospect she faces, become flatter and flatter, even as Ala's own initial complexity dissipates, perhaps losing out to Stephenson's fascination with ideas. Further, Ala's habit of becoming emotional not only undermines the idea that Erasmas' restraint is culture based but also makes her stereotypically "female."

Still, these flaws seem minor in the context of the triumphs on display here. As Stephenson writes in his introduction, *Anathem* "is best read in somewhat of the same spirit as John L. Casti's *The Cambridge Quintet*, which is to say that it is a fictional framework for exploring ideas that have sprung from the minds of great thinkers of Earth's past and present." In this sense, then, *Anathem* is a worthy successor to the ambitious Baroque Cycle. Such a reading of *Anathem* doesn't excuse some of the baggy-ness of the 900-page novel, or the impassive qualities of Erasmas; but the ideas are so attractively presented, the context so perfect for their exploration, that it's hard to find too much fault.

In the last act, *Anathem* also provides some unbelievably intricate space adventure—some of it attaining the audaciousness of a Roger Moore—era James Bond movie—wedded to spectacular scientific extrapolation and speculation about alternate universes. This action-oriented reprise in-the-flesh of the abstract hypotheticals discussed during the novel's first half has the satisfying feel of watching blueprints turn into aesthetically pleasing real-world objects.

Perhaps, then, what Stephenson has accomplished with *Anathem* is the ultimate synthesis of techno-fascination/Geek-SF sense-of-wonder with the far more ancient general quest for knowledge about the world, and what lies beyond our grasp of it.

The Books of the Decade

Omnivoracious, January 2010

In general, "Best of Decade" book lists are arbitrary and too close to the period they pretend to cover. At point of impact, the pool of visible worthies has been reduced due to environmental factors that (sadly) include lack of the right push by the publishers, lack of charisma or some other quality on the part of the author, or a writing style or subject matter that bravely pushes against the grain of what's acceptable for the time. A decade from now many "best of" books will no longer be seen as such, while some lucky few will be re-evaluated and resurrected—becoming visible in a way they did not upon publication. Hype and the ever-greater domino effect of commentary on the Internet will fade and the excited crushes of yesteryear will give way to a more mature and lasting love.

For this reason, I haven't applied anything approaching a scientific method to my picks for the books of the decade. This doesn't mean I didn't have a process, however. First, over a period of days, I thought about the books I've read that I still intensely remember. Second, to supplement my memory, I went back over a good many of the reviews and features I've written over the past decade. As I re-read these pieces, some elicited an emotional reaction and some did not. More than a few connected with me on several levels—as a reader, certainly, but also as a writer whose principal accomplishment in the aughts was to finish the Ambergris Cycle: *City of Saints & Madmen*, *Shriek: An Afterword*, and *Finch*. Thus, there was a weird doubling effect of seeing the books from several angles, because many of them made me think about my own fiction in a new way.

The resulting list is in alphabetical order by author. Some of these books received the appropriate amount of attention upon publication. Some did not. Some choices readers will easily see as legitimate and others, due to their obscurity or to the perception of the genre in which they are categorized, will not. But each, it seems to me, does something unique and not easily replicated by other books. Each, in its own way, creates its own universe.

The Elegance of the Hedgehog by Muriel Barbery (2008) – Delightful and bittersweet, this translation of a bestseller in France creates lovely portraits of an eccentric concierge and a melodramatic but gifted twelve-year-old girl. It lazes along at a leisurely pace, interjecting bits of philosophy and character background until the arrival of a Japanese gentleman at the apartment complex. From there, the plot begins to quicken and the various pieces of the story become luminous and at times devastating. It's the kind of novel that could easily have become precious, and it's a testimony to Barbery's strengths as an author that instead it's a quietly effective and lasting achievement.

What It Is by Lynda Barry (2008) – As I wrote as part of an Omni feature, Barry's extraordinary book is "An exploration of the imagination, an invitation to create, and a moving autobiographical account... one of those rare books that offers solace for the soul and brilliant commentary on the artistic impulse. The images by themselves would be amazing, the text by itself wise and luminous yet pragmatic. The combination of text and art provides new insight that feels three-dimensional and oddly soothing. I cannot over-emphasize the therapeutic effect of *What It Is*."

Fun Home by Alison Bechdel (2007) – In this story of her dysfunctional family, Bechtel perfects and showcases the ways in which graphic novels can offer as much or more than novels or movies. It is the perfect synthesis of image and text, with the visual impact of a film and the easy ability to slip through time, double back, and return to the present that typifies the best fiction. The illustration style is perfect for the subject matter, making the settings, from old gothic house to funeral parlor, evocative and real.

2666 by Robert Bolanos (2008) – Powerful, haunting, profane, political, and simultaneously wide and personal in scope, *2666* may well prove to be the novel of the decade. Bolanos keeps turning inward and outward, his narrative riddled through with ancillary stories that seem to digress but in some luminous way hint at hidden patterns. The recitation—the endless and unrelieved repetition—of the details of murders of women in a Mexican city is unsettling, brilliant, and makes the crimes impossible to ignore, or, ultimately, to comprehend. Most impressive, perhaps, is how equally comfortable Bolanos is writing from such varied perspectives as a former Black Panther, a Mexican congresswoman, or the German novelist whose mysterious life provides just one of the many puzzles of human existence explored in *2666*.

Observatory Mansions by Edward Carey – As I wrote in a review for Locus at the time, this novel is "simply the best Gothic fantasy of the new century… stunning in its use of a dark fantasy atmosphere even though, as in Mervyn Peake's Gormenghast books, nothing fantastical happens. Francis Orme narrates this story of an ancestral mansion converted to apartments, of a place in the country become a virtual island, surrounded by urban traffic. But Carey, at every step, raises the stakes; he isn't interested in just portraying eccentric characters in an eccentric setting. He wants nothing less than Mastery—of technique, of characterization, of setting, of memory, of resonance." *Observatory Mansions*, with its critique of our modern attachment to things, its portraits of damaged but sympathetic characters, and its beautiful, incisive writing, is another novel that deserves more attention.

About Writing: 7 Essays, 4 Letters, and 5 Interviews by Samuel Delany (2006) – One of the best books on writing I read in the aughts, *About Writing* features a few reprints from books like *The Jewel Hinged Jaw*, but mostly collects previously uncollected nonfiction. The letters, which I thought would be slight turn out to be one of the best things about the book—insightful, focused, and consistently fascinating. The interviews are sometimes a little too detail oriented, but still wonderful to read, and the essays are, of course, magnificent. I love that when Delany talks about even the most basic details of writing, it resonates with me in a way that makes me see certain technique and approaches in a totally new light.

One Day the Ice Will Reveal All of Its Dead by Clare Dudman (2004) – A closely observed, passionate, and complex historical fiction centered on the discoverer of continental drift, Alfred Wegener, Dudman's novel delivered a perfect blend of science, characterization, adventure, and pathos. As I wrote in my review of the book for *Publishers Weekly*, "Dudman…displays an astute gift for characterization. Wegener's complex relationship with his brother Kurt and his love for his wife, Else, as measured against his lust for meteorological expeditions, is expertly, often heartbreakingly portrayed. The emotional yet understated final scenes are particularly fine. Above all, Dudman shows us one incontrovertible truth about her Wegener: he loved the world, in all of its riotous complexity. Some may say the same of Dudman after reading this wise, beautiful novel." Criminally underrated, this book deserves much more attention.

Zeroville by Steve Erickson (2007) – Erickson is a writer whose sense of history and the absurd suffuses his books. *Zeroville*, about an eccentric, damaged man who stumbles into film directing, is primarily set in the Los Angeles of the 1970s and 1980s. As I wrote in my *Washington Post Book World* review, "Over his entire career Erickson has challenged readers with a fiercely intelligent and surprisingly sensual brand of American surrealism that can, at times, seem impenetrable. For this reason, it surprised me that almost everything in Erickson's new novel *Zeroville* entertains so readily without seeming watered down or slight. Zeroville is funny, sad and darkly beautiful, built around short chapters that allow the author to capture the essential moment and move effortlessly through time."

The Book of Prefaces by Alasdair Gray (2000) – The great Scottish writer who produced such classic novels as *Lanark* and *Poor Things* endeavored early in this decade to publish…a book of prefaces. The eccentric, brilliant result is nothing less than an exploration of the evolution of the English language. Divided into sections including "The First English," "English Reforms," "A Great Flowering," and "Between Two Revolutions," *The Book of Prefaces* reprints prefaces from books by everyone from Chaucer to Darwin—all of it annotated and illustrated by Gray. In the groupings and analysis, we learn more about language than from any more conventional history.

Light by M. John Harrison (2002) – Winner of the James Tiptree Award, *Light* shares some similarities with Bolanos' *2666* in its willingness to give sometimes brutish depictions of human behavior while also demonstrating mind-blowing depth of vision. A present-day thread involving a killer meshes with a future narrative centered around the mysterious Kefahuchi Tract in deep space. As I wrote at the time in a SF Site review, "*Light* is a book to make both Iain M. Banks and Vladimir Nabokov blush with envy, a book that uses hard SF concepts like poetry and is merciless in its assault on the irrelevant. I cannot think of a SF novel in recent memory that has both mocked the stereotypical 'sense of wonder' and yet simultaneously created a sense of wonder."

The Summer Book by Tove Jansson (1976, 2008) – The reprinting of this sublime classic about a girl's adventures under the tutelage of her grandmother on an island off of Finland confirmed Jansson as one of the twentieth century's greatest humanists. Wise, touching without being sentimental, intensely magical, and vibrant, *The Summer Book* refreshes and restores the reader at every turn. It succeeds at that most difficult of tasks: to build interest and depth without resorting to conventional conflict. The depictions of nature, wedded to great characters, are also phenomenal. (The reissue of Jansson's Moomin comics by Drawn & Quarterly also deserves mention.)

Tainaron by Leena Krohn (2004) – A translation from the original Finnish, this short novel consists of thirty letters written by an anonymous narrator visiting the city of Tainaron, a metropolis populated by human-sized intelligent insects. Krohn is a writer of the first rank, comparable to Kafka, and the novel contains scenes of startling beauty and strangeness. Krohn also effortlessly melds the literal with the metaphorical, so that the narrator's explorations encompass both the speculation of science fiction and the resonant symbolism of the surreal. In addition to the sometimes horrifying images—self-immolating insects; a funeral subculture centered on dung beetles—*Tainaron* contains a strong undercurrent of emotion. Krohn's genius is to use the homesickness and oblique personal information in the letters to substitute masterfully for more conventional character development. While *Tainaron* received good reviews upon publication, the novel has been criminally ignored since. Hopefully some publisher will republish and relaunch Tainaron, as it deserves resurrection.

Cloud Atlas by David Mitchell (2004) – Spanning 200 years, Mitchell's brilliant novel concerns nothing less than the end of history using several diverse storylines. The virtuoso stylistic performance would be pointless, however, if not for the complexity and compelling nature of the characters—-some of them doomed, some of them hopeful, some of them deluded about their place in the world, and some of them, like the vanity publisher in one section, possessing a keen sense of the absurd. *Cloud Atlas* is a sprawling yet tightly controlled novel that manages to explode the traditional structure of the novel without being gimmicky or merely clever. (In a similar vein, Jeanette Winterson's lesser but still worthy *The Stone Gods* echoes these concerns.)

Dungeon Twilight, Vols. 1 and 2: *Dragon Cemetery* and *Armageddon* by Joann Sfar and Lewis Trondheim (2006) – The French geniuses Sfar and Trondheim delivered perhaps their most sublime reading experience in the guise of a swords-and-sorcery graphic novel about an immortal lizard king's relationship to his mother and father. Stunning visuals are matched by exciting and compelling plot lines about the end of the world and its rebirth. But none of this would mean anything without the compelling characterization.

The Arrival by Shaun Tan (2006) – As I wrote in my Bookslut review: "Wordless yet containing worlds, Shaun Tan's *The Arrival* demonstrates the power of fantasy to show us our reality. The story is simple: an immigrant arrives in a strange city and tries to make a life for himself so that one day he can send for his family. He encounters strange, fantastical creatures that are as natural as breakfast, lunch, and dinner to the native inhabitants. He learns the stories of other immigrants who have come to the city....The complexity and the richness of *The Arrival* come entirely from the painstaking and effortless execution of the central idea, using a myriad of panels that, mostly in warm sepia tones, convey not just movement but *the moment*." A wordless classic as central to the new century as Bolano's *2666*.

Far North by Marcel Theroux (2009) – Theroux's post-apocalyptic novel provides a good example of critical reevaluation, even in the short term. When I first read it, I had reservations about some of the plot devices used by the author; to some extent, I still feel the structure is flawed. However, the protagonist, Makepeace, has haunted me ever since I read *Far North*; I can't shake her, and therefore I can't shake the novel. Ultimately, that immersive experience—of deeply believing in a fictional person—means I cannot shake *Far North* from this list, either. As I wrote in *The New York Times Book Review*, "Deep into this unbearably sad yet often sublime novel, Makepeace says: 'Everyone expects to be at the end of something. What no one expects is to be at the end of *everything*.' There's nothing left to say after that—yet Makepeace keeps going, and the reader follows her, if not hopefully then in the hope that she will win out and that her life will have meaning to someone, somewhere."

The Wizard of the Crow by Ngugi Wa Thingo (2007) – Chaotic and absurd, satirical and wise, *The Wizard of the Crow* is set in the imaginary African country of Abruria. The plot concerns, among many other things, a sick tyrant with a ridiculous plan to create the tallest building in the world to celebrate his glory. Scheming ministers, a rebel group called The Movement of the Voice of the People, figure prominently. So does the wizard of the title, an educated, unemployed man named Kamiti who joins the rebels. He's not a wizard, even though many mistakenly think he is, but Ngugi Wa Thingo is definitely a wizard for juggling all of the elements of this madcap romp of a novel. The sublime and the silly coexist within *The Wizard of the Crow*, but ultimately the message is as serious and cutting as the text is nimble and uproarious.

Maps of the Imagination: The Writer as Cartographer by Peter Turchi (2004) – This brilliant exploration of creative writing through the metaphor of the map makes you see craft and form from a different perspective. Chapters like "Projections and Conventions" and "A Rigorous Geometry" provide insightful analysis of various short stories and novels in the context of topography. The copious illustrations not only enliven and explicate the text, they often suggest new approaches to fictional structure, characterization, and description.

Rising Up, Rising Down by William T. Vollman (2004) – Even in the abridged one-volume version, Vollman's history of violence is a formidable and eccentric accomplishment. This exploration roams from the first world to the third, from an image outside his apartment window to the catacombs beneath Paris. Vollman's clear-eyed analysis, his continual questioning of ideas and of situations results in a fascinating and essential guide to both barbarity and the pillars of our so-called civilization.

The Jerusalem Quartet by Edward Whittemore (1977-1987/2002) – Old Earth Books did the world a tremendous favor by reprinting the four novels of Whittemore's Jerusalem Quartet: *Sinai Tapestry*, *Jerusalem Poker*, *Nile Shadows*, and *Jericho Mosaic*. As I wrote in an article for Locus Online at the time: "With his Jerusalem Quartet, Whittemore set out to do nothing less than map a secret history of the world, focusing on the Middle East, where a welter of religions converge, sometimes with tragic results. The novels are loosely related, in that several memorable protagonists appear in all four, slipping in and out of the narrative as walk-on, secondary, and main characters. Inasmuch as The Jerusalem Quartet tells one story, it follows the exploits of a man named Stern Strongbow, who hopes to create peace in the Middle East. It also covers the years 1900 through 1975, weaving together different times and places for a thematic resonance that far exceeds anything Thomas Pynchon accomplished in his excellent book *V*."

Conversation #3:

The Monstrous Capybara of Austin Texas

Ecstatic Days, June 2009

My first encounter with a capybara was sad and strange: I saw one in a cramped cage at a county fair as a teenager. In amongst the rides, the shooting galleries, and the weird food, just this tiny cage and this incredibly peculiar creature that I'd never seen before, or even imagined existed. It had unbelievably beautiful eyes. Ever since then, I've been fascinated with capybaras because they seem so fantastical and they also have this gruffly wise look to them. (I only wish I had found some way to rescue that first one from what couldn't have been a great life.)

Recently, I had a dream about capybaras. I dreamt of a land of talking capybaras and their guinea pig minions. They were in a war against a land of meerkats and their vole minions. It was not cute. It was not whimsical. I was their secret weapon. But although I could describe advanced weapon tech I could not build it. Funny thing about the dream…we were in the General capybara's command-and-control tent the whole time with the guinea pig suborbs running in and out of the flap while the capybaras plotted strategy around a map of their world on a table. The capybaras were human-sized. All very serious and gruff. It was pretty musky and muddy in there—just planks on the floor and then the dirt/mud. It must've been raining outside. So I never saw the world, just the inside of this tent with these serious capybaras asking my advice on strategy and weaponry. Some of them wore helmets with spikes coming out of them like the Kaiser's soldiers during WWI. They had little colored pins stuck in the maps and little plastic models of their capybara infantry and some cavalry, although I never did find out what a capybara might ride. The dream ended because I kept getting smaller and smaller and eventually I fell through the eye of one of the capybara officers and into a vortex of black light.

Astoundingly, a capybara named Caplin Rous responded in the comments thread when I posted a blog entry about my dream. This led to further investigations, and the discovery that Caplin Rous lives in Texas, and that Melanie Typaldos dons the Caplin Rous (Rodents of Unusual Size, if you remember your *Princess Bride*) persona for her website devoted to her capybara. Not only that, Typaldos has just released a kid's book called *Celeste and the Giant Hamster,* which does include appearances by a capybara. It seemed only natural, given the topics that crop up on Ecstatic Days, to interview Melanie Typaldos about Caplin Rous, as wonderful a capybara as I've ever seen. The answers about capybaras may surprise you, including what sounds they make! It's just a great interview.

How did you wind up with a capybara in Texas? And had you ever had one before?

Six months before we got Caplin Rous, I went to the Los Llanos region of Venezuela with my two grown children, Philip and Coral. One of our goals was to see capybaras in the wild. We were lucky enough to see quite a few of them... actually hundreds, maybe thousands. Our most amazing experience was holding a three-month-old capybara that our guide simply picked up off the road one evening. The docile nature of that capybara in our first up-close experience started us thinking that a capybara might make a good pet. When we got back to Texas we researched capybaras on the web and found surprisingly little information on their suitability as pets. However, we did note that some sites stated something along the lines of "commonly kept as pets" with absolutely no data to back the claim.

What kind of a pet is a capybara? How smart? And what kind of temperament?

When we questioned locals in Venezuela, they stated in no uncertain terms that capybaras are the dumbest animals on the planet. Our experience is quite the opposite. Caplin is at least as smart as a dog, although differently motivated. He won't do anything if there isn't something in it for him. It seems like he recognizes every person he's ever met and reacts differently to them. In general, he is a very sweet and affectionate animal. He likes to sit on the couch next to me or in my lap while I feed him treats. Since he weighs 100 lbs, I can only have him in my lap for a few minutes before it starts cutting off circulation in my legs. At night, Caplin likes to sleep under the covers if the weather is cold, or on the floor beside the bed in warmer weather.

In a single word, I would describe him as needy. He always wants to be with me and can "eep" loudly if he knows I am nearby but he can't get to me. He follows me around the house and the yard and expects me to watch him while he swims or grazes. He panics if he doesn't know where I am. When he thinks it's time for me to come home from work, he will go to the gate and wait for me.

How on earth did you train Caplin Rous?

Like many rodents, capybaras are very smart and Caplin is no exception. When he was a month old I taught him to shake hands by saying "shake" and tapping his paw until he picked it up. It took 15 minutes for him to figure it out. The last trick I taught him was to go in a circle when I signal. I saw a video of a capybara in a zoo in Japan that could do this trick. There aren't many other capybaras that can do any tricks at all and I didn't want the Japanese capybara to one-up Caplin. To teach this I used one of his favorite foods, a fruit popsicle. Keeping the popsicle just out of reach, I led him in a little circle, rewarding each correct step. After two popsicles, he knew the trick.

What is it that you like so much about capybaras?

What I love most about Caplin is how much he loves me and how smart he is. I also love his noises. When people hear him they are always amazed. His voice is often mistaken for a birdsong. When he's nervous he sounds like the dinosaurs in *Jurassic Park*. When he's happy he sounds like a Geiger counter.

Do people do double-takes when they see Caplin Rous for the first time? I shared photos with friends and they thought they had been Photoshopped.

I take Caplin out in public a lot just because I like to have him with me. It is fun to watch people's reactions. Most people have no idea what he is and some take that as a personal affront, angry that such an animal could even exist. But most people are excited and enthusiastic about him, often referring to him as a giant hamster. That usually means they like him. Those who refer to him as a giant rat are more likely to be afraid. He is confused with a variety of animals such as tapirs, wombats and peccaries. One thing that amazes me is that very small children in strollers who can hardly speak a dozen words will point at him and say, "Mouse!" They are almost better at making that connection than adults are.

How many other animals do you have? Does Caplin get along with all of them?

We have four horses, three rainbow boas, two leopard tortoises and a rabbit. Caplin and the rabbit are great friends although we constantly worry that he'll step on her. The tortoises sometimes invade Caplin's corner of the yard and he will do his threat display of clicking and barking to try to drive them off. They ignore him. He is scared to death of the snakes, probably imagining they are anacondas. Of the four horses, only the oldest and gentlest one is allowed near Caplin. I don't trust the others not to paw him out of curiosity.

Does Caplin Rous roam free? And do you need a permit to keep Caplin?

I treat Caplin just like a dog. He goes in and out of the house at will and has pretty much free roam of the fenced area. I don't let him out at night because we have coyotes that sometimes come near the house. When we're outside the yard I always keep him in his harness and leash. Catching a capybara is something like catching a greased hog with their similar body shape and his tendancy to be wet and covered with mud.

Where I live in Texas, no permits are required to own a capybara but this is not true in many places. State and local restrictions may apply. New York and California have particularly stringent rules concerning rodents.

What's your favorite thing about Caplin Rous?

It's hard to pick just one aspect, but I think I love his noises the most. Since I used to do pharmaceutical research and had frequent occasion to use a Geiger counter, I never would have thought that sound could bring a smile to my face the way it does now.

Did Caplin play a role in the writing of your book?

Caplin was the inspiration for my book. My granddaughter wanted a book about cats but I soon found the capybara taking over the story. The cats mimic human reactions including fear, anger, curiosity and surprise, finally resulting in friendship and acceptance when they get to know the capybaras in the book. Without Caplin, I would not have known about these reactions or about capybara behavior, which is very poorly documented.

When did you start pretending to be Caplin Rous? What do you find interesting about inhabiting the persona of a giant rodent?

One day as I explored MySpace I noticed that a surprising number of guinea pigs had their own pages. Just for fun, I created a Caplin page. He immediately attracted friends, either people or "anipals," who were interested in capybaras. Since I'd had so little luck finding information about pet capybaras, I wanted to do my part to contribute to the knowledge base. Even though the blog entries are written in Caplin's voice, they contain a lot of information about his behavior, both good and bad. The day Caplin bit me I posted a blog expressing both of our confusion over the event and his subsequent hostility. Over time, I realized he intended me to be part of his herd and I was not cooperating. Eventually we worked through this. I also kept a chart of his growth and had him discuss his medical issues, which included a brief period of paralysis following neutering. New capybara owners now have a little more information about what they are getting into than I did when I got Caplin.

What about capybaras do you think would come as a surprise to someone who doesn't have one as a pet?

The existence of capybaras surprises people more than anything else. Once they get over the shock of a giant rodent, they tend to admire his calm demeanor. When Caplin does a trick, such as shaking hands, they are surprised by his intelligence, frequently claiming that he is smarter than their dog. I think he is just better trained.

People with some prior knowlege would be most surprised by what active and agile swimmers they are. If you see capybaras in the zoo, they are almost always doing nothing. Caplin is a very graceful in the water, more like an otter than a dog. He has an above ground swimming pool that is about 15'x10'x5' and he zips around underwater, putting his forepaws against his stomach and pushing off with his hind feet. I love to watch him play with his pool toys. He especially loves to swim through hoops.

PERSONAL MONSTERS

The Hannukah Bear

I first moved up to Tallahassee to be with my now-wife Ann in October of 1992. At the time, Ann's daughter was six or seven years old and as accepting of the situation as she could be, most tension assuaged by the fact she saw her father on a regular basis. But I was still anxious to show her that life as she knew it wasn't going to change too drastically, and that it might even be fun. Hannukah was coming up, so I suggested we go shopping for Ann at the local mall. Erin agreed and we set off for the mall in high spirits. Erin, in those days, was a mischievous little sprite of a girl with dark eyebrows and a glint in her eye that was either piratical or good natured depending on her mood. She would say things like, "I want to be a taxi driver, but if that doesn't work out I'll be a doctor or lawyer. And if that doesn't work out I'll just be a plain old beauty queen and live at home with my mom." Once, she said she'd like to be a "scientist of crayons." For awhile, she used to say twenty minutes was "churney midgets." She was the cutest little kid I'd ever met, but also tough as all get out. I enjoyed telling her impossible things as fact and getting that little indignant half-smile out of her and the folded arms, which told me she was entertained but she wasn't buying any of it.

I should perhaps mention now that at the time I didn't know anything about Hannukah. I had not come across any traces of Hannukah learnin' in any books I'd read or through any people I'd met. But, being an agnostic, I had no organized faith for Judaism to come into conflict with, and I was eager to learn everything I could. So I was in perhaps an overly receptive state of mind as we entered the mall.

As we shopped for Ann, we eventually encountered the inevitable Santa Claus display, complete with the man in the fake beard ho-ho-ho-ing for the kids. Erin looked at the Santa without comment, but a little later, when we passed a display showing a huge white animatronic bear holding a red wrapped present, she said, "Oh—look. It's the Hannukah Bear!"

A certain madness seized me. Here was an opportunity to learn something about Jewish culture.

"The Hannukah Bear?" I said. "What's the Hannukah Bear?"

"You know," she said, "the Hannukah Bear. It's the bear that helps light the menorah. It helps with the cooking, too, sometimes."

"Really?" I said. "What else can you tell me about the Hannukah Bear?"

The glint in Erin's eye intensified and as we walked toward a Walden's Bookstore, she told me all about the Hannukah Bear. A lot of what she said is lost in the farthest reaches of my sieve-like memory, but I remember that she went into a complex explanation of the Hannukah Bear's relationship to Hannukah, what it symbolized, where the reference had come from, and a lot of other stuff. Wonderful was the Hannukah Bear! Excellent in all of its intentions and abilities! Why, it even appeared in the night sky sometimes as points of light! It was a beautiful and brilliant concentrated flow of bullshit, of smartassery, that fooled me utterly. I don't think before or since I've heard anyone feed me such a wonderful line of sustained, extemporaneous crap. And I bought it. I bought into it completely.

By the time we got home, I was stuffed full of facts about the Hannukah Bear, and feeling very pleased with myself. I had learned something about Hannukah. It was knowledge I could use when meeting Ann's synagogue members for the first time. I could even show Ann that I was trying hard to learn about her religion and culture!

Alas, of course, there were instead looks of puzzlement, even concern. When I realized how completely I'd been fooled, I laughed my ass off. Since I'd arrived in Tallahassee, I'd been fabricating little stories for her off and on. She'd just returned the favor, in spades...with a shovel, so I could dig my own grave. It was, as I say, one of the most amazing extemporaneous displays of applied imagination that I've ever been privileged to witness.

From then on, it was no-holds barred. Whether it was the pet iguana Erin and I pretended lurked around the house when her timid friends came over to play or the extended "incident" at Chucky Cheese involving the giant rat mascot and an ill-timed kick, we had a series of adventures based almost entirely on riffing off of each other's imaginations.

Eventually, she became too old to have fun with parental units and those times faded into memory. But the Hannukah Bear story is still a staple of family lore and legend—the event that started it all.

Fantasy and the Imagination

Introduction to *Best American Fantasy*, Volume 1 (2007)

In her extraordinary creative writing book *The Passionate, Accurate Story*, Carol Bly presents a hypothetical situation. One night at dinner a girl announces to her father and mother that a group of bears has moved in next door. In one scenario, the father says (and I paraphrase), "Bears? Don't be ridiculous," and tells his daughter to be more serious. In the other scenario, the father says, "Bears, huh? How many bears? Do you know their names? What do they wear?" And his daughter, with delight, tells him.

The imagination is a form of love: playful, generous, and transformative. All of the best fiction hums and purrs and sighs with it, and in this way (as well) fiction mirrors life. This is how we think of the fiction collected in this first volume of *Best American Fantasy*. There's a flicker, a flutter, at the heart of these stories that animates them, and this movement—ever different, ever unpredictable—makes each story unique.

Does it matter if the imaginative impulse is "fantastical" in the sense of "containing an explicit fantastical event"? No. It matters only that, on some level, a sense of fantastical play exists on the page. *Bears have moved in next door.*

We often disregard this sense of play. Why? In part, the idea of "play" seems immature or frivolous, especially in a society still blinkered by its Puritan origins. However, we also tend to discount play because it speaks to an aspect of the imagination that defies easy measurement. It brings yet another level of uncertainty to an endeavor already supersaturated with the subjective.

During Medieval times, the imagination was often associated with the senses and thus thought to be one of the links between human beings and the animals. Only with the Rennaissance was the imagination firmly linked to creativity and thus the intellect. Both views, however, and modern ideals of *functionality* and *utility*—even, sometimes, the idea in modern fiction of *invisible prose*—ignore or have no place for the sense of play that precedes and infuses creative endeavor.

This is perhaps no surprise, given that you cannot *teach* imagination in a creative writing workshop. As Bly explicitly states in *The Passionate, Accurate Story*, by the time a person reaches the age where they want to write and be taught to write fiction, that particular muscle, that particular manifestation of the soul, is firmly locked in place. A good instructor can perhaps draw out an imaginative impulse in a timid student but cannot instill it as other, more empirical aspects of fiction can be instilled with patience and a firm hand.

To pull out a hoary old quote, Jung once wrote: "The dynamic principle of fantasy is play, which belongs also to the child, and as such it appears to be inconsistent with the principle of serious work. But without this playing with fantasy no creative work has ever yet come to birth. The debt we owe to the play of imagination is incalculable."

In the stories contained in *Best American Fantasy*, events continually challenge and surprise our own imaginations. In this anthology, you will find talking alligators, a man as big as a county, baboon playwrights, a flying woman, sordid superheroes, men who marry trees, the fragments of a storyteller, and the very edge of the world. You may even find the end of narrative.

What you will not find is a set definition of "fantasy." If you enter into reading this volume eager for such a definition or searching for the fantastical event that you believe should trigger the use of the term, you will overlook the many other pleasures that await you. These are the same pleasures you can find in non-fantastical stories: deep characterization, thematic resonance, clever plots, unique situations, pitch-perfect dialogue, enervating humor, and luminous settings. The extraordinary depth of imagination in the best stories affects not merely their content but their form, the form shaping the content, until we realize the two are not separate, that they are, in the best writing, united by the same imaginative act.

In a sense, defining "fantasy" in the context of fiction is a losing proposition—simply not worth the effort. We do not really talk like people talk in fiction. Lives do not have the kind of narrative arc or denouement often found in fiction.

Therefore, we should not look askance at writers who change the paradigm, who have no interest in replicating reality if it does not suit their purposes. (A more interesting discussion of fantasy, beyond the scope of this introduction, might be to define it in the context of metaphor, because a writer's voice may be described as fabulist rather than mimetic based solely on metaphor, regardless of the nature of the events occurring in the story.)

In all of this, it is important to remember that even flights of fancy must have anchors to be successful. The fantastical has no reality without its characters. The alligator knows the plot of the tale better than anyone. The man as big as a county is weeping for a reason. The flying woman has an admirer. The failed superhero has bills to pay. The edge of the world isn't the end of *everything*. Even baboon playwrights and men who marry trees may have hidden depths. The fragments of the storyteller collect themselves long enough to tell one last story.

There's no *real* end to narrative, just as there is no real end to the ways in which "fantasy" elements can be put to use in the service of narrative. Every time someone reads Bly's *A Passionate, Accurate Story* and comes to the part where the father asks his daughter about the bears, there's the tantalizing possibility in the reader's mind that she'll say something different—something wonderful or horrible or bittersweet.

There's every possibility that what she says will *be* different for every reader, depending solely on the generosity of the individual imagination.

My Father's Pipe

Los Angeles Times, "Off the Shelf," October 18, 2009

When I was growing up, my dad had a family heirloom that fascinated me: a small tobacco pipe with a glass-covered pinhole in the side. If you looked through the hole you could see a microfiche-like photograph: four rows of stern-looking men and women, along with names and other information in German or Dutch.

My dad explained that the photograph depicted a group of dissidents from the days before World War I. He didn't know whether the image was intended as a "hit list" for the secret police or a way for the radicals to keep track of their own. But those kinds of details didn't register with me anyway. For me, the pipe was a compelling oddity, a window that delighted me because I could look through a tiny hole and see so much.

Over the years, I kept thinking about that pipe—my mind just wouldn't leave it alone. Then, while working on my noir fantasy novel *Finch*, it resurfaced as belonging to the father of my detective hero, John Finch. Finch's father is a mysterious figure with shifting allegiances between various factions in my war-torn imaginary city of Ambergris.

In a scene in the novel, Finch is shown the pipe as a child, much as I was shown the real pipe by my dad. Here, though, there is an added layer: that Finch's father is trying to communicate something about his real role in Ambergris that he cannot state directly without endangering his son. Finch looks through the pinhole and sees "[a] whole map of the known world. There was a dot for Ambergris. The line of the River Moth…. The Kalif's empire covering the west beyond the Moth. Exotic city after exotic city marked in that vast desert, the plains and hills beyond."

But my fictional pipe also has a pinhole on the other side, which shows "black-and-white photos of twelve men and women." Finch's father tells him,

"The owner of this pipe ran a network of spies. The map…is really a code. It tells the owner something about the spies whose pictures you're looking at."

A secret history of the world. A topography of the imagination in which cities become shorthand for people's lives. For me, writing fantasy has always had that element. Each novel has contained autobiography tied to setting—with details taken directly from the exhilarating and mundane aspects of my past and my family's past. Do readers see those elements as personal, as transposed from reality? Probably not in most cases, and it certainly isn't necessary.

But it's this hidden element, this strand of subtext, that—unseen by readers but felt by them—breathes life into fiction and is especially important for fiction set in imaginary places, which might otherwise be so disconnected from reality as to become meaningless. A novel that isn't anchored to some aspect of the human condition, to some universal aspect of our disparate experiences, is usually a novel inert and lifeless on the page.

This subtext acknowledges that what's private is also public, that the world beyond our immediate experience has an impact on us and thus on our fiction. As a kid, my father's pipe represented a potent possibility for adventure, a sense that the world was deeper and wider than I could then know. It also represented a way of bonding with my dad.

But as an adult, it became a different kind of mystery, with a different set of questions. Who were these people trapped inside the pipe? What had they lived for? What had they been willing to die for?

Slowly, the political mixed with the personal, and yet I didn't want the real answers. My mind was seeking fictional ones instead.

I found them in writing *Finch*. The novel is set in a failed state run by a dictatorship that doesn't understand the people it is governing. The consequences are both tragic and absurd. Although *Finch* has a mystery plot wedded to a surreal fantasy element, the context, the setting, the lives of the characters are informed and shaped by the last eight years, from Sept. 11 to occupation to torture to suicide bombings.

Writers often mention the need to get distance from events in their lives before they deal with them in fiction, but I find a similar need for distance from history and politics. Without that—and the transformative power of the imagination—a fiction writer risks creating an unsubtle polemic. Writing in a fantastical setting helps me, as it immediately changes the paradigm, while retaining the intellectual arguments and questions, the tone and texture, of the original events.

To me, then, fantasy continues to be highly personal because the political, the historical always takes a toll, even on those of us who occupy the sidelines. As a writer, you cannot remain unaffected by that, even if you sometimes can't see how to work with it. Ambergris enables me to write about it. Fantasy enables me to write about it. That prism is like putting my eye to the hole in the pipe and seeing this fragment of another world that's still part of our own, no matter how distant in time or space.

The truth is, Ambergris has always been porous: There's no barrier between me and it, and thus no barrier between it and the world. The world continually horrifies, moves, elates, bores and changes me—and, in a very organic, intimate way, Ambergris is continually being colonized and redrawn in my imagination as a consequence. There are no maps of Ambergris because there can be no maps of Ambergris, no matter what an image in a pinhole tells you. In *Finch*, it is a beleaguered city, linked by psychic distress to places like Baghdad, Beirut, even occupied Paris during World War II. But what will it be tomorrow?

The Novella: A Personal Exploration

Originally presented at the
2004 Associated Writing Programs Conference in Vancouver, Canada

The novella has always been a very personal form for me because it was through the novella form that I came into my own as a writer. Even today, it speaks to me in a more personal way than either the short story or the novel. Perhaps this is because although I have not written nor ever want to write the perfect novel, I have come close to, for me, writing the perfect novella. Similarly, although I love the short story form, it is too restrictive in its miniaturization and compression—I have created short stories that were too perfect for their own good, in a sense.

The novella also has a personal resonance for me because it marked the beginning of a long journey in the wilderness after years of having built up a reputation as a writer of short stories. I soon found that writing novellas might best serve my progression as a writer, but it did not best serve my career. For several years in the mid to late 1990s, after I began to write almost exclusively novellas, I found that I had difficulty getting them published, and when I did, it was in venues that had more limited circulations and reputations.

Suddenly, I went from being an up-and-coming talent to being a kind of sequestered hermit or eccentric, or at least that's how I felt. Publications that were happy to risk a limited number of pages to a new writer were less interested in devoting a lot of pages to that same writer.

For five years, I labored in utter obscurity, writing...novellas. It was perhaps the most liberating experience of my life. Although I had not considered publication while writing the short stories, I had come to expect that I could place them, and would continue to place short fiction, even if it was in the longer form of the novella. When that expectation turned out to be false, I retreated further from the idea of "audience" and "market."

In a way, this preserved and protected me. Free of any expectation of success or of career, I matured as a writer in ways that I would not have otherwise—and all almost exclusively through the novella form. I became more original. I invested more in my characters. I invested more in the prose. This was in part because of the form. There couldn't be the instant gratification of completing a rough draft in a day, as with most of my short stories. There also, I knew, wouldn't be the semi-instant gratification of a nice acceptance letter in the mail once I sent it out, either. So, I was content—and even happy—to simply spend each day held by the vision and promise of whatever novella I was working on. In short, I wrote more intrinsically for myself than ever before.

Now, for some writers this might have been self-indulgent and the lack of audience might have resulted in lack of focus or in lack of progression. But for me it worked because it re-established a high wall between art and commerce. It gave me the distance and the space to rediscover myself as a writer. I had some vague idea of "the reader" who might encounter my novellas at some point in the future, well after my death, the manuscript found in some aunt's attic and resurrected with appropriate introduction, afterword, and tragic endnotes, but for the most part this shadowy reader had my own face.

The novella became, ultimately, deeply confessional in a way, exploring what writing meant to me as well as the nature of the imagination, obsession, and love. I think I can say with certainty that I was never happier than during that period when I had no prospects and no hope of a career.

Eventually, most of the novellas were collected in a book entitled *City of Saints & Madmen*, which went on to be a *Publishers Weekly* and *Amazon.com* year's best pick and has been, to date, translated into five languages, indicating ironically enough that sometimes the best career move is to write unpublishable novellas until they become publishable.

But why the novella? What about the novella was so attractive? Was it just that I couldn't write novels yet? That I didn't have the marathon endurance to do so?

Reflecting back on this period before I wrote novels, I think the novella seemed so attractive because when you deal in images charged with a magic realist or surrealist sensibility, when your style, as a reflection of your worldview, is naturally fantastical at the level of metaphor, whether anything fantastical occurs in your fiction, then the novella provides the perfect form for what is, at base, visionary literature.

By a naturally fantastical worldview, I mean that the style itself is suffused by it, so that on the level of metaphor a novel like Mark Helprin's *A Soldier of the Great War* is more intrinsically fantasy or fabulist in nature than J.R.R. Tolkien's *Lord of the Rings* or J.K. Rowling's Harry Potter series.

This concept goes beyond the clichéd idea of suspension of disbelief. It's true that fabulist novels can be harder to sustain because the implications of the fantasy element are harder to sustain (generally) in a believable manner than the implications of a realistic setting or realistic events—at least in part because readers are already familiar with the here and now. However, I don't believe this is the primary reason I attempted novellas before novels. After all, every writer, as they say, creates his or her own reality when sitting down to write fiction, and this can be just as difficult a task for the writer of "realistic" fiction.

It's more that there is a deep anti-rational or irrational element to the best fantastical or visionary fiction, something that speaks to the intuition and the subconscious. Many times it comes out of the resonance of images connected to characters—or the way in which setting and style attain a hyper-realism. As Michael Moorcock writes in his collection of essays *Wizardry and Wild Romance*, this kind of fiction "may not be judged by normal criteria but by the power of [the writer's] imagery and by what extent their writing evokes that power, whether trying to convey wildness, strangeness, or charm; whether like Melville, Ballard, Patrick White, or Alejo Carpentier, they transform their images into intense personal metaphors."

While such elements can be sustained in the short story or novella form, at the novel length, they often become diluted, and thus more ordinary, robbing it of its intrinsic power. In a novel, some elements of plotting or other "business"— even practical considerations like moving characters from scene to scene or the need for dialogue as narrative—can undermine the surrealistic vision.

It isn't about the suspension of disbelief on the reader's part—it's about the inevitable decaying orbit on the part of the writer, the succumbing to the mundane. Sometimes "filler" can take a form other than the wasted scenes in a typical commercial paperback. Sometimes too much focus on the rational can also be filler. (I'm tempted to say that it's about the difference between a 25-year-old scotch straight up and one on the rocks.)

Another element that entered my novellas at the time was postmodern technique. Very little that I used of postmodern technique hadn't been done before in so-called realistic fiction. I wrote a fictional essay about my fantastical city at novella length, which more or less compressed plot and character. Another novella inserted the author into the text. A third used an annotated bibliography to convey plot.

I found that using these techniques to support fiction set in a fantastical city changed the context of the postmodern technique considerably. Which is to say, those techniques that might be said to break the fourth wall instead reinforced the reality of the fantasy.

But postmodern technique can be perilous in more than small doses. Although certain narrative techniques can be deployed successfully over the novel length, I do believe the novella length is the upper limit for the success of *some* of these approaches to fiction. (That said, someone will always come along to prove you wrong...)

So I believe this is also why I wrote novellas—the combination of the visionary and the postmodern made the novella length perfect, in that the visionary element didn't become diluted and the postmodern element didn't begin to annoy or seem affected. Certainly, it is even more difficult to sustain postmodern technique and visionary qualities over novel length when you are also trying to support the reality of a secondary world without allowing pure description/exposition to take over—in other words, trying very hard for the hull of your ship not to become so encrusted with barnacles and other extraneous matter that it affects your speed and manueverability.

And, in fact, when I moved to the novel length, as with my new novel, *Shriek: An Afterword*, I found that I was writing in a slightly more conventional mode, jettisoning some elements of the fantastical and the postmodern in favor of strategies that work better at the novel length.

Now, at the same time I'd been writing novellas, I'd started an original fiction anthology called *Leviathan*. The purpose of *Leviathan* was to map the continuum of short fiction, recognizing that works tackling the same themes would generally have more similarities regardless of "genre" than just, say, "fantasy" stories versus "mainstream literary" stories. *Leviathan* mixed works of realistic and non-realistic fiction, using theme and other elements as a guide for coherence.

Because I'd found so few publications willing to even consider novellas, I decided that the second volume of Leviathan would be devoted to them. (The irony of editing an anthology of novellas that I couldn't submit to myself wasn't lost on me.)

So, for over six months, I read more than four thousand novellas of all varieties, in all genres. This was an instructive if exhausting exercise. I was able to observe all of the myriad permutations from a wide range of beginning-to-experienced writers—from writers who had been published in *The New Yorker* or *Omni* to those who hadn't published anywhere at all.

The most common reason, besides inadequate grasp of technique, for rejecting novellas during that reading period came from the realization that many of these so-called novellas were actually short stories. Many of them had unnecessary scenes or scenes that dragged on too long, or scenes that did not operate at the multiple levels necessary to make them "real," thus necessitating the writing of additional scenes to make up for this lack, and just perpetuating a general *slackness*.

In short, many of the novellas read to me like rough draft short stories, and seemed to lack the recognition that a novella might be longer than a short story but that this didn't mean you could simply write something longer than usual and it would magically become a novella. It still had to have a pleasing form, a pleasing structure.

The other flaw that became preternaturally prevalent was the novel excerpt presented as a novella. While I do believe that the much-maligned A to B "slice-of-life" short story structure can still offer up new and delightful variation, I do not believe that, in general, it is sustainable at the novella length. And yet we received many submissions that had either been deliberately sampled from a novel or novel-in-progress, or, more interestingly, novels-in-waiting that the writers didn't realize should be longer, and at the novella length appeared to be

A to B "slice-of-life" tales. A novella is not simply an interesting stretch of novel, would be one lesson to be learned from reading slush pile novellas of this type.

Although there are obvious exceptions, therefore, I don't think that a novella justifies *apparent* plotlessness as easily as a short story can. Short stories, like poems, can be about a moment in time quite easily. But the structure of the novella seems more practical—that if you are going to stretch your canvas over that length, you should have more to say on a structural level than just here's a segment of someone's life.

Which brings me to a third problem, one that can, of course, be inherent in a flawed short story as well, but that becomes more apparent in a novella: weak ideas or characters only become *weaker* at the greater length. The nervous stylistic tic that in a short story might even seem charming becomes unbelievably annoying in a novella. The character that might stand up under the reader's jaded gaze for the length of a short story crumbles under the pressure exerted by the greater responsibilities created by the novella. Even a propensity on a writer's part to suggest setting through quick flashes of description can, in the novella form, begin to suggest a lack of commitment.

These statements might make it sound as if I think that short stories are a lesser form; not true. The ideal short story and the ideal novella are equals. I am talking about the context of slush pile submissions, the context of reading with an eye toward selecting work for publication. But it does make me think about the limits of the short story form in terms of your *average* published short story. How many writers run through the finish line, so to speak? How many of their characters really do have a life beyond the end of the story?[1]

Since *Leviathan 2*, novellas have continued to play an important role in the anthology. Both *Leviathan 3* and *Leviathan 4* contained several novellas. In

---

[1] What I did find interesting in making final selections was how many novellas used the original definition of the term—of many stories meshed together into one story cycle. That for some writers the novella was an opportunity to weave stories within stories within stories, in a way that, just for length reasons alone, would have been impossible at the shorter length. For example, a novella from Stepan Chapman, "Minutes of the Last Meeting," takes place aboard a train in Czarist Russia, as it is about to be attacked by anarchists. Chapman uses the different compartments of the train almost as separate chapters or stories in his novella, spinning stories off of the inhabitants of each that intertwine and contribute to a greater whole.

many cases, we were the market of last resort and the work would have gone unpublished otherwise. Ironically, these pieces are the ones that almost always receive the most praise from reviewers, which to my mind means there is a need for more markets for novellas. It may also be a perception issue, too. One writer I cajoled into sending in a novella had put it aside in a drawer and had no plans to send it out, having no idea of anyone who would be interested in a cross-genre piece of that length.

This attitude uncannily echoes my own experience in the mid-90s, when I ran out of markets willing to look at anything longer than a certain number of pages—or unwilling to look at anything surreal or magic realist in nature.

For my own part, I have lately focused more on short stories and on novels. But both have been greatly enhanced by working in the novella form. Because of working with novellas, I have a greater appreciation for, on a purely instinctual level, what a short story does well and what it cannot support. It has, by way of contrast, made me better understand how a short story coils and compresses information and situation.

At the same time, working with novellas has allowed me to organically transition from writing short stories to writing novels. It has allowed me to experiment with using larger casts of characters, functional digressions (the kinds of things that novels thrive on), and to discover the kinds of textures stylistically that work best at the longer lengths, without having to commit to them first for the years it takes to complete a novel.

For all of these reasons, the novella remains my favorite form of fiction, both to read and to write. I believe it will continue to be a source of innovation for a long time to come.

Two Essays on Hiking
VanderWorld Blog, June 2005, and *Ecstatic Days*, May 2009

Inspiration (Together)

My wife Ann and I have been hanging out around estuaries and pool halls. This past weekend, we took a 12-mile hike on a trail in St. Mark's Wildlife Refuge. The trail transitions from pine forest and swamp to salt marshes and freshwater ponds. At one point, you come out on the salt marsh to your left and the freshwater ponds to your right. On the left, there's what amounts to a long canal, fringed on the far side by reeds that spread out to the horizon, interrupted only by the earthen islands of clumps of trees and the byzantine maze of the estuaries that feed into the ocean. The light, even on a cloudy day, that reflects off the tan grasses, is often remarkably luminous, like a Turner painting. It's easy to imagine you've stumbled across some primordial terrain and that you're never going to make it back to the 21st century.

As we're walking along, around mile nine, we notice two straight lines coursing through the water some sixty feet ahead of us, waves rippling out from the lines.

Now, the brain is a strange and suggestible muscle, delicate as it is despite being housed in bone. It is much affected by context. We had been expecting the possibility of otters in the water. When we saw the two straight lines, we thought we were seeing evidence of two otters swimming toward us across the canal. But no, as the lines came closer, we saw that it was something much more odd for that place. In an odd, almost magic realist way, the otters morphed into the form of two dolphins, their fins cutting through the water forming the two straight lines. The canal was shallow and they were only able to submerge up to their fins. Their blowholes made surly air-expelling sounds. They roved back and forth across the brackish canal, making the alligators nervous. Some of the alligators came out of the water while others dove in, caught between the unexpected dolphins and the slightly more expected humans.

We watched the dolphins as they swam up the canal back the way we had come, until they were out of sight. It was a surreal moment for us, especially because we were in that part of the hike where you lose your bearings a little bit—not becoming disoriented, but working simply at walking, talking less, in your own thoughts, and the pristine nature of your surroundings bringing you deeply into whatever fictions the mind may deliver to you.

Later, on our way out of the refuge, we stopped at the visitor center, worried that perhaps the dolphins had gotten lost or trapped. The water there was at least partially fresh water, and the shallowness of it bothered us too. But the ranger at the center reassured us, saying that every once in awhile a few dolphins would follow high tide into the estuary system to feed in the salt marshes, and then go out to sea again at the next high tide. We were, though, lucky to see them. In the many years I've been going out to St. Marks I've never seen dolphins while walking one of the trails—only when out at the lighthouse, in the open sea. (Although, I have seen alligators swimming out at sea, the delineation between fresh and salt water becoming blurred; sometimes fishermen become a little startled, out there at low tide in their long boots, seeing a sudden reptile, sinuous and oddly close.

We followed up our hike with a sojourn to a local pool hall, for beer and a spirited dozen games. Ann and I are evenly matched in pool, and it's been fun to find a sport to share. It was the prototypical smoky pool hall, with an odd mixture of college co-eds, young professionals, older couples, geeks, freaks, scantily clad waitresses, and players. Our cue ball had a crack in it. The crack of billiard balls and the plastic smack of balls hitting pockets mingled with the distant crowd noises from the televisions tuned to sports events. The smell of cigarettes and beer had an oddly invigorating effect.

I thought about Lake Baikal while we played, and secret lives, and the role of a character named Sybel in my novel, *Shriek*. I thought about what awaited me at the day job the next day, and wondered why Ann was kicking my butt so thoroughly in some games and not in others. I wondered where Liz Williams would be taking my plastic alien baby next. I talked with Ann about the Dark

Cabal and about *Shriek*, and the International Horror Guild Awards. But mostly, for some odd reason, I thought about Lake Baikal and its freshwater seals. And about Alaska and its melting glaciers, which made me worry about St. Marks, wondering if someday, maybe when I am sixty, I'll go out to the familiar paths, and the sea levels will have risen, and the whole refuge will be under water. And once, near the end of one game, I saw the clean geometric line of cue ball to eight ball to pocket as the clean slice of a dolphin fin through water.

The Unknown and the Luminous (Alone)
(All quotes from Henry David Thoreau's *Where I Lived, and What I Lived For*)

> "The mass of men lead lives of quiet desperation. What is called resignation is confirmed desperation. From the desperate city you go into the desperate country, and have to console yourself with the bravery of minks and muskrats."

This may be so, but it doesn't feel like desperation at the trail head. It feels like adventure. It feels like you are about to test yourself against a task hard and worth doing, and even if you retreat from it back into the normal rhythms of your life, you will learn something about yourself in the process. Memories of dodging wild pigs, standing silent while a panther walked by you, and jumping over allligators—the stuff of tales exaggerated later over beers, and thus untrue even though true—melt away into another image: of having been disoriented and lost in a thunderstorm on these very same trails, and how that brought back childhood memories of walking on the reef at night in Fiji, with no way to tell sea from shore, and how, in some guise, you are hoping to recreate that experience that cannot be recreated, because in being lost in the natural world you actually feel more alive, more safe, than at any other time in your life. That's how you start at least: in the abstract, and in your recollections, rather than in the moment.

> "I went to the woods because I wished to live deliberately, to front only the essential facts of life, and see if I could not learn what it had to teach, and not, when I came to die, discover that I had not lived."

Nowhere is this sense of urgency more apparent than in passing through the swampy forest that lies a mile or two in, with woods meeting a dank blackwater gutter, the place you've most often seen bears and heard things rustling in the darkness that the imagination assigns horrible forms to. Hiking alone is a different experience than hiking with someone. The pleasures of conversation distract from the still, standing water, from the reflections of cypress knees and the oppressive Southern Gothic feel to the air, the sky blocked by scraggly pine trees. This, too, is the corridor where wild pigs once charged, and while danger is minimal, the imagination magnifies it, and in the absence of company the mind exaggerates and finds ghosts where none exist. "Nature" in this context is something aggressive that wants to cause harm, even though it's not true. Once through that gauntlet, you feel foolish, you feel dumb, you wonder why you bothered with the anxiety, or brought your senses to heightened alert. It's just a walk in the woods.

> "Time is but the stream I go a-fishing in. I drink at it: but while I drink I see the sandy bottom and detect how shallow it is. Its thin current slides away, but eternity remains."

Then the trail becomes straight and long and bright, and you're trudging across the sandy soil wondering how the Spanish invaders with their heavy hot armor ever hacked their way through the swamps. This section seems to last forever, and even as you remain vigilant, scanning the trail ahead for signs of motion, still your thoughts stray, time become elongated and porous. There's the memory of each past experience traversing this stretch, and the awareness that you've come early enough to beat the biting flies for once, and then you're somewhere else. You're driving across Hungary toward Romania in a tiny car. You're lost with your wife on a plateau in a park above San Diego, where the grass is the color of gold and reaches to your knees and the trees are blackened from fire. You're hiking up a mountain in scrubland outside of Brisbane, each breath labored, every muscle in your legs protesting even as you're possessed by a wild giddiness that keeps you moving past exhaustion. You're back in the first year of college when you wanted isolation and walked the five miles from the campus home in utter silence every day, receiving the world through a hole in your shoe and knowing you weren't lonely but just alone. These thoughts are an embarrassment to you later. They seem to give significance to the mundane, but heightened awareness combined with a strange comfort is a signature of being solitary in solitary places.

> "The life in us is like the water in the river. It may rise this year higher than man has ever known it, and flood the parched uplands; even this may be the eventful year…"

After having passed the unofficial gauntlet of bears and wild pigs, along with the stretch nicknamed "alligator alley," your stride has achieved a rhythm, and your legs are no longer tight, and you can feel the muscles moving as you move, and you come out of the scrubland into the wetlands, with the freshwater canal serving as a buffer to the salt marsh and, ultimately, the sea. You've seen dolphins there, searching for food at high tide, before being pulled out again at low tide. You've seen otters and heard the call of curlews. The water means more life than anything the woods can support, in a myriad of forms. It's also an area struck awhile back by hurricane, and you can still see the marks of that abuse, even though the water level's long since receded. Once, this section was much harder to traverse because of that violence—you had to make your way through thigh-high water, always wary of that sudden tickle that might mean contact with an alligator. Now, though, they've filled those spaces in with concrete, and you're vaguely disappointed. You're now seven or eight miles out, and yet you're confronted by this artificial bridge. No one is anywhere nearby, and yet there's no escaping the fact people were here in numbers once.

> "Men esteem truth remote, in the outskirts of the system, behind the farthest star, before Adam and after the last man."

Finally, you reach the farthest-most point, beyond which you are but returning and returning still, feeling the pull of mile markers and the road beyond. But for that moment, you're so remote that there's no one for miles—and you feel that. You feel it strongly. You've gone from being a little on edge to being a little tired. And you've come out onto this perfectly still scene that looks from the light like Turner painted it. And you just take a deep breath and relax into the landscape.

> "A lake like this is never smoother than at such a time; and the clear portion of the air above it is shallow and darkened by clouds, the water, full of light and reflections, becomes a lower heaven itself so much more important."

And so you walk along the shore of this lower heaven, in the middle of nowhere and are rejuvenated by its perfect stillness. Your legs for a time are no longer tired, and you are afraid of nothing, and you have no room for memory or thought or anything except this moment, and this one, and the next. If a place can be called perfect or pristine or timeless, this stretch of the trail has all of those qualities, and your peace of mind is absolute in its embrace of the sky's reflection.

> "In any weather, at any hour of the day or night, I have been anxious to improve the nick of time, and notch it on my stick too; to stand on the meeting of two eternities, the past and future, which is precisely the present moment."

The present moment elongates again, ignited by the heat, once past still ponds and into the eleventh mile. You live in the present by dint of blistered feet and chaffed ankles and biting flies drawn to the sweat on your ears or forehead and the parched feeling in your throat despite drinking water from the canteen. The sun has decided to lodge itself behind your eyes and shine out so that the inside of your head feels burnt. Every beautiful thing you see ahead of you you know you've already seen at least once behind you. Eternity is found in the repetition of your steps and the constant way the light grips the ground and sends its heat back up at you. There's no memory in you now. There's no room. The present has filled you up.

> "At other times watching from the observatory of some cliff or tree, to

> telegraph any new arrival; or waiting at evening on the hill-tops for the sky to fall, that I might catch something, though I never caught much…"

The larger things in this context fall away, until you revel only in small details—the dark line of a marsh hawk flying low over the water, the delicate fracture of the water where a snake bird submerged, and, between, the strangely satisfying long grass that cascades like hair from the ground.

> "By the words necessary of life, I mean whatever, of all that man obtains by his own exertions, has been from the first, or from long use has become, so important to human life that few, if any, whether from savageness, or poverty, or philosophy, ever attempt to do without it."

In the final miles, the sun is so bright and hot you actually feel a little delirious, even though you know this is a mirage—you have water and you're still hobbling through your blisters and petty aches. How can the sun be so oppressive and yet the scene so unbearably beautiful? The final mile approaches, and you bend down to tighten the laces on your boot. There's a tiny black-and-red grasshopper, symbolic as a scarab, beside your foot. From what seems like a great distance, you hear a scrambling huff from the marsh beside the trail. For an instant some odd, broad-shouldered marmot pushes its face through the reeds. Then sees you and hurriedly disappears with a plop into the water behind it—while you rise, startled, the grasshopper leaping onto your leg. Then you're walking again, laughing a little, and in a few minutes you're back at the road and your car, everything pressed out of you except a yearning for water and a clean shirt. And you're unaccountably happy, grinning even. And you feel monstrous, perhaps, but you also feel *clean*.

About the Author

Jeff VanderMeer grew up in the Fiji Islands and has had books published in over twenty countries. His books, including the bestselling *City of Saints & Madmen* and *Finch*, have made the year's best lists of *Publishers Weekly, LA Weekly, Amazon*, the *San Francisco Chronicle*, and many more. Considered one of the foremost speculative fiction writers of his generation, VanderMeer has won two World Fantasy Awards, an NEA-funded Florida Individual Writers' Fellowship and Travel Grant, and, most recently, the Le Cafard Cosmique Award in France and the Tähtifantasia Award in Finland. He has also been a finalist, as writer or editor, for the Hugo Award, Bram Stoker Award, Philip K. Dick Award, Shirley Jackson Award, and many others. The author of over three hundred stories, his short fiction has appeared recently in *Conjunctions, Black Clock*, Tor.com, and Library of America's definitive anthology *American Fantastic Tales*, edited by Peter Straub. Collections include *Secret Life* and *The Third Bear* (called essential reading by Junot Diaz). He reviews books for, among others, the *New York Times Book Review*, the *Washington Post Book World*, the *Los Angeles Times*, and the Barnes & Noble Review, as well as being a regular columnist for the Omnivoracious book blog. Current projects include *Booklife: Strategies and Survival Tips for the 21st-Century Writer*, the noir fantasy novel *Finch*, and the forthcoming definitive *Steampunk Bible* from Abrams Books. He currently lives in Tallahassee, Florida, and serves as assistant director for Wofford College's Shared Worlds writing camp for teens (Spartanburg, South Carolina), in addition to conducting workshops and guest lecturing all over the world.

www.ingramcontent.com/pod-product-compliance
Lightning Source LLC
LaVergne TN
LVHW011416080426
835512LV00005B/84